# TRANSLATION AS A FORM

This is a book-length commentary on Walter Benjamin's 1923 essay "Die Aufgabe des Übersetzers," best known in English under the title "The Task of the Translator." Benjamin's essay is at once an immensely attractive work for top-flight theorists of translation and comparative literature and a frustratingly cryptic work that cries out for commentary. Almost every one of the claims he makes in it seems wildly counterintuitive, because he articulates none of the background support that would help readers place it in larger literary-historical contexts: Jewish mystical traditions from Philo Judaeus's Logos-based Neoplatonism to thirteenth-century Lurianic Kabbalah; Romantic and post-Romantic esotericisms from Novalis and the Schlegels to Hölderlin and Goethe; modernist avant-garde foreclosures on "the public" and generally the communicative contexts of literature.

The book is divided into 78 passages, from one to a few sentences in length. Each of the passages becomes its own commentarial unit, consisting of a Benjaminian interlinear box, a paraphrase, a commentary, and a list of other commentators who have engaged the specific passage in question. Because the passages cover the entire text of the essay in sequence, reading straight through the book provides the reader with an augmented experience of reading the essay.

Robinson's commentary is key reading for scholars and postgraduate students of translation, comparative literature, and critical theory.

**Douglas Robinson** is Professor of Translating Studies at the Chinese University of Hong Kong, Shenzhen, and author or editor of 12 other Routledge books, including the recent *Critical Translation Studies*, *Translationality*, *Priming Translation*, and *The Behavioral Economics of Translation*, as well as the textbook *Becoming a Translator* and the anthology *Western Translation Theory: From Herodotus to Nietzsche*.

# TRANSLATION AS A FORM

A Centennial Commentary on Walter Benjamin's "The Task of the Translator"

*Douglas Robinson*

LONDON AND NEW YORK

Cover image: © Getty Images

First published 2023
by Routledge
4 Park Square, Milton Park, Abingdon, Oxon OX14 4RN

and by Routledge
605 Third Avenue, New York, NY 10158

*Routledge is an imprint of the Taylor & Francis Group, an informa business*

© 2023 Douglas Robinson

The right of Douglas Robinson to be identified as author of this work has been asserted in accordance with sections 77 and 78 of the Copyright, Designs and Patents Act 1988.

All rights reserved. No part of this book may be reprinted or reproduced or utilised in any form or by any electronic, mechanical, or other means, now known or hereafter invented, including photocopying and recording, or in any information storage or retrieval system, without permission in writing from the publishers.

*Trademark notice*: Product or corporate names may be trademarks or registered trademarks, and are used only for identification and explanation without intent to infringe.

*British Library Cataloguing-in-Publication Data*
A catalogue record for this book is available from the British Library

*Library of Congress Cataloging-in-Publication Data*
Names: Robinson, Douglas, 1954- author.
Title: Translation as a form : a centennial commentary on Walter Benjamin's "The task of the translator" / Douglas Robinson.
Description: Abingdon, Oxon; New York : Routledge, 2022. | Includes bibliographical references and index.
Identifiers: LCCN 2021058639 | ISBN 9781032161396 (hardback) | ISBN 9781032161389 (paperback) | ISBN 9781003247227 (ebook)
Subjects: LCSH: Benjamin, Walter, 1892-1940. Aufgabe des Übersetzers. | Translating and interpreting—Philosophy. | Language and languages—Philosophy.
Classification: LCC P306.2 .B4667 2022 | DDC 838/.91209—dc23/eng/20220316
LC record available at https://lccn.loc.gov/2021058639

ISBN: 978-1-032-16139-6 (hbk)
ISBN: 978-1-032-16138-9 (pbk)
ISBN: 978-1-003-24722-7 (ebk)

DOI: 10.4324/9781003247227

Typeset in Bembo
by codeMantra

# CONTENTS

| | |
|---|---:|
| Introduction | 1 |
| *Passages, titles, and sections* | 2 |
| *Interlinears and paraphrases* | 3 |
| *Commentaries* | 4 |
| *Previous English translations* | 6 |
| Commentary | 8 |
| *References* | *191* |
| *Index* | *199* |

# INTRODUCTION

This book is a commentary on Walter Benjamin's 1923(/1972) essay "Die Aufgabe des Übersetzers," best known in English as "The Task of the Translator," as a guide to reading it. The essay is, after all, both famously brilliant and infamously difficult, not only because to many readers Benjamin's claims seem wildly counterintuitive but because the theoretical underpinnings of those claims are systematically backgrounded, and thus "hidden" from the reader's view. Samuel Weber (2008: 56) calls those claims a "string of powerful if unargued propositions," noting wryly that this makes the essay rather overwhelming. As a result, it is quite easy to attack and dismiss what Bernd Witte (1976) calls the "elitist, esoterical, if not idiosyncratic nature" and "authoritarian and hypertrophic subjectivism" of the "Task" and other early works (both attacks as paraphrased in Gasché 1986: 69–70). It is my task in this book to explore those theoretical underpinnings by mapping out the series of claims and foregrounding their cultural and religious contexts, to help the reader frame and understand what's there.

There have been numerous earlier commentaries on the essay, at least two at book length; in fact one of the two, by Antoine Berman (2008), was published in English translation by Routledge (Wright 2018). Most, however, have taken the form of longish articles that tend to quote selectively and provide a brief interpretation of each quoted passage. Some of these are quite brilliant, in fact—notably those by Jacques Derrida and Werner Hamacher, but several others as well—and I engage them along the way, respectfully presenting their views and offering slight corrections where necessary; those that are less transformative in their readings of Benjamin appear mostly in the "Other commentators" lists at the end of the various numbered passages. The two book-length commentaries, by Berman (2008) in French (and Chantal Wright's 2018 English translation) and by Hans J. Vermeer (1996) in German, are often quite brilliant as well, and wherever relevant I also engage both. Compared with mine, however, both of those

DOI: 10.4324/9781003247227-1

are rather idiosyncratically polemical, Berman seeking explicitly to assimilate Benjamin to his own Romantic vision (downplaying Benjamin's pre-Kantian mysticism), Vermeer comparing Benjamin to his own *skopos* theory and ultimately rejecting the "Task" as utopian thinking. I seek to be more inclusive, engaging Benjamin's own and his idiosyncratic commentators' views on their own terms. (Also, neither Berman nor Vermeer deals with the entire essay. Even though both deal with the "Task" at book length, each only quotes from and comments on about half of the essay.)

None of which is to say, of course, that my reading of the essay is "right" or "accurate." Indeed the difference between Berman's and Vermeer's on the one hand and mine on the other is not that theirs are idiosyncratic and mine is neutral and accurate: mine is equally idiosyncratic. So for that matter is every other interesting commentary on the essay. The chief difference is rather that I do not seek to overturn Benjamin's theological mysticism. I am very far from a believer myself, but I find supernatural mythologies intriguing, in a literary sense, and am glad to allow Benjamin his *donnée*.

## Passages, titles, and sections

To that end I have divided the essay into 78 more or less thematically coherent passages—segments of one to several sentences—in sequence. These cover the entire essay. Reading straight through from #1 to #78, therefore, will give you an expansive experience of reading the essay.

In addition to numbering the passages, I have given them titles—sometimes omnibus titles like "38. Translation's mystical task (4): elevating the source text by transmitting its semantic content as little as possible / Translating vs. the writing of an original work (1): the essential kernel as the part of the original that is not translatable (1): stump and stalk." Each parenthetical number in that title places that part of it in a sequence that constitutes a kind of thematic section. The text seems to me to fall "naturally" into 19 such sections. Most sections consist of four to eight passages. One—"The Logos of translation (#59)"—consists of only a single passage, and that passage is only 16 words long, five of those words a Bible quotation in Greek and another five the German translation of that quotation. Sometimes the passages making up a section are consecutively sequential, as in the first—"Foreclosing on audiences (#1–6)"—and sometimes the sequence is more sporadic, more intermittent, as in "Translational fidelity (#52–58, #60–64, #70, #73)." Either way, I hope the titles will help you organize the trajectory of Benjamin's argument as you read along.

Here is the complete list of sections (and note that some sections overlap, so that a single passage may appear in two or more):

Foreclosing on audiences (#1–6)
Translatability (#7–12, #73–74)
Historicity (#13–18)

Fame (#16–17)
The relationship between languages (#19–24)
After-ripening (#25–29)
The supplementation of intentions (#30–34)
Translation's mystical task (#35–38, #47–50)
The essential kernel as the part of the original that is not translatable (#38–40)
Translating vs. the writing of an original work (#38–43, #45–46)
Hölderlin (#43, #55, #75–76)
The translator's task (#43–45, #51, #69)
Translational fidelity (#52–58, #60–64, #70, #73)
The Logos of translation (#59)
Pure language (#65–69)
Symbolizing and symbolized (#65–67)
The translational tangent touching the circle glancingly (#70, #73–75)
Pannwitz (#71–72)
Holy Writ (#77–78)

Let me underscore that those are not Benjamin's titles, but mine—and indeed that he gives no indication whatever that any part of his essay is to be thought of as sectioned off. The only divisions he provides for his text are paragraph breaks: the essay consists of 12 paragraphs (and Antoine Berman 2008/2018 writes his commentary based on paragraph structure).

## Interlinears and paraphrases

In keeping with Benjamin's overwhelming preference for literal translation (which in #62 he calls an "arcade") as well as with his assertion in the last line of the essay (#78) that *Die Interlinearversion des heiligen Textes ist das Urbild oder Ideal aller Übersetzung* "the interlinear version of the Holy Scripture is the prototype or ideal of all translation," I first present each of the 78 passages in an interlinear box, in which my literal rendition is strung out together with Benjamin's German, each German word printed directly above its English translation.[1] This will not

---

1 Scholars comparing a self-proclaimed "literal" or "word-for-word" translation against its source text often complain that it's not strictly speaking literal—and the same complaint can be lodged against mine, in the interlinear boxes. Sometimes it takes two or more words in English to render a single German word—*seines*, for example, in English can be "of his" or "of its"—and quite often a German separable-prefix verb is stretched so far across a whole sentence, with the preposition at the end, that a really strict literalism would be so difficult to parse as to be less useful.
    For example, in #1 *So setzt auch die Kunst selbst dessen leibliches und geistiges Wesen voraus* splits the separable-prefix verb *voraussetzen* (morphologically "for-out-set") between the main verb *setzen* at the beginning and the separable prefix *voraus* at the end. My "literal" translation there, "So presupposes also the art itself this's bodily and spiritual essence," is therefore not radically or "near-perfectly" literal. A *more* literal rendition would be "So supposes also the art itself this's bodily and spiritual essence pre." One step further: "So sets also the art itself

only give the English-speaking reader with no German a sense of what Benjamin is doing in the German, but will give the stereoscopic reader the kind of word-by-word juxtaposition that Benjamin expressly championed. (When he asks in #2 whether a translation has any force for the reader who can't understand the source text, for example, he is tacitly urging the kind of reading that Antoine Berman called "reading-in-translation.")

The interlinear as a genre, of course, was developed for learners of the foreign language, to make it easier for the foreign-language learner to track the foreign syntax. It has, therefore, the implicit subtext that you *want* to understand the German syntax, and are constantly tracking along from each English word up to its German source text, looking to understand Benjamin better by feeling the syntagmatic flow of his prose. This is what Benjamin himself would have wanted you to do! But of course that doesn't mean you have to do what he wanted. The interlinears have little or no functionality for readers who only want to know what the source text *says*, and have no interest in the syntax and semantics of the foreign language—and there should be no shame in that preference.

Given that this book is designed to serve a wide variety of scholarly readers, professors and postgraduates, therefore, from those with no German and no interest in German to those who can read Benjamin's German original fluently—indeed given that many readers, perhaps even most, will find themselves somewhere in between those extremes—I provide the interlinears as a Benjamin-approved guide to the German words and syntax, but also follow each interlinear up with a paraphrase that tells the reader what the source text says.

This latter of course is what Benjamin strenuously disapproved. But my assumption is that the modern scholarly reader of Benjamin's "Task" is less interested in theological correctness than in exploring the *tensions* between the word and the sentence, as Benjamin puts it—between strict interlinear literalism and a looser paraphrase of the sense. In any case, as we'll see, Benjamin himself moved from a dogmatic binary between *Treue* "fidelity" (good) and *Freiheit* "freedom" (bad) to a recognition of the fidelity that informs true freedom and the freedom that invigorates true fidelity.

## Commentaries

Following the interlinear and the paraphrase in each passage comes the commentary proper. This is of course the book's main burden, and each commentary engages a representative sampling of the relevant critical literature on that passage;

---

this's bodily and spiritual essence for-out." The point to remember is that "pure" or "perfect" literalism is indeed impossible, except in very rare short passages, often in the kind specially constructed to illustrate such perfection; and therefore that a "literal" translation is *always* an approximation, a workaround, designed above all to give the *impression* of literalism. Literalism, to put that differently, is always a phenomenology rather than an ontology.

Introduction  5

but, as I say, like every other reading of Benjamin's essay mine too is somewhat personal and idiosyncratic.

Chief among my new contributions to scholarship on Benjamin's essay, perhaps, is the one that informs my main title, *Translation as a Form*: I have never seen another scholar arguing that by *Übersetzung ist eine Form* (#7) Benjamin means that translation is a *Platonic* Form. Implicit in that reading, but made explicit in the commentaries to #9, #12–18, and other passages, is the recognition that for Benjamin the Platonic Forms of the original and the translation, and of the source and target languages, are vitalistic agents driving the "sacred history" (*Heilsgeschichte*) toward the messianic end of pure language. And, by extension, I have also never seen another scholar arguing that Benjamin's quotation of the first five words of John's Gospel (#59) tacitly invokes the Jewish Neoplatonist Logos mysticism of Philo Judaeus—the notion that the Logos is a quasidivine demiurgic being who controls the vitalistic force of Plato's Forms.

Other takes on the "Task" that you'll find here and nowhere else include:

- #5, #13, #33: Reading Benjamin's passing phenomenological remarks as a transitional bodying-forth of his transcendental metaphysics. Werner Hamacher's (2001/2012: 539) suggestion that those remarks constitute a phenomenology of the non-phenomenon, or an "aphenomenology," is similar; but, as I suggest in note 6 on pp. 21–22, he and I imagine the process running in opposite directions. My argument is more like Benjamin's remarks constituting a *trans*phenomenology of the phenomenon—turning an actual embodied, embedded, extended, enactive, and affective experience into a revelation, or at least intimation, of a transcendental and therefore disembodied truth. In the service of that reading I use J.L. Austin's performativity and, just below, Diltheyan hermeneutics and Bakhtinian dialogism.
- #13: Tracking Benjamin's account of the intertwining of the translation and the original as a *Zusammenhang des Lebens* "intertwining of life" back to Wilhelm Dilthey's coinage of that term in his expansion of Schleiermacherian hermeneutics, and exploring the semantic shift from Dilthey's to Benjamin's usage of the term.
- #13: Translating *das Überleben* as "superlife" and understanding the original's fame as a suprahistorical superpower—a vitalism powered by the Platonic Forms wielded by the Philonian Logos.
- #13, #17: Translating *hervorgehen* in #13 and *entstehen* and *entfalten* in #17 as "to emanate," in the mystical sense promoted by Philo Judaeus and other Neoplatonists in antiquity and by the Jewish and Christian Kabbalists in the Middle Ages.
- #50, #78: Building a bridge from Mallarmé's insistence on the importance of restoring body to and through translation in #50 to the embodiment of the "total text" of the Hebrew Bible in #78.
- #54: Unpacking Benjamin's term *Gefühlston* "feeling tone" through Bakhtinian dialogism.

**6** Introduction

- #60: Reading the Latin *intentio* not only as "intention," as it has usually been read, but also as a tension or a straining, an increase or an augmentation, and as the exertion or the effort that goes into increasing or augmenting.
- #65, #70: Building a "symbolized" link between Benjamin's use of the aura in "The Work of Art in the Age of Mechanical Reproduction" and the ideal translation as a tangent touching a circle only fleetingly and at a single point in #70 through the Kabbalistic text Zohar 1.15a, where we read that "Zohar-radiance, Concealed of the Concealed, struck its aura. The aura touched and did not touch this point."

Just below the commentary for every passage there is a section called "Other commentators"; there I list (without comment) the places in other scholars' work where they comment on that particular passage. If I have engaged a particular scholar's reading of the passage in the commentary just above, I do not mention that scholar again under "Other commentators," even if the remarks I have just engaged above do not exhaust that scholar's take on the passage. If the remarks that I do engage in the commentary interest you, I encourage you to find the cited place in that source and read around it in search of other illuminating analyses.

You may notice that two or three (or a dozen) of your favorite studies of Benjamin's "Task" are missing from this book. I apologize in advance for those missing titles and perspectives; I have included everything I have been able to lay my hands on, in a language I can read. And, as many scholars have noted, there are a great many such studies, probably more than for any other piece of writing on translation—I have included around 80 of them—and they almost certainly bring a far greater variety of perspectives to bear on this one shortish essay on translation than has been focused on any other theoretical study of translation. It would have been great to include every single one in every single language! But, alas …

## Previous English translations

Benjamin's "Task" has been translated into English in full four times before, by Harry Zohn (1968/2007), James Hynd and E.M. Valk (1968/2006), Steven Rendall (1997a), and J.A. Underwood (2009). In her 2018 translation of Antoine Berman's 2008 commentary on Benjamin's "Task," Chantal Wright also did a partial translation of the essay, twice, the first directly from the German, the second from Berman's and Gandillac's French translations.[2] (Note that in my References that book appears three times: in French once as *L'Âge de la traduction* [Berman 2008] and in English twice as *The Age of Translation*, as something written by

---

2 Berman selected for commentary, and Wright translated twice—once from Benjamin's German, again from Berman's French—almost exactly half of Benjamin's essay: 2271 of the total 4526 words, in 75 segments of varying lengths, from 5 to 135 words.

Berman [2008/2018] and as something translated by Wright [2018]. Whenever I discuss what Berman wanted to say, I cite Berman 2008 or 2008/2018; whenever I discuss how Wright translated, or how she commented on her own translation, I cite Wright 2018.)

Wherever one or more of those five translations differ(s) significantly from my understanding, or if they unpack a word or phrase that in my paraphrase needs unpacking, I have given their versions—sometimes in the paraphrase, more often in the commentary—and occasionally discussed the differences at some length.

# COMMENTARY

## 0. The title

> Die Aufgabe des Übersetzers
> The Task of the Translator

*Paraphrase*: The Task of the Translator.

*Commentary*: Jacques Derrida (1985: 175) comments that "the title also says, from its first word, the task (*Aufgabe*), the mission to which one is destined (always by the other), the commitment, the duty, the debt, the responsibility. Already at stake is a law, an injunction for which the translator has to be responsible." In his commentary/deconstruction Derrida directs a good deal of attention to the debt, to the translator's responsibility: "The translator is indebted, he appears to himself as translator in a situation of debt; and his task is to *render*, to render that which must have been given" (176).[1]

That is certainly what one would normally think "task" meant, but Antoine Berman (2008/2018: 40) argues that that ordinary sense of task is severely attenuated in the essay. "This is a text," he writes, "that is more preoccupied with translation than with the translator. We could perfectly well replace each occurrence of the word 'translator' with the word 'translation'." The word *Übersetzer*

---

1  Dominik Zechner (2020: 323n12) notes that "the reason Derrida calls Benjamin's translator 'indebted' lies in his understanding of the German term 'Aufgabe' ('task'), which may well be interpreted as the inheritance of a certain debt or responsibility."

DOI: 10.4324/9781003247227-2

"translator" appears 20 times in the text—one of those in the title—and, according to Berman, in not one of those cases does Benjamin specify what the translator must do to carry out his or her responsibility adequately. The ostensible task of the translator in every case is reportedly to achieve a mystical transformation of the source and target languages that no human translator could ever possibly *set out* to achieve. As Hans Vermeer (1996: 99) puts it:

> Wahrheit, Totalität aller Sinne, Verkörperung der Urideen der reinen Sprache und Hinführung auf die Vollendung und Überhöhung des Seins—das soll die Übersetzung leisten. Und nicht etwa ein Original!—möchte man hinzufügen. Oder persönlich ausgedrückt: Das ist die Aufgabe des Übersetzers, der damit weit höher gestellt wird als ein Autor eines Originalwerks.

> Truth, the totality of all meaning, embodying the primordial idea of pure language, and transporting us to the perfection and exaltation of being—that is what translation is supposed to accomplish. And not an original!—one would like to add. Or to put it in personal terms: that is the task of the translator, who is thus ranked much higher than any source author.[2]

Benjamin's idea in Berman's and Vermeer's readings would appear to be that *translation* achieves that transformation, whether the translator wills it or not, and whether the translator is aware of participating in it or not. But actually the transformation is not exactly achieved by translation either, as if that transformation were the *task* of translation; it is simply (or complexly) a kind of inevitable byproduct of translation. It is just sort of what happens when translation takes place. According to Berman there is no task, really.

Berman (2008/2018: 42–44) also goes on to argue intriguingly that in his title and elsewhere Benjamin was drawing on a German Romantic tradition going back to Novalis (1965/1981: 535) linking *die Aufgabe* "the task" with *die Auflösung* "the resolution/dissolution." "The 'task,'" Berman argues, "is always confronted with a state of affairs that needs 'resolving'" (43), including "*solution* in the logical sense (of a problem)," "*(dis)solution* in the chemical sense (of a substance)," and "*(re)solution* in the sense of musical harmony" (43). This all seems a bit of a stretch, from *die Aufgabe* to *die Auflösung*, until Berman quotes one of Novalis's fragments, to the effect that "die Poesie löst fremdes Daseyn in Eignen auf" (quoted in Berman 48n42). Chantal Wright translates that as "Poetry dissolves the foreign within itself" (43), but it could be rendered more closely as "Poetry dissolves foreign being/presence/existence in its own [being/presence/existence]." "The task of poetry," therefore, Berman concludes, "is the dissolution of the foreign in its true essence, language" (43). In the abstract, this still seems somewhat far-fetched; but see the commentary to #51 for conclusive evidence that Berman is right.

---

2  Except where otherwise indicated, all translations from the German are my own.

The other interesting challenge to the usual reading of Benjamin's title as promising to specify a "task" to be performed by a human being called a "translator" comes from Paul de Man (1986, 2000). Drawing our attention to Benjamin's self-admitted failure as a practical translator himself, of Baudelaire and Proust, de Man notes that in the normative understanding of the work the translator fails *by definition*: "The translator can never do what the original text did. Any translation is always second in relation to the original, and the translator as such is lost from the very beginning" (2000: 20). Hence de Man's suggestive re-translation of *die Aufgabe* as "the surrender, the giving up." That is, after all, what the word means morphologically, and how it is used in certain contexts:

> If the text is called "Die Aufgabe des Übersetzers," we have to read this title more or less as a tautology: *Aufgabe*, task, can also mean the one who has to give up. If you enter the Tour de France and you give up, that is the *Aufgabe*—"er hat aufgegeben," he doesn't continue in the race anymore. It is in that sense also the defeat, the giving up, of the translator. The translator has to give up in relation to the task of refinding what was there in the original. (20)

This obviously flips the whole title on its head, and from that upside-down position actually reflects the passivity that Berman, de Man, and Vermeer insist Benjamin more or less casually assigns to the translator much better than the translation of *die Aufgabe* as "the task." The only real task in the essay is performed by "the languages," as vitalistic agents with transcendental intentions; those agents are inadvertently triggered by translations, and translations are rather haplessly cobbled together by translators.

Now this reading of the title and the essay it problematically encapsulates is plausible, and attractive; I myself argued a similar case in Robinson (1996: 201). Working on this commentary, however, has directed my attention much more closely to the text than on previous readings, and that has changed my mind. The fact is that Benjamin does specify that the translator's task is to translate literally, so as to transfer source-textual syntax (rather than sense) into the target language and in that way to maximize the friction between the two languages; and he gives us several quite practical takes on that.

In #44, for example, he says that "the task of the translator lies in finding that target-language intention that awakens the echo of the source text"—a task that sounds a bit strange, perhaps, and not immediately accessible to practical application, but not impossibly mystical. The phrase could very well awaken the imaginative translator's practical sense to new possibilities.

In #69 "it is the translator's task to transcreate the source text in which pure language is imprisoned, in order to unleash in the target language that pure language that is spellbound in the source language." That sounds not only mystical but like a task set the hero of a fairy tale; but Benjamin goes on to illustrate his definition of that task with actual examples: "For pure language's sake the translator smashes through the target language's rotten barricades: Luther, Voß, Hölderlin, and George all pushed back the boundaries of the German language." Again, the reference to pure language sounds mystical, but if we read that in the opposite direction, he seems to be saying that the translator's task is to push back the boundaries of the target language, and that that *does* serve pure language. (Certainly it would seem a stretch to argue that in translating the Bible Luther was guided by a mystical translation strategy.[3])

And finally, when he tells us in #76 that Friedrich Hölderlin's German translations from the ancient Greek of Pindar and Sophocles are "prototypes of their Form," we learn that the translator's task is to do what Hölderlin did—translate not only literally but etymologically, so that the *sense* of the source text drops away and leaves only the letter, fidelity to the letter, or radical literalism. He also gives us a chilling account of the phenomenology of that task: in those brilliant translations "lurks the most appalling primal peril of all translation: that when the gates of language have been so savagely sprung they may slam shut and enclose the translator in silence. The translations of *Antigone* and *Oedipus Rex* were Hölderlin's last work. In them sense plunges from abyss to abyss until it risks losing itself in the bottomless pit of language." This would be the most radically extreme version of the translator's task; and, according to Benjamin, the willingness to incur that spiritual risk made Hölderlin's translations prototypical, better (and holier) even than "the most perfect translations."

So upon further reflection I think Berman is wrong about replacing every reference to "the translator" with "translation"; his reading works with most of those references, but not with all. I also think that de Man was partly wrong about Benjamin conceiving the translator's task as "giving up," and that I too was partly wrong to follow de Man in *Translation and Taboo*. Throughout most of the essay, yes, the agents with a "task" to perform are not translators or translations but vitalistic languages, which are only triggered indirectly by translation and more indirectly still by translators; but that is not the only approach Benjamin offers to the phenomenology of translating. It now seems to me, therefore, that Derrida was also right: Benjamin does in the end—not all the way through, but at least in the end—write "The Task of the Translator" about the task of the translator.

---

3   But see Louth (1998: 9) for the suggestion that in his Bible translation Luther extended not only elite literary German by mobilizing colloquial German for literary use but also low colloquial German by translating key passages literally—and, further, that in so doing Luther was simply putting into practice Jerome's claim in the letter to Pammachius that he translated sense for sense *except* in translating scripture, where even the word order contains a mystery. Antoine Berman (2008/2018), like Louth (13–45), correctly takes this literalism to be the core of German Romantic translation theory, from Bodmer to Hamann and Herder to the Schlegel brothers, Novalis, Schleiermacher, and Humboldt, with the first important practical application of that theory by Voß; but Louth also makes the important point that it was actually an ancient mystical practice that was later *adopted* by the Romantics, especially by the stratagem of extending the mystical veneration for the divine to human authors.

**12** Commentary

*Other commentators*: Balfour (2018: 751), Baltrusch (2010: 124), Bannet (1993: 582), Benjamin (1989/2014: 87), Fenves (2001: 161), Flèche (1999: 97–98), Gelley (2015: 170), Liska (2014: 233), Pence (1996: 87).

## 1 Foreclosing on audiences (1): the existence of the human

> Nirgends erweist sich einem Kunstwerk oder einer Kunstform gegenüber
> Nowhere proves itself to an artwork or to an artform vis-à-vis
>
> die Rücksicht auf den Aufnehmenden für deren Erkenntnis fruchtbar. Nicht
> the look back at the receiver for its recognition fruitful. Not
>
> genug, daß jede Beziehung auf ein bestimmtes Publikum oder dessen
> enough, that every relationship to a specific public or its
>
> Repräsentanten vom Wege abführt, ist sogar der Begriff eines
> representatives from the way leads away, is in fact the concept of an
>
> ›idealen‹ Aufnehmenden in allen kunsttheoretischen Erörterungen vom
> "ideal" receiver in all art-theoretical discussions from
>
> Übel, weil diese lediglich gehalten sind, Dasein und Wesen des
> evil, because these merely held are, presence and essence of the
>
> Menschen überhaupt vorauszusetzen. So setzt auch die Kunst
> human in general to presuppose. So presupposes also the art
>
> selbst dessen leibliches und geistiges Wesen voraus – seine Aufmerksamkeit
> itself this's bodily and spiritual essence – his attention
>
> aber in keinem ihrer Werke.
> however in none of its works.

*Paraphrase*: In the appreciation of art, no orientation to the receiver is ever fruitful. It's not just that every invocation of a specific public or its representatives is a wrong turning; it's also that in all art-theoretical discussions the concept of an "ideal" receiver is "from evil," since all such discussions do is stipulate the existence and essence of human beings. Yes, art does assume that humans exist, body and soul; but it does not require their attention.

*Commentary*: This radical foreclosure on the response of audiences to art lies at the core of Benjamin's argument in the piece. His contention throughout is that art, and specifically high verbal art, great literature, is a force unto itself, and does not need a human response. In fact Betsy Flèche (1999: 96) goes further and suggests not only that translations "are not intended to enable the reader to comprehend a piece of writing," but also that "the translation is an object distinct from the original—even distinct from the translator—which survives by living away from the original (temporally, spatially, and linguistically)." More generally, she adds that "the object of Benjamin's essay is to re-evaluate literary work away from authorship and originality, and away from polemical determinism (meaning, message, content). The original's content, its author's intention, its translator and the translator's understanding of the original are not significant to the afterlife of the translation" (96).

Any attempt to drag literature down into the informational marketplace of communication, therefore—the transmission of messages from one human to another—will only distort and demean the true essential power of the verbal arts. We will see in #9 that the study of language and literature can only achieve its greatest possible heights if it is not limited to the efforts of human beings; in #11 that translatability is an essential intrinsic property of any great work of literature even if no human being is ever able to translate it; and in #26 that studying how human beings use the language of a source text to explain the temporal changes in that language over the centuries is "the crudest psychologism," in that it confuses the *Grund* "ground" or "root cause" of the change with its *Wesen* "Essence," which is "the ownmost life of language and its works."

Werner Hamacher (2001/2012: 487) rephrases Benjamin's point here with the kind of philosophical circumspection that Benjamin the metaphysician tended to eschew: "Just as thinking in terms of speakers and addressees is insufficient—since speakers and their audiences occur only *because of* language, and as its functional extreme—so, too, must we move beyond the propositional content of a language." "Insufficient" is obviously far more reasonable than *von Übel* "from evil"—for which Zohn has "detrimental," Rendall "spurious," Underwood "an evil," Hynd and Valk "vitiates." (Note that *das Übel* in German is not an active, demonic evil—not a vitalistic agent of evil, which would be *das Böse*—but rather whatever isn't good.) The pragmatist might argue that while moving beyond the communicational nexus of speakers and addressees ontologically we can, and indeed should, still pay attention to the phenomenology of communication; but Benjamin, at least this early in the essay, is having none of that. (See note 6 on pp. 21–22 for an account of the shifts to come.)

Note also in passing that Benjamin's supposed justification for this foreclosure on readers—that imagining an ideal reader entails nothing more than recognizing the existence of human beings—might be read anachronistically as a misreading (*avant la lettre*) of phenomenological response-oriented criticism and theory. It's obviously not the *existence* of audiences that those theorists posit, but the *mutual shaping* of art by artists and audiences, and that entails far more than the mere existence of human beings. It entails what Mikhail Bakhtin (1934–35/1981) calls the dialogicality of human communication, and more generally the post-Kantian social-constructivist view that what seem like truths and realities are constructed in and by groups. But this is a model of human knowing with which early mystical Benjamin would have had no patience.

Another trenchant analysis of Benjamin's "utopian" project in the "Task" comes from Hans J. Vermeer (1996), the founder of the *skopos* theory of translation, who not only limns in that theory throughout his book but cites or paraphrases such fellow *skopos* theorists as Justa Holz-Mänttäri and Christiane Nord. One would of course expect Vermeer to be ill-inclined to read Benjamin sympathetically: if one believes as he does that the *skopos* or professional purpose of a translation for the target reader in a specific use-situation is the key to the translator's ability not only to translate but to construct the source text as meaningful and to mobilize the target language as communicatively available for target-textualization, Benjamin's foreclosure on the target reader will not inspire confidence. But in fact Vermeer does due diligence. He devotes 250 pages to a close, thoughtful examination of every apparently counterintuitive claim Benjamin makes in the essay, testing it for even minimal applicability to *die reale Welt* (199) "the real/tangible world"—and comes, almost apologetically, to the conclusion that "Benjamins Theorie ist Utopie" (199): "Benjamin's theory is utopia."[4]

Antoine Berman (2008/2018) reads the Benjamin of the "Task" as a Romantic: "In putting it this way, we are aligning Benjamin's thought with Romantic thought, which conceived of criticism and translation as ensuring the in-finitization of the literary text. We will see if this interpretation is truly licit" (108). And it is certainly true that early Benjamin shared many views in common with the Romantics. The early Romantics, however, were Kantians, and their intellectual and artistic progeny over the past two centuries have been post-Kantians, insistent that their metaphysics is grounded in the imagination rather than accurate perception/understanding.[5] The Benjamin of the "Task" by contrast is a traditional essentializing metaphysician, confident that he possesses an accurate understanding of the transcendental underpinnings of universal reality. Berman's

---

4   Thanks to Dilek Dizdar not only for mailing her spare copy of Vermeer (1996) to me in China but also for providing anecdotal background from her years as Vermeer's colleague at Germersheim.

5   Berman (2008/2018: 129) agrees with Benjamin's non-Kantianism here: noting that *rein* "pure" is a very Kantian term, signaling the non-empirical or *a priori*, including "the pure forms of intuition, the categories of understanding, the concepts of reason"; and, noting further that "extending Kantianism ... was Benjamin's project in the years 1919–1920," Berman states that the Benjamin of the "Task" is doing something very different. What that different thing was from Berman's point of view, however, was Romantic, tied to Hölderlin, who, he admits, "could also have borrowed from Kant whom he viewed as the 'Moses' of the German nation." But then all of the early Romantics read Kant that way. Indeed Kant was the Moses not only of the German nation, and of the Romantic Nationalists who became increasingly militant in their promotion of that nation—which wasn't to exist as a political entity until nearly three decades after Hölderlin's death—but of modern (aka "post-Kantian") philosophy, as the formulator of the so-called Copernican Hypothesis: just as Copernicus hypothesized that humans on earth do not stand still and watch the heavenly bodies revolving around them, but are in motion and see the planets and stars from a variety of distorting perspectives, so too did Kant hypothesize that we do not view empirical reality objectively but rather make objects conform to our *a priori* knowledge (1787/1929: 22). Insisting that Benjamin was not a Kantian Idealist but a Romantic is just a way of saying that he shared the same philosophical orientation but applied it to poetry rather than reasoning. And indeed Berman's project is to rescue Benjamin from the pre-Kantian and pre-Romantic essentialism of his mystical/magical/religious thinking.

See also Tanaka (2002), Homburg (2018: ch. 5), and Weber (2008: 63–65).

project of rescuing Benjamin from that "religious" essentialism for Romanticism is admirably quixotic in a double sense, namely that Don Quixote is himself both absurdly wrong and a Kantian *avant la lettre*. We love Don Quixote precisely because he is so passionately convinced of his absurd views that he transcends madness and comes to embody and exemplify the state of fallible human cognition (let's say Peircean fallibilism) in a post-Kantian universe.

The fact that early Benjamin is a pre-Kantian a full century and a half after Kant published his revolutionary works does, however, create problems for his reception. He sounds so much like a Romantic that we expect him to be a Romantic; and when he makes claims that are patently pre-Romantic, even apparently *naively* pre-Romantic, we expect him to justify himself, explain himself, critically engage the Romantic/Kantian views that he is so puzzlingly flouting—and he doesn't. He never does. Typically he argues by mere assertion—dismissing both superficial common sense and deeper and more transformative views, grounded in what for us are now two-plus centuries of post-Kantian epistemology, not by engaging them thoughtfully but with an irritated aside.

One is tempted to say that he wrote the piece for readers who already agree with him; but then he would retort that taking the reader into consideration is never fruitful.

One quite common strategy in citing Benjamin, in fact, is to quote him piecemeal, out of context—or even to build a thinly plausible accommodation of some vaguely remembered point and claim that he said it, without quoting. The same, of course, has long been widely done with the Bible. I had the idea early in my planning for this commentary that I would collect such absurdities and devote paragraphs in specific passages to showing in detail how wrong they are; but I decided in the end that the less said about such solecisms the better.

*Other commentators*: Bellos (2010: 208), Britt (1996: 53), de Man (2000: 16–17), Flèche (1999: 102), Hamacher (2001/2012: 535), Jacobs (1975: 755–56), Pan (2017: 36), Porter (1989: 1067), Smerick (2009: np), St. André (2011: 112–13), Steiner (2010: 48), Vermeer (1996: 144), Wurgaft (2002: 379), Zathureczky (2004: 202).

## 2 Foreclosing on audiences (2): the author–reader relationship tracked by *gelten*

Denn kein Gedicht gilt   dem Leser, kein Bild   dem   Beschauer, keine
For   no   poem   yields to the reader, no   image to the viewer,   no

Symphonie der   Hörerschaft. Gilt   eine Übersetzung den   Lesern, die
symphony  to the audience.   Yields a   translation   to the readers that

das Original nicht verstehen?
the original  don't understand?

*Paraphrase*: For no poem has value or force for a reader, no picture for a viewer, no symphony for an audience.

Does a translation have value or force for a reader who cannot understand the source text?

*Commentary*: João Ferreira Duarte (1995: 273) reads these opening salvoes against audiences—against taking the receivers of art into consideration in the evaluation or other understanding of art—as modernist slogans. No poem is written for the reader, because (#4) no poem has anything to say to the reader. Compare Archibald MacLeish saying in "Ars Poetica" that "A poem should not mean / But be," and Wallace Stevens titling a poem "Not Ideas About the Thing But the Thing Itself." In #8 we will see Benjamin assuring us that "translation's law is the translatability of the source text": this too, Ferreira Duarte argues, is derived from modernist precepts, in particular

> what we could call the low rate of informational content of a literary work. A passage towards the end of the essay [#73] makes it clear that for Benjamin predominance of content in a work renders it untranslatable (81; 20). Translatability, then, belongs to a poetics that aims ultimately at redefining literature in accordance with a modernist standpoint, reminding us of the very similar role played in the Russian formalist context by the concept of literariness. (273)

Liska (2014: 243) similarly refers Benjamin's conception of the literary text to "a central value of modernist poetics: the transgression of conventional meaning in view of a singular literary creation."

But this reading rests on a rather naïve binary, according to which a source text either *says something to the reader* (and thus is a non-literary text that for Benjamin wallows in the gutters of the marketplace) or *says nothing to the reader* (and thus is a literary text that exists primarily on a superhuman or transhuman plane). The German verb for what I paraphrased in the previous paragraph as "is written for" is *gelten*, here in the third-person singular indicative, *gilt*: *Kein Gedicht* **gilt** *dem Leser*. *Gelten* is an extremely important and extremely problematic keyword for Benjamin in this essay. Chantal Wright (2018: 53) argues that "The relevant meaning in 'The Task of the Translator' is that of *gelten* as an intransitive verb meaning 'to be addressed to or destined for' with an overtone of one of its other meanings 'applies to'"; and indeed Zohn (69) and Hynd and Valk (298) translate *kein Gedicht gilt dem Leser* as "No poem is intended for the/its reader," Rendall as "No poem is meant for the reader" (151), and Underwood as "no poem is aimed at the reader" (29).

Antoine Berman (2008/2018: 50) dismisses as utterly misleading Maurice de Gandillac's similar French translation, "Une traduction est-elle faite pour les lecteurs qui ne comprennent pas l'original?", which Wright translates into English as "Is a translation made for readers who do not understand the original?" (2018: 59). Berman's own preferred French translation is "Une traduction *vaut-elle* pour les lecteurs qui ne comprennent pas l'original?" (51), which Wright translates as "Does a translation *apply* to readers who do not understand the original?" (59). Wright herself favors "pertain" as a translation of *gelten*: "Does a translation pertain to readers who do not understand the original?" (2018: 53).

In #4, however, Benjamin himself paraphrases *gelten* along considerably narrower lines: *der Gedicht* **sagt** *dem Leser nichts* "the poem *says* nothing to the reader." For Benjamin, *gelten* is all about conveying a message, "constating," communicating propositionally. This is unmistakably a strawman argument. If the poem *says* nothing—if it has no constative *message* or *meaning* to communicate to readers—it doesn't communicate at all. And if it doesn't communicate to readers, the reader is irrelevant to any literary work as an autonomous artwork.

One significant challenge to this train of thought might come from J.L. Austin's (1962) notion that even ordinary language is not for conveying or constating semantic information (saying things) but for performing actions (doing things). What action, we might ask, is the poem performing to or for the reader? What does a translation *do* to the target reader with words? Asked that way, Benjamin's *gilt*-question becomes less of a strawman and so harder to dismiss. We could also push that reframing one step further through Jacques Derrida's (1972/1988) deconstruction of Austin, which is all about the communication not of *messages* but of *force* (see Robinson 2013a: 89–103 for discussion): one billiard ball striking another obviously communicates not verbal messages but force. Derrida starts his deconstruction there in order to read Austin's performativity precisely as a communication of force. Thus perhaps: "No poem communicates a force to a reader"; "Does a translation communicate a force to the reader who doesn't understand the original?" Asked that way, the question is harder to answer with a "no, never."

Wright also usefully defines *gelten* more broadly as including the semantic fields "'to be valid,' 'to count,' 'to be worth,' 'to apply'; or 'to be considered as', for example *die Fahrkarte gilt in allen Bussen* (the ticket is valid on all buses), *ihre Stimme gilt* (her vote counts), *das Geld gilt nicht viel* (the money isn't worth much or doesn't carry much weight); *hier gilt die StVO* (the Highway Code applies or is applicable here); *er gilt als Fachmann* (he's considered an expert)" (53). But now rethink those usages through the lens of Derrida's remarks on the communication of a force: *die Fahrkarte gilt in allen Bussen* could also be translated as "this card *has the force* of a ticket on all buses"; *ihre Stimme gilt* could be "her vote *wields force*" (or perhaps "her vote *has the force* of a voice"); *das Geld gilt nicht viel* "the money doesn't *have much force*"; *hier gilt die StVO* could be "the Highway Code is *in force* here"; and *er gilt als Fachmann* could be "he *is assigned the force* of an expert."

Etymologically *gelten* is related to *das Geld* "money"; both derive from a more narrowly focused Old High German sense of the verb *geltan* as "to pay." Hence the range of value-related usages in Modern German like "to be valid" and "to be worth": various objects and social activities *have the force* of money, even when no money changes hands. If you have a ticket, you can be broke and still board any bus. You don't need money for your vote to count; your choice in the ballot box has the same *value* or *worth* (or force) as a rich person's vote.

English "gild" and "gilt," however, are not cognates: both come not from *geltan* but from "gold." The English cognate of *gelten* is actually "to yield," and that is what I have used in the interlinear. Since as Wright notes *gelten* tends to work both ways, A having an effect on B or B having an effect on A, *gelten* as "to wield force" can also be *gelten* as "to yield to force." One more trial translation of "Gilt eine Übersetzung den Lesern, die das Original nicht verstehen?", then, would be either "Do readers who don't understand the original yield to (the force of) a translation?" or "Does a translation yield to (the force of) readers who don't understand the original?"

These retranslations, of course, would no longer be Benjaminian strawman questions, rhetorical questions designed, with an implicit "no" answer, to protect the autonomy of the literary work from the depredations of reader-response theory.

*Other commentators*: Bellos (2010: 208), Benjamin (1989/2014: 87), Berman (2008/2018: 56–57, 59–60), Biti (2019: 251), Britt (1996: 53), Chapman (2019: 17), Cohen (2002: 102), Hamacher (2001/2012: 535), Jacobs (1975: 756), Johnston (1992: 44), Rendall (1997b: 187), Smerick (2009: 57), St. André (2011: 112–13), Weber (2008: 56), Zathureczky (2004: 202).

## 3 Foreclosing on audiences (3): against translation as repetition of the same

| Das scheint hinreichend den Rangunterschied im | Bereiche der | Kunst |
| That seems amply the status difference in the realm | of the art | |

zwischen beiden zu erklären. Überdies scheint es der einzig mögliche
between both to explain. Beyond this seems it the only possible

Grund, ›Dasselbe‹ wiederholt zu sagen.
reason "the same" repeatedly to say.

*Paraphrase*: That would seem to explain the difference in status between original works and translations. It also seems to be the only possible reason for saying "the same thing" over and over.

*Commentary*: There is a puzzling syntactic jump somewhere here. *Das* "That" at the very beginning of the first sentence would seem to refer to the rhetorical question about the value or force of monolingual readers of translations in the second sentence of #2. But it's difficult to imagine how that question might explain the difference in status between original works and translations. In fact the progression from the first to the second sentence in #2 would almost seem to *equate* originals and translations: if readers don't wield any force for source texts, they obviously don't wield any force for translations. That is a structural parallel that may not definitively equate them, perhaps, but doesn't distinguish one from the other, either (see #6 for a similar structural parallel). *Es* "it" in the second sentence refers back to the same rather vague antecedent—and there is nothing there that would provide a possible reason for saying the same thing over and over.

Best guess: Benjamin is hinting at the wrong-headedness of people who don't agree with #1 and #2. If you're stupid enough to think that art is made for audiences, you're stupid enough to believe the normative notion that translation is just repeating or reproducing the semantic content of the source text, and therefore that translations are inferior to originals.

Of course he says nothing explicitly about such people in #1 or #2, which is why it is so difficult to identify an antecedent for "that" and "it."

There is also the uncomfortable fact that Benjamin himself argues in #38–40 that translations are intrinsically and therefore universally inferior to source texts. That would seem to throw up obstacles in the path of reading the two sentences of #3 along the implied tonal lines of contempt and ridicule for people who believe such things.

Here Carol Jacobs' (1975: 756) comment is germane: "'Die Aufgabe des Übersetzers' dislocates definitions rather than establishing them because, itself an uncanny translation of sorts, its concern is not the readers' comprehension nor is its essence communication."

*Other commentators*: Bellos (2010: 208), Sandbank (2015: 215), Smerick (2009: np), Vermeer (1996: 152).

## 4 Foreclosing on audiences (4): literature says little or nothing to the reader

| | | | | | | | |
|---|---|---|---|---|---|---|---|
| Was | ›sagt‹ | denn eine Dichtung? Was | teilt | sie mit? | Sehr wenig | dem, |
| What | "says" | then a poem? | What shares | it with? | Very little | to him |

der sie versteht. Ihr Wesentliches ist nicht Mitteilung, nicht
that it understands. Its essentiality is not with-sharing, not

Aussage. Dennoch könnte diejenige Übersetzung, welche vermitteln
constating. However could that very translation that to convey

will, nichts vermitteln als die Mitteilung – also Unwesentliches. Das
wants, nothing convey but the with-sharing – i.e., inessentiality. This

ist denn auch ein Erkennungszeichen der schlechten Übersetzungen.
is then also a recognition-sign of the bad translations.

*Paraphrase*: If we think of a poem as written for readers, what does that poem "say" or "communicate" to those readers? Very little to readers who understand it. Its essence is not communicational. And a translation of that poem that seeks to convey the source text's semantic content accurately to a target reader can convey nothing but a message, which has nothing to do with the source text's Essence. This is how you can recognize bad translations.

*Commentary*: Benjamin here echoes Philip Sidney's famous dictum in his *Defence of Poesy* (1595), in response to the Puritan charge that poets are liars, that "The poet never lieth, for he nothing affirmeth." The commentary in #2 casts a very different light on this line of argument, of course. Benjamin wants us to believe that the choice is between (a) the poem "saying" something to the reader and (b) the reader being completely irrelevant; but if what the poem *does* to readers is wield some kind of force, and that doing is reciprocal, so that readers are also doing something forceful to the poem, then the dynamic takes on a very different cast. It's interesting to note that in retheorizing language as doing things to people with words, and not as conveying information, in the 1955 William James lectures at Harvard, three decades after Benjamin's "Task," J.L. Austin himself fell into exactly the same constative trap, in arguing that "Walt Whitman does not seriously incite the eagle of liberty to soar" (1962: 104): no, but Walt Whitman *is doing something* with those words, performing an indirect speech act with them, such as encouraging his readers to cherish and promote democracy.

The interesting follow-up question to that reframing, of course, would consider what indirect speech acts translators perform in translating. Annie Brisset (1991) offers an interesting example of that kind of translatorial indirect speech act in her reading of Michel Garneau's 1978 translation of *Macbeth*, the first play to be written and performed in *joual*, the Québécois dialect of French. When Macduff says

> I cannot but remember such things were,
> That were most precious to me. Did heaven look on,
> And would not take their part!

and Garneau translates

> C'que j'ava's d'plus précieux dans l'monde, chu t'oblige d'commencer
> A m'en souv'nir. Comment c'est que l'bon dieu peut laisser fére
> Des affe'res pareilles? Sans prende la part des faibes!

Brisset notes that "The wording of this resolution [to remember, in *m'en souv'nir*] echoes the declaration *Je me souviens* ('I remember') which is such a prominent feature of Québécois social discourse. (It is on every vehicle's license plate.) Injunctions such as this, that closely link words to deeds, are called *performatives* in speech act theory" (126). The indirect performative or perlocutionary force of *m'en souv'nir* is to make the audience remember the slogan and the political conditions that it was designed to recall.

According to Benjamin, of course, this would be a bad translation—or else, if he were to dismiss Annie Brisset's reading of *m'en souv'nir* as just her imagination, and to argue that Garneau never intended to remind his audiences of local politics, it would be an irrelevancy.

*Other commentators*: Bellos (2010: 208), Benjamin (1989/2014: 88), Berman (2008/2018: 57–59), Britt (1996: 51), Chapman (2019: 17), Cohen (2002: 102), Derrida (1985: 179), Engel (2014: 3), Ferris (2008: 62), Jacobs (1975: 756), Liska (2014: 236), Pan (2017: 36), Sandbank (2015: 215–16), Smerick (2009: np), Vermeer (1996: 152), Weber (2008: 56), Zathureczky (2004: 148).

## 5 Foreclosing on audiences (5): what is truly essential in a literary work

| | | | | | | | |
|---|---|---|---|---|---|---|---|
| Was aber | außer der | Mitteilung | in einer Dichtung steht | – und |
| What however | outside of the | with-sharing | in a poem | stands – and |
| auch der schlechte Übersetzer gibt zu, daß es das Wesentliche ist – gilt es |
| also the bad translator admits that it the essential is – yields it |
| nicht allgemein als das Unfaßbare, Geheimnisvolle, ›Dichterische‹? das |
| not generally as the ungraspable, mysterious, "poetic"? that |
| der Übersetzer nur wiedergeben kann, indem er – auch dichtet? |
| the translator only reproduce can, insofar as he – also poetizes? |

*Paraphrase*: Apart from a message, though, what is there in a poem? Even bad translators will admit that it is an intangible, mysterious, "poetic" thing, which the translator is supposedly only capable of translating if "he" is also a poet.

*Commentary*: It's hard to tell whether Benjamin is stating what he believes to be true here, or caricaturing what he takes to be the established view. The "intangible, mysterious, 'poetic' thing" is definitely the standard normative view, and it seems that Benjamin accepts it too; but the requirement that the translator of that thing must also be a poet is one that he explicitly rejects in #42–43, and here at least implicitly places in question.

We might in fact take the performativism of Austin and Derrida broached in the commentaries to #2 and #4–5, especially the idea that a poem might wield a performative force that is not necessarily propositional or generally verbal, to be a phenomenological working out of what Benjamin here mystifies as "an intangible, mysterious, 'poetic' thing."[6] By the same token, what Chantal Wright identifies

---

6   In my reading Benjamin begins the essay with a strong and rigid binary between the (refused) phenomenology of communication as grounded in the situated embodiment of social animals

as the reciprocity of *gelten* makes it possible to explore the ways in which the "intangible, mysterious, 'poetic' thing" that Benjamin identifies "in" a poem might actually be part of a performative force that readers project *onto* or *into* the poem.

*Other commentators*: Bellos (2010: 208), Rothwell (2009: 260), Smerick (2009: np).

## 6 Foreclosing on audiences (6): the translator should not serve the target reader

| | | | | | | |
|---|---|---|---|---|---|---|
| Daher | rührt in der Tat | ein zweites Merkmal der | | schlechten | | |
| Thence stirs | in the deed | one second feature | | of the bad | | |
| Übersetzung, welche man demnach als eine ungenaue Übermittlung eines | | | | | | |
| translation, | which one therefore as an | | imprecise transmission | | of an | |

and the (embraced) theology or metaphysics of ideal form and vitalistic growth as posthuman or transhuman mysticism, but as he progresses increasingly realizes that his mysticism too is phenomenologically grounded—that the phenomenology of reading and writing and speaking and translating and so on is either an earth-bound metaphor for the transcendent or simply how we humans experience the transcendent.

This is not a common reading of Benjamin, but it is one that I also find at work, in somewhat different terms, in Werner Hamacher (2001/2012: 539):

> The philosophies of language, the theories of cognition and philosophies of history with which Benjamin was confronted in his work were, whether programmatically recognized under this title or not, all phenomenologies. They were arranged following the logic of possible phenomena, their laws and constraints. As minimally empirically as they might have proceeded, as phenomenologies, the domain of that which could not become phenomenon or contribute to it had to be suspect or else remain buried for them. In the domain of languages, there is prima facie nothing that could not qualify as a phenomenon—as a morphological, semantic, syntactical, or rhetorical phenomenon. When Benjamin turns his attention to translation as the irreducible structure of language, he turns to it as a form that is without doubt a linguistic phenomenon, but that as language presents a liminal phenomenon between languages, encompassing no independent content.

A phenomenology of the non-phenomenon: hm. "For this reason," Hamacher adds, "Benjamin's philosophy of language is an aphenomenology; it holds for a dimension that does not enter into appearance and a law that designates not the constraints on possible appearance but rather structural buriedness [*Verborgenheit*]" (539).

Yes, but what we take to be "structurally buried" may be an intuitive projection arising out of preverbal/preconscious *Andeutungen* "intimations" (#20) that are indeed phenomenological in the usual sense of lived/situated/embodied experience. As my reference to the *Intensität* "intensity" of *Andeutungen* "intimations" in the previous sentence suggests, in fact, we find that very formulation in Benjamin as well: see #19 for his insistence that "it is impossible for translation to lay bare that hidden relationship, or to manufacture it; but to body it forth, to make it real germinally or intensively, that it can do," and the commentaries to #19–20 for the argument that "body[ing] it forth" and "mak[ing] it real germinally or intensively" is precisely the kind of preconscious phenomenological embodiment that Hamacher wants to call "aphenomenological" but to my mind is more like "transphenomenological."

> unwesentlichen Inhalts definieren darf. Dabei bleibt es, solange die
> inessential content define may. At that remains it, so long the
>
> Übersetzung sich anheischig macht, dem Leser zu dienen. Wäre sie
> translation itself an effort makes to the reader to serve. Were it
>
> aber für den Leser bestimmt, so müßte es auch das Original sein.
> however for the reader determined, so must it also the original be.
>
> Besteht das Original nicht um dessentwillen, wie ließe sich dann die
> Stands the original not for that's sake, how let itself then the
>
> Übersetzung aus dieser Beziehung verstehen?
> translation out of this relationship understand?

*Paraphrase*: Bad translation is a sloppy transfer of a trifling content. And as long as we think of translation as intended to serve the target reader, we will never get past that. After all, making the translation serve the target reader would also make the source text serve the source reader. And if the source text was not created for the source reader, how can the notion of serving the reader help us understand translation?

*Commentary*: There is nothing new here that either has not been spelled out clearly in #1–5 or else is not a truism with which it would be difficult to argue. The truism, of course, would be the first sentence defining bad translation. The difference between what we usually mean by "Bad translation is a sloppy transfer of a trifling content" and what Benjamin wants to say with it, however, is that the commonsensical truism highlights the word "sloppy," while Benjamin would highlight the word "content." For Benjamin a translation is bad if it (a) seeks to transfer semantic *content*, which (b) is *trifling* not in the abstract but in comparison with what Benjamin considers "the essential" in translation, and (c) tends to get done *sloppily* because translators who imagine their task along these commonsensical lines are for him by definition bunglers.

*Other commentators*: Bellos (2010: 208), Britt (1996: 53), Pfau (1988: 1083), Rothwell (2009: 260), Smerick (2009: np), Weber (2008: 56).

## 7 Translatability (1): translation is a Form

> Übersetzung ist eine Form. Sie als solche zu erfassen, gilt es zurückzugehen
> Translation is a Form. It as such to grasp, yields it to go back
>
> auf das Original.
> to the original.

*Paraphrase*: Translation is a Form, and to understand it as such, we are compelled to revert to the source text.

*Commentary*: *Übersetzung ist eine Form* has proved difficult to parse. Zohn and Rendall both translate it as "translation is a mode"; Andrew Benjamin (1989/2014: 89) renders it "translation is a model." The question that one might put to all three of them, "a mode(l) of what?", might also be put to a translator (like Underwood, Hynd and Valk, or Wright—or me) inclined to render it literally, as "Translation is a form." A form of what?[7]

Fortunately, (Walter) Benjamin recurs to that claim throughout the essay, with enough contextual variation to enable us to guess at the meaning. In #41, for example, he tells us that the great work the Romantics did as translators was informed by "a feeling for the Essence and worth of this Form"—translation *felt*, Romantically, as a Form. In #43 he tells us that "After all, given that translation is a Form in its own right, so too is the translator's task its own Form, which must be distinguished from that of the poet."

In #28 it seems to mean something like "genre"—translation as a genre—but a boosted sense of genre, an augmented and transcendentalized sense that soars high above the professional marketplace of literature professors and booksellers, indeed that in effect launches the literary category or type called "genre" up into the ionosphere of the Platonic Realm of Forms. In secular social-semiotic terms, a genre is a grouping or class organized by social conventions that have developed over time and vary across space; in Plato's mystical terms, which the early Benjamin of the "Task" would certainly have favored, a genre is simply the first earth-bound copy of the transcendental Form of that type of literature. *Übersetzung ist eine Form* as "Translation is a Form."

This Platonic reading seems particularly pressing in #8, up next, where he says that the translatability of a literary work can be understood in two ways: as depending either on whether any human is able to translate it (the pedestrian pragmatism that he attacks throughout) or, *eigentlicher* "more properly, more authentically," on whether its *Wesen* "Essence" allows translation and its *Form* "Form" demands it. (If "Form" meant genre, it wouldn't be "demanding" anything.) In #9 Benjamin hints at the importance of excluding human engagement from consideration, and that would strongly suggest the validity of a Platonic mysticism in the Essence of translation as a Form. In #10 he offers a roundabout analogy that similarly hints at the Platonic Realm of Forms: the translatability of a great literary work is like the unforgettability of a person, in that even if the person has been forgotten by every living human, s/he may still be remembered by God. And #11 rounds that out by asking rhetorically whether we should not regard a work as translatable even if no human translator ever proved able to translate it.

---

7   Indeed Rendall (1997b: 167) begins his article on the "Task," which immediately follows his translation in the special Benjamin issue of *Traduction, Terminologie, Rédaction* (*TTR*), with precisely an amalgamation of this question: "A form or mode of what?"

In #73 we find a similar formulation: "How well a translation can assimilate itself to the Essence of this Form depends objectively on the source text's translatability." If "the Essence of this Form" is transcendental, no human translation will ever fully correspond to it: in Platonic copy theory every successive copy is worse than the previous one, and no earthly copy can ever attain the pristine perfection of the transcendental Form (which is of course "objective" in a pre- or proto-scientific sense). And when he says in #76 that "Hölderlin's translations are prototypes of their Form," we may take him to be setting Hölderlin's radical etymological/morphological translations of Sophocles and Pindar up as the greatest *human* copies of the transcendental Form of translation; study of those prototypes, therefore, will give us the strongest possible sense of what that true mystical Form must be like.

*Other commentators*: Bellos (2010: 209), Berman (2008/2018: 62–64), Derrida (1985: 179), Engel (2014: 7), Ferris (2008: 63), Hamacher (2001/2012: 487, 499), Kohlross (2009: 98–99), Smerick (2009: np), St. André (2011: 113), Vermeer (1996: 154), Weber (2008: 56–58).

## 8 Translatability (2): whether it depends on a human translator's skills

Denn in ihm liegt deren Gesetz als in dessen Übersetzbarkeit beschlossen.
For   in it   lies  this's law   as in this's    translatability   decided.

Die Frage   nach der Übersetzbarkeit eines Werkes ist doppelsinnig.
The question after the translatability  of a  work  is double-sensed.

Sie kann bedeuten: ob    es unter  der Gesamtheit seiner Leser   je
It can  mean:    whether it among the totality    of its readers ever

seinen zulänglichen Übersetzer finden werde? oder, und eigentlicher:
its    adequate     translator  find   will?  or,  and more properly:

ob     es seinem Wesen nach   Übersetzung zulasse und demnach – der
whether it its   essence toward translation   allows and thereby  – to the

Bedeutung dieser Form gemäß    – auch verlange. Grundsätzlich  ist die
significance of this form according – also demands. Fundamentally is  the

erste Frage    nur problematisch, die zweite apodiktisch zu entscheiden.
first question only problematic,  the second apodictic   to settle.

*Paraphrase*: Translation's law is the translatability of the source text, and it lies hidden inside the source text. A work can be translatable in either of two senses: whether among all of its readers a translator able to translate it is ever found, or, more authentically, whether its Essence allows it to be translated and its Form demands that it be translated. Answering the first question is problematic; answering the second is apodictic.[8]

*Commentary*: What makes the question of finding a human translator capable of translating a given literary work problematic can also be thought on two levels: on the more superficial one, it has to do with the relative difficulty of the source text and the relative translation skill of the human translator, and the impossibility of being 100 percent certain of either. How difficult does a text have to be to translate for that to count as a problem? How good does a translator have to be at translating that specific text for the translation that results to count as a translation? This is the commonsensical level on which we typically think about translatability. On a deeper level, what makes the question of finding a good enough translator problematic is that the whole event occurs on the human level. For early mystical Benjamin that guarantees that it will remain mired in complications that are ultimately irrelevant to the transcendental Essence of the Form.

The "apodictic" answer to the question of the translatability of the Essence and Form of translation is of course even more problematic to readers who care deeply about the empirical basis of human life, and scoff at apodictic claims; but it is clear that the apodictic voice is the voice of a true believer.[9] (Hynd and Valk render "apodictic" as "a matter of demonstration" [299], which tends to talk Benjamin's apodicticism down off the platonizing ledge into precisely the kind of deductive reasoning that early Benjamin despised.) If the Platonic reading of #7 is at all accurate, and Benjamin's idea is that the translatability of the source text is the law of translation as a transcendental Form, his passionate conviction in the absolute truth of that law is akin to the one powering Plato's Socrates in his many recountings of the eschatological myths that later shaped Christian theology (see e.g. Annas 1982).

The interesting question would then be whether Benjamin gives us enough information to sketch in the details of this transcendental Form of translation. We do know that translatability is the *Gesetz* "law" of translation but not a characteristic of its Form; indeed it is only when the Form of the great original *Dichtung* "poem" (any prototypically great literary work) demands translation that translatability becomes the law of translation. We also know that reproducing the semantic content of the source text is *not* a characteristic of the Form of translation.

In the next two dozen passages Benjamin does sketch in many details of the translational Form. In #13–18 he explores the historicity of the translation as the superlife or ongoing life of the source text, which as it were (#17) "emanates"

---

8  Incontrovertibly and absolutely true; not subject to question or challenge.
9  It may be, of course, that the passionate conviction that the essay evinces in the absolute truth of the law of translatability is embodied not in the author but in some unnamed and uncharacterized narrator who is *not* the author; because Benjamin gives no direct indication of such a split subjectivity, however, a reading of that sort must remain speculative.

good translations when it reaches the age of its fame. ("Emanates" is not Benjamin's term, though in the paraphrase of #13 I've translated *hervorgehen* "to arise from, to go forth from" with that mystical verb, and in #17 I've done the same with *entstehen* "arise, emerge, come into being"—and hinted in the commentary there that *die Entfaltung* "the unfolding" could also be an emanation.) In #19–24 we learn that translation bodies forth and propels into motion the relationship between languages, leading toward the messianic end of pure language. In #25–29 he explores the *Nachreife* "after-ripening" of both the source text and the translation after the era of the former's genesis, and warns specifically against reducing such changes in both the source language and the target language to changes in human social practices (he calls that reduction "the crudest psychologism"). In #30–34 he covers the ways in which translation precipitates and agitates the supplementation of intentions in the source and target languages, and thus contributes to the messianic movement toward pure language, and in #35–38 he defines translation's mystical task as probing languages to see how close they are to the messianic end of their history. In #38–40 he explains that the source text contains that aspect of the translation that does not transmit a message, which is the kernel that cannot be translated: translatability may be the *law* of translation, but *un*translatability is a critical aspect of its Form.

The importance for Benjamin's thought of the *-bar* "-able" and *-barkeit* "-ability" suffixes (here in "translatable" and "translatability") from his earliest works to his last has received notable attention, most prominently perhaps in Samuel Weber's 2008 monograph *Benjamin's -abilities*, but also in Alexei Procyshyn's (2014) nuanced response to Weber through the lens of the affordance theory of meaning developed by Chemero (2009). Procyshyn's point is that Weber explores the grammatical surface structure of Benjamin's -abilities without delving more deeply into the cognitive deep structure of the affordance as "an organism-relative feature of an environmental niche that provides an opportunity for, and structures action" (380n10). Of the four types of affordance model that Chemero discusses, Procyshyn finds the dispositional model most appropriate for Benjamin, as it sees "the manifestation of affordances [a]s always relative to the 'interactivity' of properties distributed among environment, things, and organisms" (380n10).

This is a productive rethinking of Weber—who, to be fair, does delve much more deeply into Benjamin's -abilities than the grammatical surface. The only problem with Procyshyn's affordance-theoretical reading is that he never identifies the Benjaminian agent whose reciprocal/participatory (extended, embedded, enactive) perception of the source text generates and mobilizes the affordances to translate it. Indeed in Procyshyn's two sentences that essay a translational application of affordance theory—"Some texts thus *afford* translation" (377; emphasis Procyshyn's) and "a translatable text bears within itself a transformative potential (as yet unschematized) that can be made manifest" (378)—*there is no agent* to participate in the animal–environment relationality that generates and mobilizes affordances. There is only an environment, namely the source text, and its static properties "that can be made manifest"—a phrase that echoes Chemero's account of the disposition model, which he specifically rejects because it *lacks* "the 'interactivity' of properties distributed among environment, things, and organisms."[10]

Benjamin's own discussion of translatability and mediability suggests that the agent is actually the Platonic Form (#7), or perhaps the Logos that manages the Form (#59); but can we really track the development of affordances in demiurgic entities or vitalistic Essences? The most interesting possibility, of course, would be the one suggested in Benjamin's title: the *translator* is the agent whose dynamic interactivity with editors and readers and writers and texts and languages and cultures generates and mobilizes affordances that lead to the creation of a target text that "bears within itself a transformative potential" that advances the sacred history toward its messianic end of pure language. See Robinson (forthcoming-a) for a more detailed account.

*Other commentators*: Baltrusch (2010: 118), Bellos (2010: 209), Berman (2008/2018: 64–66), Derrida (1985: 179–80), Gelley (2015: 20), Hamacher (2001/2012: 487–88), Smerick (2009: np), Steiner (2010: 48), Vermeer (1996: 91).

## 9 Translatability (3): the value of excluding the human

> Nur das oberflächliche Denken wird, indem es den selbständigen Sinn
> Only the superficial    thinking will, in that  it  the self-sufficient sense
>
> der    letzten leugnet, beide für gleichbedeutend erklären. Ihm gegenüber
> of the last   denies,  both for synonymous     explain. To it opposing
>
> ist darauf     hinzuweisen, daß gewisse Relationsbegriffe   ihren guten,
> is thereupon to point out that certain relational concepts their good,
>
> ja     vielleicht besten Sinn  behalten, wenn sie  nicht von  vorne
> indeed perhaps best   sense keep    if   they not from outset
>
> herein ausschließlich  auf den Menschen bezogen werden.
> on     exclusively    to  the humans   tied    become.

*Paraphrase*: Given a choice between defining translatability in terms of the capabilities of human translators and in terms of the transcendental Form of translation, only the superficial thinker will deny the independence of the latter and claim that both come to the same thing. Certain relational concepts are best served by pulling back from an exclusive focus on human beings.

10 Among the several significant points Procyshyn misses in his reading of Chemero is that for Chemero (2009: 145) it is precisely the misguided notion that there are static "properties" in the environment and the animal, and that the properties in the environment simply "become manifest" in any animal that enters it, that fatally wounds the disposition model.

*Commentary*: This passage might be read as a cautious way of urging us to ignore human beings altogether, and focus exclusively on translation as it stands in the Platonic Realm of Forms; but it's more complicated than that. Benjamin does want to engage human history; he just doesn't want to attribute what Aristotle would have called translation's efficient cause (the antecedent condition that brought translation about) to human activities. The efficient cause is a transcendental vitalism that mobilizes humans as its lower-level agents. For that matter, Benjamin is also constantly at pains to attribute translation's material cause (the stuff out of which translation is made), formal cause (translation's defining characteristics), and final cause (translation's purpose) to transcendental vitalisms; but not only does he recognize throughout that humans are involved in some way, at some stage, but also as he moves through the essay he focuses more and more attention on what humans contribute, indeed what one particular human, Friedrich Hölderlin (#75–76), contributed brilliantly to the prototypicality of human translation.

Hans J. Vermeer, whose *skopos* theory is focused on the practical professional final cause of translation, concludes from this exclusion of the human from causality that

> die Theorie [Benjamins] erweist sich als Utopie. Sie ist nicht realistisch, zumindest deshalb nicht, weil der Glaube verlorengegangen ist, der die ermöglichen könnte, jene Mischung aus jüdischer hartnäckiger Beharrlichkeit und Mystik mit einem messianischen Erlösungs- als Vollendungsglauben, den es einfach nicht mehr gibt. (1996: 91)

> [Benjamin's] theory turns out to be a utopia. It is not realistic, at the very minimum because the faith that could have made it possible has been lost, that mixture of Jewish stubborn persistence and mysticism with a messianic belief in redemption-as-perfection that simply no longer exists.

Paul de Man (2000: 26) rather gleefully called Harry Zohn (70) out for his mistranslation of the last line in the passage as "It should be pointed out that certain correlative concepts retain their meaning, and possibly their foremost significance, if they are referred exclusively to man." It should of course be "if they are *not* referred, etc." But then de Man himself resorted to surprising extremes in his campaign to debunk Benjamin's mysticism. Hans Vermeer may be wrong to claim that *der Glaube verlorengegangen ist* "the faith has gotten lost"—just as "es ist doch der Mensch, der zählt, nicht die Sache der Übersetzung" (1996: 199), "it is to be sure the person who does the counting, not the fact(-s/-uality) of translation," so too is it *der Mensch, der glaubt* "the person who does the believing," not the belief or the faith that either "exists" or "gets lost"—but Paul de Man was emphatically a person in whom the believing had gotten lost. Reading Benjamin, he couldn't even summon up the literary scholar's as-if belief in fairy tales, but must debunk everything he read by putting absurdities in Benjamin's mouth.

It is tempting to link this attack on two Jews—the debunking of Benjamin and the repeated crowing about Zohn's mistranslations—to de Man's war-time Nazi anti-Semitism; but the "Conclusions" piece on Benjamin came at the end of his life, after three-plus decades of brilliant theorizing and the friendship and admiration of many prominent Jewish scholars, notably Geoffrey Hartman and Jacques Derrida. His motivations for the skewed response to Benjamin and Zohn must, perhaps, remain an open question.

*Other commentators*: Balfour (2018: 755), Biti (2019: 252), Ferris (2008: 64), Hamacher (2001/2012: 488), Liska (2014: 234), Procyshyn (2014: 377), Weber (2005: 74, 2008: 90).

## 10 Translatability (4): as existing in the mind of God

> So dürfte von einem unvergeßlichen Leben oder Augenblick gesprochen
> So might of an unforgettable life or eyeblink spoken
>
> werden, auch wenn alle Menschen sie vergessen hätten. Wenn nämlich
> become, even if all humans it forgotten had. If namely
>
> deren Wesen es forderte, nicht vergessen zu werden, so würde jenes
> this's essence it required, not forgotten to become, so would be that
>
> Prädikat nichts Falsches, sondern nur eine Forderung, der Menschen
> predicate nothing false, but only a requirement that humans
>
> nicht entsprechen, und zugleich auch wohl den Verweis auf einen Bereich
> don't meet, and likewise also well the reference to a realm
>
> enthalten, in dem ihr entsprochen wäre: auf ein Gedenken Gottes.
> comprise, in which it met were: to a memory of God.

*Paraphrase*: Translatability is like unforgettability: even if a life or a moment had been forgotten by every living human, it could still be considered unforgettable if its Essence demanded that it be remembered. It would only be a (transcendental) demand to which humans had been unable to respond. What makes that demand manifestly transcendental, in fact, is that the failure of humans to respond to it also constitutes a reference to a kingdom in which it would be fulfilled, namely God's memory.

*Commentary*: God's memory is important here because the translatability-analogue in this passage is specifically unforgettability. Even if humans don't remember, God does. The transcendental Form of translation doesn't necessarily entail a divine memory; divine memory is an analogue for transcendental translatability. Hence Rendall's translation, which cuts a semantic corner in order to make the passage's analogical implications for the Form of translation explicit: "a reference to a *thought* in the mind of God" (1997a: 152; emphasis added).

This is in fact the only mention of God in Benjamin's essay; note, however, that in what Theodor Adorno titled the "Theological-Political Fragment" (date contested, but Gershom Scholem insisted it was written in 1921,[11] the same year as the "Task") Benjamin wrote of "das Reich Gottes" (the kingdom of God) and "das Gottesreich" (God's kingdom; quoted in Jacobson 2003: 21). See also Zathureczky (2004: 185n425) for the suggestion that this image of God's memory is an allusion to "the Jewish tradition according [sic] which only God remembers perfectly."

Werner Hamacher (2001/2012: 492) notes that Benjamin first broached the image of the life that is *in essence* unforgettable (as opposed to "in human memory") four years before the 1921 writing of the "Task," in his essay on Dostoevsky's *The Idiot* (written in 1917, published in 1921). He also adds trenchantly that, "just as the unforgettability of a life overtaxes every remembrance, so the translatability of a language overtaxes every translation" (492).

*Other commentators*: Derrida (1985: 182), Gelley (2015: 21), Jacobs (1975: 765), Liska (2014: 234), Pan (2017: 42), Pfau (1988: 1086), Sandbank (2015: 215), Smerick (2009: np), Steiner (1975/1998: 66), Weber (2008: 59–61).

## 11 Translatability (5): a work is essentially translatable, even if untranslatable by humans

| Entsprechend bliebe | die Übersetzbarkeit sprachlicher Gebilde | auch dann |
| Accordingly remains | the translatability of linguistic structures | even then |

| zu erwägen, wenn diese für die | Menschen unübersetzbar wären. Und |
| to consider, if these for the | humans untranslatable were. And |

| sollten sie | das bei einem strengen Begriff | von Übersetzung nicht |
| should they that | by a strong concept | of translation not |

---

11 "According to Adorno," Jacobson (2003: 23) reports, "he and his wife met Benjamin for the last time at the end of 1937/1938 in San Remo, Italy. Benjamin reportedly read them the text aloud, referring to it on that occasion as the 'Newest of the New.' Adorno dated the text 1937 accordingly." Gershom Scholem smiled indulgently at that dating:

> I rest assured that these pages were written in 1920–1921 in conjunction with the Critique of Violence and did not entertain a relationship with Marxism at the time. It exhibits a metaphysical anarchism that corresponded to the author's ideas before 1924. Adorno dates the text from 1937. My response is that the date is a jest, to see if Adorno would mistake a mystical-anarchist text for a recently composed Marxist one. Benjamin, by the way, engaged from time to time in such experiments. (quoted in Jacobson 23)

> | wirklich | bis | zu einem | gewissen | Grade | sein? | In solcher | Loslösung | ist die |
> |---|---|---|---|---|---|---|---|---|
> | really | until | to a | certain | degree | be? | In such | detachment | is the |
>
> | Frage | zu stellen, ob | Übersetzung bestimmter Sprachgebilde | zu |
> |---|---|---|---|
> | question | to pose, | whether translation of specific language structures | to |
>
> | fordern sei. Denn es gilt | der Satz: | Wenn Übersetzung eine Form |
> |---|---|---|
> | require be. For | it yields the proposition: | If translation a form |
>
> | ist, so muß Übersetzbarkeit gewissen Werken wesentlich sein. |
> |---|
> | is, so must translatability of certain works essential be. |

*Paraphrase*: The implications of the unforgettability-analogue in #10 for translation as a Form would be, then, that verbal expressions must be translatable even if they prove untranslatable by human beings. Indeed if we define translation rigorously, should they not be that to a certain degree? We must in fact ask whether the translation of some verbal expressions be demanded—for if translation is a Form, it follows that the translatability of certain works must be part of their transcendental Essence.

*Commentary*: Werner Hamacher (2001/2012: 491) glosses this passage: "Translatability is not a demand made by some subject, determinate as ever, on a work or an utterance, but is rather a demand of the essence of every work and, moreover, of language itself, in which it is constituted." The implication—perhaps only arguably, from one perspective—is that the Essence of the work or the language is itself an agent capable of placing demands on the humans involved.

Because the question *sollten sie nicht das?* "shouldn't they be that?" in the second sentence is a bit vague—shouldn't they be what?—Zohn and Rendall both explicitate it, in opposite directions: Zohn has "Given a strict concept of translation, would they not really be translatable to some degree?" (70) and Rendall has "And mustn't they actually be untranslatable to a certain degree, if a rigorous concept of translation is applied?" (153). As I read that line, both are wrong. Each gets only one part of the antecedent. Syntactically, the antecedent to "shouldn't they be *that*" would be the entire previous clause: "[1] verbal expressions [a] must be translatable even if they [b] prove untranslatable by human beings." Rendall is clearly unpacking (1b), the closest bit; Zohn is unpacking (1a), the arguably "truer" bit. But Benjamin needs the whole comparison: (1ab) translatable-by-God-even-if-untranslatable-by-humans. That is the "that." In addition, without the specification of the two levels or layers, transcendental and human—translatable on the former, untranslatable on the latter—both Zohn's "translatable to some degree" and Rendall's "untranslatable to a certain degree" collapse into ambiguity. Translatable by whom? Untranslatable by whom? (Hynd and Valk and Underwood both refrain from specifying what should be: Hynd and Valk have "should this not be the case" [299], Underwood "ought they not … truly to be so" [31].)

*Other commentators*: Benjamin (1989/2014: 89), Berman (2008/2018: 67), Britt (1996: 54), Chapman (2019: 16), Hamacher (2001/2012: 531–32), Kohlross (2009: 104), Smerick (2009: np), St. André (2011: 109), Steiner (1975/1998: 66, 257), Vermeer (1996: 168), Weber (2005: 74, 2008: 59).

## 12 Translatability (6): essential to certain works

> Übersetzbarkeit eignet gewissen Werken wesentlich – das heißt   nicht, ihre
> Translatability   suits    to certain works    essentially  –  this means not,   their
>
> Übersetzung ist wesentlich für sie selbst,    sondern will    besagen, daß
> translation   is essential   for themselves, rather   wants to say    that
>
> eine bestimmte Bedeutung, die    den   Originalen innewohnt,   sich  in
> a   specific    significance, which in the originals    inwardly lives, itself in
>
> ihrer Übersetzbarkeit äußere.     Daß eine Übersetzung niemals, so gut   sie
> their translatability   expresses. That a    translation   never,   so good it
>
> auch sei, etwas    für das Original zu bedeuten vermag,  leuchtet ein.
> also  be, something for the original to signify    could be, is evident.
>
> Dennoch steht   sie mit  diesem Kraft    seiner Übersetzbarkeit im
> Therefore stands it   with this      power of its   translatability    in the
>
> nächsten Zusammenhang. Ja,    dieser Zusammenhang ist um   so
> next      together-hang. Indeed this    together-hang    is that much
>
> inniger,   als er für das Original selbst nichts    mehr bedeutet.
> inwarder, as  it for the   original  itself nothing more signifies.

*Paraphrase*: Translatability is built into the Essence of certain works. This does not mean that it is essential for the source text that it be translated; rather, it means that a certain significance resident in source texts expresses itself in translatability. Obviously no translation, no matter how good it is, can have the slightest significance for the source text. Still, the translation is closely intertwined with this power of the source text's translatability. Indeed the two are the more closely intertwined precisely because that intertwining no longer means anything for the source text.

*Commentary*: There is a part–whole dynamic running all through Benjamin's imagery in the "Task"—one that we might call synecdochic, in the sense that the part in question, in this case that "certain significance resident in source texts," is the most important part, the defining part that in some sense stands in for the whole. His other terms for that part are *der Kern* "the kernel" and *das Gehalt* "the tenor," especially in #38–40, where the kernel/tenor "contain[s] that aspect of the translation that does not transmit a message," and is therefore "the element toward which the true translator's work is stirred," but that in the translation becomes "untranslatable, because the relation between the tenor and language is different in the source text and the translation." See also #66, which describes the etiology of that kernel—"that generative impulse in the becoming of languages that seeks to body itself forth is the very kernel of pure language"—and the commentary to #76.

Note also the agentive language of "no translation, no matter how good it is, can have the slightest significance for the source text" and "that intertwining means nothing for the source text." It's not clear why anyone would imagine the source text as an agent that either cared or did not care about the translation or its "intertwining" with the kernel of translatability in the source text; but Benjamin clearly needs to underscore the great extent to which the source text *does not* care. At this early stage in the "Task" the powers that care about such matters are transcendental vitalisms operating at a metaphysical level high above the texts and far from the puny humans involved in translating or reading them. Gradually (#52–58, #60–64, #70, #73) he begins to devote more attention to the desirable and undesirable states of the target text as an emptying out of the source text, and then even to individual translators: (#43, #69) Martin Luther, Johann Heinrich Voß, A.W. Schlegel, Friedrich Hölderlin, and Stefan George, but especially, prototypically, (#55, #75–76) Hölderlin.

The interesting slippage in this passage is *gewisse Werken* "certain works." There is a Platonic Form of translation, and that Form is built into the Essence not of the prototypical literary work, say, but of "certain works"—presumably the ones that J.A. Underwood calls "pieces of fine writing." This seems a bit *ad hoc* for a Platonic cosmology of literary translation—and that observation would in turn seem to justify Zohn's and Rendall's mundanization of *Die Übersetzung ist eine Form* as "translation is a mode": translation is a way of proceeding, a way of getting things done. Perhaps translation is not a Platonic Form after all? Perhaps *das Original* "the original" is not another Platonic Form? Do we need to posit the existence of a Platonic Form for each individual instance of "certain works"? Should we assume that there is a Platonic Form for a certain great work like Joyce's *Finnegans Wake*, say, with translatability built into its Essence? Must each one of those "certain works" be a prototypical copy of its own Platonic Form? Or would it make more sense to posit a Platonic Form for the class of "great literary works," so that, say, Homer's *Iliad*, Dante's *Divina Commedia*, Shakespeare's *King Lear*, Melville's *Moby-Dick*, and Joyce's *Finnegans Wake* are all prototypical copies of that Form? If so, how do we identify the boundary beyond which literary works no longer belong to that elevated category? Do we simply accept the current hypercanon (Damrosch 2006) as transcendentally ordained?[12] Benjamin does finally make his (here quite vague) assumptions clear in #73.

---

12 For a discussion of Benjamin's apparent transcendentalization of the hypercanon of world literature in his *Habilitationsschrift*, published in 1928 as *Die Ursprung des deutschen Trauerspiels* and in

*Other commentators*: Bellos (2010: 209), Berman (2008/2018: 67–68, 77–84), Chapman (2019: 17–19), Gasché (1986: 76), Hamacher (2001/2012: 494), Jacobs (1975: 764–65), Kohlross (2009: 104–5), Procyshyn (2014: 377), Smerick (2009: np), Weber (2008: 62), Wright (2018: 74–75).

## 13 Historicity (1): translation as the superlife and ongoing life of source texts

> Er darf ein natürlicher genannt warden, und zwar genauer ein
> It may a natural named become, and in fact more precisely a
>
> Zusammenhang des Lebens. So wie die Äußerungen des Lebens
> together-hang of the life. So as the expressions of the life
>
> innigst mit dem Lebendigen zusammenhängen, ohne ihm etwas
> inliest with the living together hang, without to it something
>
> zu bedeuten, geht die Übersetzung aus dem Original hervor. Zwar nicht
> to signify, goes the translation out of the original forth. In fact not
>
> aus seinem Leben so sehr denn aus seinem ›Überleben‹. Ist doch die
> out of its life so much as out of its "overlife." Is after all the
>
> Übersetzung später als das Original und bezeichnet sich doch bei
> translation later than the original and betokens itself after all by
>
> den bedeutenden Werken, die da ihre erwählten Übersetzer niemals
> the significant works, that there their chosen translator never
>
> im Zeitalter ihrer Entstehung finden, das Stadium ihres Fortlebens.
> in the era of their emergence find, the stadium of their forthliving.
>
> In völlig unmetaphorischer Sachlichkeit ist der Gedanke vom Leben
> In fully unmetaphorical factuality is the thought from the living
>
> und Fortleben der Kunstwerke zu erfassen.
> and forthliving of the artworks to grasp.

*Paraphrase*: That intertwining can be called natural; more precisely it is an intertwining of life. For in the same way as expressions of life are intimately intertwined with living beings, without having any significance for those beings, so does a translation emanate from the original—not from its life so much as from its "superlife." After all, the translation comes later than its source text, and when

---

John Osborne's English translation as *The Origin of German Tragic Drama* in 1977, see Robinson (2017a: 2–15).

one arises out of a truly significant work—the kind that never finds its chosen translator in the era of its genesis—that indicates that the work has reached the stage of its ongoing life. And when we speak of the life and ongoing life of an artwork, that manner of speaking should be understood as fully unmetaphorical objectivity.

*Commentary*: This is deservedly one of the most famous passages in the essay. As Werner Hamacher (2001/2012: 494) summarizes it,

> it must be said of the language of the original that it does not live [*nicht lebt*] in the translation—already in the original it did not live as itself, but only as its transition toward another—but rather that it lives on or survives [*überlebt*], and that relative to its "own" life and distanced *a priori* from itself, it lives forth or goes on living [*fortlebt*]. Translation is the *a priori* form of a language's living on and living forth in another. (Ira Allen's insertions)

The image of translation as emanating (in German *hervorgehen*, literally "to go forth [in the direction of the speaker]"[13]) from the survival[14] or superlife (in German *Überleben*, literally "overlife" or "overliving") of the original is a powerful one. Both Zohn and Rendall translate *Überleben* as "afterlife" (Rendall adds the gloss "survival"), which has the unfortunate implication that the source text has died and is now a ghost or spirit;[15] Benjamin expressly goes on to talk about *das Leben und Fortleben der Kunstwerke* "the life and ongoing life of the artworks," and contrasts that life with (#27) the dead equivalence theory of translation and

---

13 See Flèche (1999: 97) for the suggestion that *geht die Übersetzung aus dem Original hervor* should actually be translated "the translation wins out over the original, 'comes off victorious from' the original, diminishes the original, apparently, but does not quite kill it." This reading pointedly backs off from de Man's (2000: 24) claim that the translation kills the original, but is in the same imagistic realm of depredations: "The movement to translation from the original is dialectical rather than organic, discontinuous and interruptive rather than progressive. The life of the original cannot be said to be 'continued,' as Zohn's translation would have us think. The translation's life is quite apart from the depleted original—maybe even on another level." Depleted, diminished: not killed.
14 Underwood and Wright give us "survival"; Hynd and Valk give us "surviving life."
15 James St. André (2011: 111) problematically refers to "the terms that Benjamin uses to describe translations (Nachleben and Überleben, both translated as 'afterlife' in the English edition)"—as if (a) there were only one English translation, and (b) it were not a translation but an "edition," authored or at least authorized by Benjamin himself. In fact of course *two* translators render *Überleben* "afterlife," Zohn and Rendall, but St. André only cites a reprint of the one by "Howard Zohn" (118), though he also cites Rendall (1997b), the article that immediately follows Rendall's translation in the special Benjamin issue of *TTR*.

Chapman (2019) also uses "afterlife," but, he notes, "under erasure" (7), with an eye to Spivak's (1976/1997: xiv) "overliving," which he defines along Derridean lines as "constant translation" (16): "not 'after' anything, but a present perfect movement of change, where for a text to exist is for that text to go beyond itself and exceed itself continually" (30).

(#28) the *erstorbene* "having-died" languages posited by that theory. Translating *Überleben* as "superlife," as I do, suggests instead that, so far from dying, the great source text is supercharged, develops superpowers. In #16–17, that superlife is expressly identified as *Ruhm* "fame"—the famous work not as hyped by sheep-like readers (that would be what #26 calls "the crudest psychologism") but as a superhero with God-given powers.

The fact that everything I have said about the original's superlife in the two previous paragraphs seems metaphorical, however, puts that line of thought in tension with Benjamin's claim that "when we speak of the life and ongoing life of an artwork, that manner of speaking should be understood as fully unmetaphorical objectivity." The idea there is that metaphysics is not myth or metaphor or imagination but objective truth, the truest truth. Plato's own mystical metaphor for that reversal in the Allegory of the Cave (*Republic* 514a–520a) is that what we take to be empirical reality on earth is but the flickering of shadows cast in a cave by a fire onto the wall opposite the one to which we are fettered; in order to experience true reality we have to break free of our fetters and go up to the surface of the earth and view the sun—which tropes divinity. The ongoing life of a work of art, in that sense, is more real, more objective, than the life of the human artist who created it, because the life of the artwork is metaphysical—its very Essence as a Platonic Form is real—and the human artist as "copyist" is mere animated matter. Dust to dust. In the mystical underpinnings of Platonic copy theory, the earthly copies of transcendental Forms are the metaphors; the Forms themselves possess fully unmetaphorical objectivity.[16] And what Benjamin is discussing here is not actual literary originals and translations but their transcendental Forms. The original with the ongoing life that is an unmetaphorically objective reality is the Form of the great literary work. The empirical literary work, by contrast, is a dead copy: a book, a commodity, an inert thing made of paper with black marks on it.

James St. André (2011) is on the right track with this, but to my mind oversimplifies it: for his Benjamin "the work of art is alive" (112). Yes, in a sense—but only insofar as the actual physical work of art is a low-level emanation of the transcendental Platonic Form of the work of art, which in Kabbalistic terms is a Kelipot shell that encases and conceals the divine spark it embodies but also can and should be broken to reveal that spark (see the commentary to #57). St. André's error arises from the fact that he sees no connection between the "life" in a work of art and its "form." Since "form" in literary terms tends to be understood as dead structure, and St. André doesn't think to seek out a more vitalistic conception of form, he gives us this: "Benjamin's decision to call translation a 'form' obviously relates to his discussion of the Romantics as concerned

---

16 Presumably the reason Plato has Socrates present the transcendental truth in the form of an allegory—a narrativized metaphor—is so his human interlocutors will be able to *imagine* the transcendental truth. The metaphor is not the truth; it points upward to the transcendental Realm of the Truth.

first and foremost with the form of the work" (113). Benjamin does not write "Translation is artistic form," or "Translation is the form of a work of art"; he writes "Translation *is a Form*." The transcendent Platonic Form is the living spark in the translation; to the extent that translation has a mystical task, that task is performed by the living spark, not by the words on the page that conceal the vitalistic agent living in and working through them.

I agree with St. André that it is precisely because Benjamin's admirers find it so ludicrous to believe that a statue or a painting or a printed poem is alive that they read the fully unmetaphorical "life" of a work of art as a metaphor (115); I just don't think Benjamin ever attributed objectively unmetaphorical life to actual physical works of art. To the extent that they *seem* to be alive, life lives *in* them. They are the material shells for spiritual life—and Platonic Form, especially as read through Philo's Neoplatonist Logos mysticism (#59), is the perfected vitalistic shape, function, and impact of that life. That kind of essentializing spirit–matter dualism is not particularly popular any more; but it is very active in early Benjamin.

The only real difference between this metaphysics and the view of most secular intellectuals today, in fact, is that for secular intellectuals the "transcendental" literary work is an imaginative projection that is sustained by intersubjective agreement among the group of such intellectuals. When we talk about the greatness of *Finnegans Wake*, for example, we don't mean the physical book; we mean the image of Joyce's novel that we hold in our head. That is more or less what Benjamin is talking about as well. For Benjamin, though, it is not a collectively organized and stabilized projection; it is an unmetaphorically objective reality that exists—lives—on a transcendental plane.

One apparent syntactic hitch in the articulation of this position here in #13 is that Benjamin introduces the notion of the supposedly unmetaphorical life of the original analogically, with the conjunction *wie* "as": *So **wie** die Äußerungen des Lebens innigst mit dem Lebendigen zusammenhängen* "So *as* the expressions of life are intertwined with living beings." That telltale *wie* "as" sets the expressions of life up as an analogue of the intertwining of the translation and the source text's translatability.[17] The argumentative trajectory of this analogue is that (1) "the

---

[17] Werner Hamacher (2001/2012: 495) argues that Benjamin puts quotation marks around "Überleben" because he means "living on in citation," which would arguably be another kind of reified analogicality: "This is living on in citation and thus no living on at all, a 'living on' that is only linguistic and yet that still means living on. Language first lives in 'living on,' no longer signifying only its own life in the life of another." In a footnote he also draws our attention to the *Überleben in Zitat* "living on in citation" deployed explicitly by Nietzsche in aphorism 262 of *Beyond Good and Evil*—the source of his suggestion that Benjamin is doing the same (which would effectively be "'living on in citation' in citation")—and directs us to his essay on that subject, Hamacher (1996).

My reading of *das "Überleben"* as "superlife" takes a different tack: the source text's superlife is not linguistic but transcendental, and the quotation marks around it are scare quotes, designed to warn us not to equate it with ordinary biological life on earth.

translation is closely intertwined with this power of the source text's translatability" (#12), (2) "that intertwining can be called natural," (3) "more precisely it is an intertwining of life," (4) "*as* expressions of life are intimately intertwined with living beings, ... so does a translation emanate from the original," (5) "not from its life so much as from its 'superlife'" (#13). The analogy, that is, is primarily between "the intertwinings of translations with their source texts" and "the intertwinings of expressions of life and living beings," secondarily between "translations and expressions of life" and between "source texts and living beings." Hence just as expressions of life emanate out of living beings, so too does a translation emanate out of its source text.

But then comes the definitive shift: "not from its life so much as from its 'superlife'." The source text is an earthly thing; its life transpires on earth as well; the intertwinings of its life with the translation are "natural." But its superlife is supernatural, superhuman, supernal—and it is out of the "fully unmetaphorical objectivity" of that transcendental superlife that the translation emanates.

The *Zusammenhang des Lebens* in the first sentence is a hermeneutical term that Benjamin borrowed from Wilhelm Dilthey (1833–1911), the German philosopher responsible for reviving the hermeneutical thought of Friedrich Schleiermacher (who in turn revived the hermeneutical thought of Johann Gottfried Herder). For Dilthey the *Zusammenhang des Lebens* "intertwining of life" or *Erlebniszusammenhang* "intertwining of experience" was the "autobiographical" phenomenology of one's entire life as experienced historically, not just one moment at a time but one hermeneutical interpretation of life at a time. Morphologically "the together-hang of life," the phrase is traditionally rendered "the coherence of life" (Carr 1986: 76) or "the nexus of life" (Dilthey 2002: 241); but Dilthey is writing about the cohering of experiential interpretations of life, and arguably the abstract philosophical or linguistic image of a "nexus" or a "coherence" is not really adequate for the relationality of disparate entities in translation about which Benjamin is writing. (Also, "nexus" does not give us a convenient verb form for *zusammenhängen* in the second sentence.) The historicity of texts and their hermeneutical interpretations was another key Diltheyan concept that Benjamin borrowed here (#13–18); the fact that in the "Task" he escalated historicity into a mystical vitalism but continued to call it historicity is almost certainly another tacit nod to Diltheyan hermeneutics.[18] To the extent that over the course of his short life that phenomenological historicity became increasingly politicized as a vitalistic basis of fascism, in his middle and late periods Benjamin

---

18 Benjamin does not of course mention Dilthey in the "Task"; nor does he in his *Habilitation* dissertation *Ursprung des deutschen Trauerspiels* (1928)/*The Origin of German Tragic Drama* (1998), written three years after the "Task." In his introduction to John Osborne's English translation of the *Ursprung*, however, George Steiner (1998: 20) notes that in his *Erkenntniskritische Vorrede* (9–44)/"Epistemo-Critical Prologue" (27–56) Benjamin "is working consciously in the current of Schleiermacher and Dilthey"—and it is true that the section of that prologue that Benjamin titles *Idee als Konfiguration* "Idea as Configuration," pp. 34–35 in English, follows Dilthey's hermeneutic closely.

distanced himself from it, and from such elite advocates of it as Ludwig Klages and Carl Jung (see Ulrich 2001: ch. 3, esp. 156–70).

Dilthey's term was picked up by Martin Heidegger in that phenomenological historicizing sense toward the end of *Sein und Zeit/Being and Time* (§77, in the fifth chapter on *Zeitlichkeit und Geschichtlichkeit* "timeliness and historicity"); it also influenced the emergence of Edmund Husserl's phenomenological concept of *die Lebenswelt* "the life-world" (see Carr 1986: 56–57 and 74–77, and, on Heidegger, 80, 86–87, and 107–8). *Sein und Zeit* was of course not published until 1927, six years after the writing of the "Task," and the phenomenologists' overriding concern with the experience of life in the body was alien to early mystical Benjamin; as a result, Dilthey's thought lurks very much under the surface of Benjamin's argument in the "Task," and without blindingly obvious explanatory power.

The transcendentalizing turn by which Benjamin steps away from Dilthey comes in the second sentence: for Dilthey "expressions of life are intimately intertwined with living beings," but (in Benjamin's rereading) "without having any significance for those beings." In Dilthey in fact the phenomenological intertwining of expressions of life does have every possible significance for the living beings who form them, but Benjamin has his theoretical sights set higher: so too, he says, filling out the translation-theoretical target of the hermeneutical analogy, "does a translation emanate from the original—not from its life so much as from its 'superlife.'" We should think of the famous source text as emanating the translation out of its superpowers. In Benjamin's Diltheyan analogy, the source text is the "living being," and the translation is the "expression of life" that has no significance for the source text. Quite a significant turn.

It is perhaps not surprising, therefore, that I have seen no attempt in the literature on the essay to explore the proto-phenomenological legacy in it of Dilthey's *Zusammenhang des Lebens*. (Phelan 2002 comes close, but, like Benjamin himself, does not mention Dilthey.) I have, however, had occasion to speculate—notably in the commentary to #33, but see also the commentaries to #20, #31, #41, #51, and #54—that phenomenology plays a surreptitious role in the "Task," as the source of embodied orientations that Benjamin either projects onto the transcendent or, as he would doubtless prefer to put it, deploys as a material channel of revelation.

The word *Zusammenhang* appears 11 times in the essay, in a variety of different contexts—and indeed "context" is one of its primary translations in the dictionary. In #31 in fact I follow Hynd and Valk in translating it as "context" (301); but, as I read him, Benjamin only uses the word in that linguistic sense when he is writing dismissively of the traditional "dead" theory of translation as a striving for semantic equivalence—i.e., there in #31. He mostly uses it in support of his souped-up Diltheyan suprahistoricizing/vitalistic account of languages as living agents, and in those places (#12–13, #44, #56, #65), as mentioned, I have translated it as "intertwining." In one connection (#29), where he seems to be vacillating between the two interpretive modes, I have followed Underwood in rendering it "connection." Interestingly, Chantal Wright (2018: 74–75) recommends a blanket use of "interrelation" for *Zusammenhang*; because Berman did not select either #29 or #31 for translation and commentary, she was not brought twine to twine with contexts and connections in which "interrelation" not only wouldn't work right but would confuse Benjamin's binary argumentation. (Also, of course, Berman did not notice the unattributed citation of Dilthey.)

*Other commentators*: Bannet (1993: 582), Bartoloni (2004: np), Bellos (2010: 209), Benjamin (1989/2014: 90, 105–8), Berman (2008/2018: 83–89, 94–95), Britt (1996: 50n39, 53), Cohen (2002: 103), Derrida (1985: 178–79), Flèche (1999: 96–97), Gasché (1986: 78), Gelley (2015: 21, 23), House (2017: 41), Johnston (1992: 55n5), Kohlross (2009: 105), Liska (2014: 237), Menke (2002: 94, 96, 223n6), O'Keeffe (2015: 378), Pan (2017: 38–39), Pence (1996: 87), Procyshyn (2014: 380n15), Rendall (1997b: 169–70), Steiner (2010: 48), Uhl (2012: 456), Vermeer (1996: 89), Weber (2005: 74, 2008: 65–67, 90), Weigel (2002: 202), Wright (2018: 75–76), Zathureczky (2004: 201).

## 14 Historicity (2): steering life between organic corporeality and the soul

| Daß  man nicht der    organischen Leiblichkeit    allein Leben zusprechen |
|---|
| That one   not   to the organic      embodiment alone life      attribute |
| |
| dürfe, ist  selbst in Zeiten des     befangensten Denkens vermutet worden. |
| might, has itself  in times of the most biased    thinking surmised become. |
| |
| Aber       nicht darum     kann es sich  handeln, unter dem schwachen |
| However not    thereabout can    it itself handle,  under the   weak |
| |
| Szepter der      Seele dessen Herrschaft auszudehnen, wie es Fechner |
| scepter of the soul   this's    dominion to extend,     as it Fechner |
| |
| versuchte; geschweige daß Leben aus den     noch weniger maßgeblichen |
| sought;     let alone      that life    out of the still   less      substantial |
| |
| Momenten des     Animalischen definiert werden  könnte, wie aus |
| factors      of the animalistic    defined  become could,   as out |
| |
| Empfindung, die    es nur  gelegentlich kennzeichnen kann. |
| sensation,    which it only incidentally characterize   can. |

*Paraphrase*: Even eras beset by the most cramped and closed minds have suspected that life is not to be attributed to organic corporeality alone. On the other hand, however, life's dominion cannot be augmented under the shaky scepter of the soul, as Fechner tried to do, let alone defined based on the less definitive impulses of animality, such as sensation, which is only incidentally found in living things.

**42** Commentary

*Commentary*: That last exclusion, *Empfindung*, is usually translated "sensation," but can also be translated "feeling" (as Underwood has it) or "emotion"; Rendall has "sensitivity." Benjamin is manifestly seeking to steer a middle course between body and soul: animals have bodies and bodies have sensations, and denying that those things are only *gelegentlich* "incidentally" found in living things makes it seem as if he is putting all his life-eggs in the basket of the soul (or, in Underwood, the mind)—but he isn't. The interesting problem he faces is that he wants to attribute life (and especially superlife) to literary works, in "fully unmetaphorical objectivity," though they have neither bodies nor souls. His solution in #15–18 is to associate life with Diltheyan history, or rather historicity, the quality of having a history. That solution serves his purposes well, in that the historical tensions he tracks through translations and their source texts are highly plausible; the only problem is that just invoking history doesn't sufficiently ground his claims about (#13) the "fully unmetaphorical objectivity" of the "life and ongoing life" of original literary works. Yes, literary works have histories; but how does that make them alive? The answer is presumably lodged again in Plato's Realm of Forms—those Forms have neither bodies nor souls, and they are not normally taken to be alive; but in some versions of Renaissance Neoplatonism (especially say Marsilio Ficino, Giordano Bruno, and Tommaso Campanella) they do have vitalistic powers, and thus a vital force that *powers* life (and its historicity). It seems likely that what Benjamin (cryptically) meant by "history" is "vitalism"; why he didn't just come out and say "vitalism" is not clear.[19] As we saw in the commentary to #13, too, the Kabbalistic mythology adumbrated in #57 would suggest that for the early mystical Benjamin the "life" that lived inside great literary works was made up of low-level emanations of the divine, trapped/protected in the Kelipot shells that sheltered revelation from profane eyes.

*Other commentators*: Chapman (2019: 31), Derrida (1985: 179), Gelley (2015: 22), Hamacher (2001/2012: 522).

## 15 Historicity (3): according life to everything that has a history

| Vielmehr nur wenn allem demjenigen, wovon es Geschichte gibt und |
| Rather only if to all that every, wherefrom it history gives and |
| |
| was nicht allein ihr Schauplatz ist, Leben zuerkannt wird, kommt dessen |
| what not alone its scene is, life conferred will be, comes this's |

19 See the commentary to #13 for the observation that with the rise of fascism in the years following the publication of the "Task" Benjamin would have had increasing reason to avoid theorizing Diltheyan historicity vitalistically; at the 1921 writing of the essay, however, the term was still largely associated with Renaissance and Enlightenment esoterics and the German Romantics.

| | | | | | | |
|---|---|---|---|---|---|---|
| Begriff | zu seinem | Recht. Denn von | der Geschichte, nicht von | der Natur | | |
| concept | to its | right. For | from the history, | not from the nature | | |

| | | | | |
|---|---|---|---|---|
| aus, geschweige von | so schwankender wie | Empfindung und Seele, | ist |
| out, let alone | from so shaky | as sensation | and soul, | is |

| | | | | |
|---|---|---|---|---|
| zuletzt der Umkreis des | Lebens zu bestimmen. Daher | entsteht dem |
| finally the circle | of the life | to determine. | Thence emerges to the |

| | | | | |
|---|---|---|---|---|
| Philosophen die Aufgabe, | alles natürliche Leben | aus dem |
| philosopher the task, | all natural life | out of the |

| | | | |
|---|---|---|---|
| umfassenderen | der | Geschichte zu verstehen. |
| more all-encompassing | of the history | to understand. |

*Paraphrase*: It is far truer that it is only when we attribute life to everything that has a history, and is not just history's setting, that full justice is done to the concept of life. For it is on the basis of history rather than nature, let alone such tenuous affairs as sensation and soul, that the circle of life must be defined. Hence the philosopher's task of understanding all natural life in the more all-encompassing terms of history.

*Commentary*: Benjamin's idea in contrasting "things that have a history" with "things that serve as history's setting" would appear to be not to *ex*clude human beings from the category of "natural life," as he seems to be hinting in #8–11, but to *in*clude works of art in the category. The commonsensical assumption would be that literature and the other arts are mere decorations or diversions for living human beings with a history; Benjamin opposes that view.

The slippage between what he calls *alles natürliche Leben* "all natural life" and the supernatural life he calls *das "Überleben"* "superlife" is somewhat problematic here: there is no clear demarcating line between natural life on earth and superlife in the transcendental Realm of Forms. It seems plausible to speculate, however, that Benjamin is working very hard to flesh forth a whole continuum of emanations, as in the creation myth of Kabbalah (see the commentary to #57), where even at the lowest levels the apparently "natural" and "earthly" emanations leak the revelatory light of the higher (transcendent, divine) ones. See also #17, where he refers to the unfolding *eines eigentümlichen und hohen Lebens* "of a characteristic and high life," and it's not clear whether he means one of the highest "natural" earthly levels/forms of life or the supernatural superlife: whatever it is, it's up there somewhere, really high. And in #18 we read about seeking "the purpose toward which all of life's individual purposivenesses strive … not in its own sphere but in a higher one," which would presumably be one (or more?) of those high lives mentioned in #17; but in #18 it's no longer a *Leben* "life" but a *Sphäre* "sphere," and we read on that "All purposive vital phenomena, like their overall purposiveness, are in the end purposive not for life but for the expression of its Essence, for the bodying forth of its meaning." *Not* for life *but* for the expression of life's Essence in that higher sphere: is that Essence of life its superlife?

*Other commentators*: Berman (2008/2018: 101–2), Chapman (2019: 24, 103), de Man (2000: 22–23), Derrida (1985: 179), Ferreira Duarte (1995: 277), Hamacher (2001/2012: 496–97), O'Keeffe (2015: 378), Pfau (1988: 1083), Smerick (2009: np), Vermeer (1996: 90, 161).

## 16 Historicity (4): fame (1): the ongoing life of creative works

> Und ist nicht wenigstens das Fortleben der    Werke unvergleichlich viel
> And is   not   least       the forthliving of the works incomparably   much
>
> leichter zu erkennen als    dasjenige der   Geschöpfe? Die Geschichte der
> easier   to recognize than that       of the creature?  The history    of the
>
> großen Kunstwerke kennt ihre Deszendenz aus den  Quellen, ihre
> great  artworks   knows its  descent    from the sources, its
>
> Gestaltung im     Zeitalter des    Künstlers und die Periode ihres
> formation  in the era      of the artist    and the period  of their
>
> grundsätzlich ewigen Fortlebens bei den nachfolgenden Generationen.
> fundamentally eternal forthliving in  the following       generations.
>
> Dieses letzte heißt,   wo    es zutage tritt,   Ruhm.
> This   last   is called, where it to light comes, fame.

*Paraphrase*: And is it not incomparably easier to recognize the ongoing life of creative works than that of creatures? The history of the great works of art knows their descent from their precursors, their formation in the artist's own era, and the periods of their—in principle eternal—ongoing life among later generations. Wherever that last emerges, it's called fame.

*Commentary*: It is difficult to imagine in what sense it is "incomparably easier to recognize the ongoing life of creative works than that of creatures"; indeed one might be justified in surmising that there might only arise some kind of difficulty in recognizing the "ongoing life" in living creatures if the phrase implied "after death." But of course Benjamin not only never says that the translational *Überleben* "superlife" or *Fortleben* "ongoing life" of a great work of literature begins after the death of the work, but that assumption would be wildly out of alignment with everything else he says about it. As he says here, the life of the work is "in principle eternal," and, as we'll see in #29, for him the ideally eternal life of works is in stark contrast with the "death" of languages and works as imagined in the "dead" theory of translation.

His comparison of that life with the life of creatures here is, however, somewhat problematic. If the ongoing life of creative works begins not after their death but after their "birth"—"their formation in the artist's own era"—the analogous ongoing life of creatures after their birth is quite easy to recognize. It is, after all, what we call "life." What Benjamin seems to be trying to do is to set up the "superlife" and "ongoing life" of creative works on the ancient model of the creaturely afterlife—the "in principle eternal" (because supernatural) life after death—and then to deny that creative works ever die. Because he neglects to explain just how it becomes more difficult to recognize the ongoing life of creatures, of course, this reading—that it is only difficult if creatures die before their lives supposedly go on—must remain speculative.

Antoine Berman (2008/2018) asks pointedly "What bestows 'fame' on a work if not its readers?" (90), and while admitting that "perhaps there is a risk of this here," he suggests an alternative way of understanding that line: what "if 'fame' indicates not so much the author's celebrity as *the sheer glory of the original text*" (90). His suggested translation is *Cette dernière s'appelle, lorsqu'elle vient au jour, la gloire* (89): "The latter is called, when it comes into being, glory" (90). In other words, *der Ruhm* "fame" "glory" is not a social phenomenology but a metaphysically objective quality of the source text. *La gloire/glory* is in fact an accepted translation of *der Ruhm*, though usually only when *la gloire/glory* is understood as a social phenomenology like fame or stardom; in the objectified sense of "splendor" or "magnificence" it would usually be a translation of *die Glorie* or *die Herrlichkeit*. But Berman's suggested translation does tacitly correct for an apparently misleading association in Benjamin's text.[20] See also the commentary to #13 for an intensification of that correction: "the famous work not as hyped by sheeplike readers ... but as a superhero with God-given powers."

Rendering *Im Zeitalter des Künstlers* "in the artist's own era" as *à l'époque de l'artiste* (89) "in the epoch of the artist" (90), Berman also reads that as stipulating that the artist must be dead before the source text's "glory" can possibly generate its ongoing life through translation: the artist's own era, apparently, ends on the day of his or her death. This seems a bit extreme. There is nothing in Benjamin's rather vague sketch of the history of this unfolding that suggests such strict demarcations between the artist's own era and the ongoing life of the work in translation.

Another take on that is offered by Jacques Derrida (1985: 183), who suggests that the author is "dead insofar as his text has a structure of survival even if he is living." This in turn points us down another interpretive path: that the author is "dead" in the sense of Roland Barthes's "The Death of the Author" (1967),

---

20 "Misleading," of course, in the sense of relying too heavily for Benjamin's metaphysics on the opinions of human readers. When Chantal Wright translates this passage directly from Benjamin's German, she makes *der Ruhm* "fame."

dead for the reader of the readerly text. Derrida's continuation of that line of thought—"What is the proper name if not that of the author finite, dead or mortal of the text?" (183)—seems to direct us back to Michel Foucault's riposte to Barthes, "What Is an Author?" (1969/1979), where the author's sociological reduction to a name and the name to a function is another kind of symbolic death.

*Other commentators*: Bannet (1993: 582), Bellos (2010: 209), Benjamin (1989/2014: 90), Berman (2008/2018: 66–67), Britt (1996: 53), Ferreira Duarte (1995: 277), Gelley (2015: 23, 105), Hamacher (2001/2012: 496–97), Menke (2002: 223n60), Smerick (2009: np), Steiner (2010: 48), Vermeer (1996: 79, 155–56), Weber (2008: 67–68).

## 17 Historicity (5): fame (2): good translations emerge when a work has reached the age of its fame

> Übersetzungen, die  mehr als   Vermittlungen sind, entstehen, wenn im
> Translations    that more than transmissions are   emerge   if     in the
>
> Fortleben  ein Werk das Zeitalter seines Ruhmes erreicht hat. Sie   dienen
> forthliving a  work the era      of its  fame    reached has. They serve
>
> daher     nicht sowohl diesem, wie schlechte Übersetzer es für ihre Arbeit
> therefore not  as well this,   as  bad       translators it for their work
>
> zu beanspruchen pflegen,  als daß sie ihm ihr   Dasein   verdanken.
> to claim         tend,    as that it  to it their presence owe.
>
> In ihnen erreicht das Leben des    Originals seine stets erneute  späteste
> In them reaches the life    of the original  its   ever renewed latest
>
> und umfassendste          Entfaltung. Diese Entfaltung ist als die  eines
> and most comprehensive unfolding.  This  unfolding  is  as that of a
>
> eigentümlichen und hohen Lebens durch   eine eigentümliche
> characteristic  and high  life  through a    characteristic
>
> und hohe Zweckmäßigkeit bestimmt.
> and high purposiveness   determined.

*Paraphrase*: Translations that do more than convey a message emanate from the source text when it has reached the age of its fame. This means that they don't exactly serve the source text, as bad translators tend to claim, but rather owe to it their very existence. In them the source text unfolds—in its most all-encompassing unfolding, which is constantly being renewed.

This unfolding constitutes one form of the most distinctive and elevated life, and it is achieved through a distinctive and elevated purposiveness.

*Commentary*: The purposive *Entfaltung* "unfolding" that Benjamin theorizes here is core vitalism. His idea is that the source text is not a dead husk that translators serve by reproducing its semantic content but a living agent that drives the process—emanates the translation during the age of its fame. The translation "owes its very existence" to the source text not by being passively dependent on it, in the sense that there can be no translation if there is no source text that the translator renders into the target language, but rather in the active sense that the source text *brings it into existence*. The source text's superlife brings the power of its vitalistic Platonic Form to bear on the age of its fame and emanates the translation. Indeed "emanation" works as an English translation of *Entfaltung*: the source text *unfolds* the translation. The source text experiences a supervital unfolding in the age of its fame, and that unfolding *is* the translation.

And the unfolding or emanation of the translation out of the source text's superlife is not a mere flowing of energy out of one state and into another: it is *purposive*. It is agentive, vitalistic. What Benjamin is outlining here is not a mere theory of translation, but a cosmogony.

*Other commentators*: Bannet (1993: 582), Bellos (2010: 210), Berman (2008/2018: 93–95, 101), Cohen (2002: 103), Hamacher (2001/2012: 496–98), Jacobs (1975: 757), Kohlross (2009: 106), O'Keeffe (2015: 377), Smerick (2009: np), Steiner (2010: 48), Vermeer (1996: 161), Weber (2008: 62), Zechner (2020: 319).

## 18 Historicity (6): the convergent higher purpose of all the single purposivenesses of life

Leben und Zweckmäßigkeit — ihr scheinbar handgreiflicher und doch
Life and purposiveness — their apparently more tangible and yet

fast der Erkenntnis sich entziehender Zusammenhang erschließt sich
almost the knowledge-self-foreclosing intertwining discloses itself

nur, wo jener Zweck, auf den alle einzelnen Zweckmäßigkeiten
only where that purpose towards which all single purposivenesses

des Lebens hinwirken, nicht wiederum in dessen eigener Sphäre,
of the life work not in turn in this's own sphere,

sondern in einer höheren gesucht wird. Alle zweckmäßigen
rather in a higher sought become. All purposive

Lebenserscheinungen, wie ihre Zweckmäßigkeit überhaupt sind letzten
life's phenomena, like their purposiveness in general, are of last

> Endes zweckmäßig nicht für das Leben, sondern für den Ausdruck
> end purposive not for the life, rather for the expression
>
> seines Wesens, für die Darstellung seiner Bedeutung.
> of its essence, for the representation of its significance.

*Paraphrase*: The intertwining of life and purposiveness seems tangible, yet nearly defies understanding; it is tapped only when that purpose toward which all of life's individual purposivenesses strive is sought not in its own sphere but in a higher one. All purposive vital phenomena, like their overall purposiveness, are in the end purposive not for life but for the expression of its Essence, for the bodying forth of its meaning.

*Commentary*: What seems *handgreiflich* "tangible" is most likely something like a personal sense of purpose—I'm alive and I feel driven to fulfill some purpose in life—or else a collective purpose, as when a group to which one belongs strives to achieve a goal. These would be "life's individual purposivenesses." Benjamin wants to direct our attention not to the fulfillment of such earthly human purposes but to the "higher" sphere that involves the vitalism of Platonic Forms and Essences: "All purposive vital phenomena ... are in the end purposive not for life but for the expression of its Essence." The phenomena pervading the translation of great literary works are of course humanly purposive—finishing this translation, getting paid, getting the translation into print, disseminating it to ever broader audiences, etc.—and those purposes are "of life" and therefore "vital"; but "in the end," which is to say teleologically, they are purposive not for *life on earth* but for the expression of life's Platonic Essence, which is operated out of the transcendental Realm of Forms.

One might feel inclined to read "*not* for life *but* for the expression of its Essence" as setting up a binary whose earthly pole, called "life," is foreclosed in favor of that higher realm far above "life." That reading would seem to overturn the emanational-layering-of-life line Benjamin has been following in the previous passages, where (#13) a translation is not only the life but the superlife of its source text, (#14) life is not to be attributed to organic corporeality alone, (#16) the ongoing life of creative works is much easier to recognize than that of living creatures, and (#17) the source text unfolds in and as the translation, an all-encompassing and ever-renewed unfolding that constitutes one form of the most distinctive and elevated life. But that would be a mistaken impression. In "not for life but for the expression of its Essence" the antecedent of "its" is "life." Benjamin isn't disparaging life; he's layering it metaphysically.

To reiterate the final paragraph of the commentary in #17: the translator's task is "in the end purposive" not for the translator, nor for the target reader, and ultimately not for the translation itself, nor even for the source text, but for the transcendental Essence of the Platonic Form of life. The vital(istic) purpose of translation is, again, to accelerate the holy growth of languages toward pure language; and that purpose is driven by translators only very indirectly, at three removes. At the top it is driven directly by the vitalistic Essence of the Form of life; at one remove it is driven by the vitalistic Essence of the Form of the source text; at two removes by the vitalistic Essence of the Form of the translation; and only at a third remove by the translator, who can at best, through radical literal translation, activate the clashing of languages that fuels and drives the entelechy.

This is the metaphysical model that leads Paul de Man, Antoine Berman, and others to read "The Task of the Translator" as not really about the task of the translator. As I noted in #0, though, that impression is only locally true—not throughout the essay.

*Other commentators*: Bellos (2010: 210), Benjamin (1989/2014: 90), Berman (2008/2018: 102–3), Derrida (1985: 186–87), Hamacher (2001/2012: 500), Wright (2018: 99–100).

## 19 The relationship between languages (1): actualized and represented by translation

> So ist die Übersetzung zuletzt zweckmäßig für den Ausdruck   des
> So is the translation   finally  purposive     for the  expression of the
>
> innersten Verhältnisses der    Sprachen zueinander.    Sie kann dieses
> innermost relationship  of the languages to one another. It  can   this
>
> verborgene Verhältnis  selbst unmöglich offenbaren, unmöglich herstellen;
> hidden        relationship itself  impossibly reveal,       impossibly produce;
>
> aber     darstellen, indem  sie es keimhaft  oder intensiv    verwirklicht,
> however to perform, in that it  it germinally or     intensively realizes,
>
> kann sie es. Und zwar  ist diese Darstellung  eines Bedeuteten durch
> can   it  it.  And in fact is this   performance of a    significance through
>
> den Versuch, den Keim seiner Herstellung ein ganz    eigentümlicher
> the trial,     the germ of its  propagation an entirely characteristic
>
> Darstellungsmodus, wie er im    Bereich des   nicht sprachlichen Lebens
> performance mode,  as   it in the realm  of the not   linguistic       life
>
> kaum angetroffen werden mag.
> hardly met with     become may.

*Paraphrase*: In the end, then, translation is purposed for the expression of the innermost relationship among languages. It is impossible for translation to lay bare that hidden relationship, or to propagate it; but to body it forth, to make it real germinally or intensively, that it can do. And that bodying forth of an *intendendum* through the trial or the germ of its propagation is a thoroughly unique performative mode, one that can hardly be found outside the life of language.

*Commentary*: Dominik Zechner (2020: 319) warns against misunderstanding here:

> It is critical to underscore that Benjamin here refers less to the plurality of languages as such, as a measurable spectrum of multilingualism or a quantifiable number of languages, than to a certain affinity, a kinship among languages through which individual languages enter into a relation with one another. This kinship of languages is what motivates translation's reach, which can only be performed proleptically, as linguistic intensity. It is not presentable extensively, as concretely expressible form, but lies intensively concealed in a manifest translation.

Note that Zechner uses three English keywords there for Benjamin's two German ones, only one of which appears in this passage: "affinity," "kinship," and "relation (with one another)" in Zechner, and *Verhältnis* (#19) and *Verwandtschaft* (#21–23 and #29–30) in Benjamin. Arguably *Verhältnis* is "relation(ship)" and *Verwandtschaft* is either "kinship" or "affinity"; but the concepts bleed into each other. Two siblings can have a relationship based on kinship, and two lovers can have a relationship based on affinity; but people related by blood can feel a mutual affinity as well as kinship, and soulmates may feel related by a spiritual kinship. Benjamin will be at some pains to distinguish the spiritual or transcendental *Verhältnis/Verwandtschaft* of languages from the language families that philologists study; but, as we'll see in #29, he can't let go of philological relatedness entirely. In his view etymological equivalencies were the wormhole through which Friedrich Hölderlin summoned up the wind that strummed the Aeolian harp of his translations of Pindar and Sophocles (#75).

In using "proleptic" to translate Benjamin's term *vorgreifende* "anticipatory," Zechner is drawing on Hamacher's (2001/2012: 513) account of Kant defining anticipation as the basis of all cognition, and basing that account on Epicurus calling the same anticipatory stance πρόληψις/*prólēpsis*.[21] As we'll see in #20, *vorgreifende* "anticipatory" is a pillar of Benjamin's definition of *intensiv* "intensive": what intensifies the performance of translation's reach in and through the affinity or kinship or relatedness of languages is specifically the anticipation of the advent of pure language. In other words, here in #19 *dieses verborgene Verhältnis* "this hidden relationship" is *not* the kind of philological kinship of the sort postulated for language "families," related through etymological/morphological

---

21 Hamacher (2001/2012: 513n19) speculates that Kant knew the Epicurean *prolepsis* from Cicero's *De natura deorum*, where he refers to Epicurus and mentions the term in Greek before translating it into Latin as *praenotio* and *anticipatio*.

"blood," that Benjamin will seem to favor (at least terminologically) in #29. One cannot demonstrate that kinship linguistically. One can only *sense* its concealment in translations—and what one is sensing is the intensity of anticipation.

In terms of the three removes outlined in the commentary to #18, "translation is purposed for the expression of the relationship among languages" at the second remove, from which it is incapable of either "lay[ing] bare that hidden relationship" or creating, producing, propagating, manufacturing it. Those opcrations can only be performed at the top level, in the Realm of Forms, by the vitalistic Essence of the Form of (super)life—specifically, as we'll see in #59, by the Logos. What makes translation significant in this transcendental cosmogony, however, is that even at that second remove, by engaging the source language embodied in the source text at the first remove, it can body it forth. The German verb there is *darstellen*, which is traditionally translated in philosophical contexts as "to represent"—and indeed Zohn, Hynd and Valk, and Rendall all write of *representing* the relationship. But that makes it sound very abstract; morphologically *darstellen* is putting it (out) there, putting it forth, making it widely available (Underwood renders it morphologically as "setting-forth" [33]). As we've seen, Berman translates it *présenter*, which he expressly narrows down to performance (and Chantal Wright translates accordingly). My translation, "body forth," is in the same performative neighborhood, and I shift to "perform(ance)" in the next sentence. I am, in other words, pushing on the German verb a bit: there is no "body" or embodied "performing" in its morphology. But it does seem to me that at this second remove Benjamin would imagine life as embodied, as opposed to the spiritual/transcendental Form of superlife at the top. (Underwood, in fact, renders *Herstellung*, which I make "propagation" and Chantal Wright makes "production," as "bodying-forth" [33].) It would not have a physical body, perhaps, let alone a human one; it would not have sensation. But it would nevertheless be a body in fully unmetaphorical objectivity (perhaps what Deleuze and Guattari call a "body without organs").

The idea would be that by embodying the relationship between the source and target languages the translation doesn't just make it "visible" (as Zohn has it) or "real"—as Benjamin himself hints with the verb *verwirklichen*, "to realize" (as Hynd and Valk, Rendall, Underwood, and Wright have it) or "to make real" (as I have it)—but makes it *active*. The embodied translation *activates* the relationship between languages. Making it real means giving it a bodily channel by which it can contribute materially to the vitalistic growth of languages toward pure language.

What he means by "making it real *germinally* or *intensively*" is less clear, but he hints at his construction of *keimhaft* "germinally" here in #19 and at his construction of *intensiv* "intensively" in #20. His unpacking of "germinally" is subtle: *durch den Versuch, den Keim seiner Herstellung* "through the trial, the germ of its propagation," he writes, with the implication that the germ is a paraphrase of the trial—a restatement or repetition with a figurative shift. Treating *der Versuch* "the trial, test, attempt" as an anticipatory gloss of *der Keim* "the germ" first tropes translation as a sketch, a first draft, a dry run, and then tropes that "beta version" (as it were) botanically as a "germ," the embryo of a seed (and indeed both Zohn and Underwood give us "embryo"). The propagation and ripening of that seed will continue throughout the essay to shape Benjamin's figuration of the messianic growth of languages toward pure language, in the movement from *der Keim* "germ or embryo" (#19, #50) to *der Samen* "seed" (#36) to *der Kern* "kernel or grain" (#38) to *Frucht und Schale* "fruit and skin" (#39). The propagation and growth of a plant as the manufacture of a device, as the growth of languages toward pure language; translation as the germ or trial that kicks it all off.

*Im Bereich des nicht sprachlichen Lebens kaum angetroffen werden mag*—which Zohn (72), Rendall (154), and Underwood (33) translate as "is rarely met with/seldom encountered in the sphere/domain/realm of nonlinguistic life," and Hynd and Valk as "[is] virtually confined to the linguistic province of life" (300)—is paraphrased just above as "can hardly be found outside the life of language." The idea would seem to be that physically embodied life without language, life with sensation but no ability to do things with words—the life of nonhuman animals and plants, obviously, but also the human life of nonverbal communication—is neither germinal for the messianic growth of language nor intensive (for which latter see #20).

Eric Jacobson (2003: 106) tracks Benjamin's early Jewish theology of language in "Über Sprache überhaupt und über die Sprache des Menschen" (1916/1991)/"On Language as Such and on the Language of Man" (1978/1986), noting that "The word was given a divine insignia. It receives the nameless in the name as the translation of languages that pertain to things in human language. For Benjamin, translation is the mode of reception most capable of receiving revelation." But "language as such" does not inevitably or entirely exist on the plane of "the language of [hu]man[s]":

> Daß jede höhere Sprache (mit Ausname des Wortes Gottes) als Übersetzung aller anderen betrachtet werden kann. (Benjamin 1916/1991: 151; quoted in Jacobson 273n96)

> Every higher language (with the exception of the word of God) can be considered a translation of all the others. (Jephcott 325; quoted in Jacobson 106 with an edit of Jephcott's translation, replacing "evolved language" with "higher language")

*Das Wort Gottes* "the Word of God" is of course the Logos, a single word that not only contains all truth and all knowledge but, as Benjamin hints in #59, in the Jewish Logos mysticism of Philo of Alexandria is a divine being, a demiurgic agent that may be imagined as the vitalistic force powering the holy growth of languages. Obviously that "language" is not translatable. It's not clear what all "every higher language" entails; Jacobson (106) assumes that it refers only to a divine language, but there may be several divine languages, and it is plausible to consider the human languages whose intentions are activated by translation as higher languages as well, each translating the others, and with each translation those "higher" languages moving a step or two higher:

Die Übersetzung ist die Überführung der einen Sprache in die andere durch ein Kontinuum von Verwandlungen. Kontinua der Verwandlung, nicht abstrakte Gleichheits- und Ähnlichkeitsbezirke durchmißt die Übersetzung. (151; quoted in Jacobson 274n98)

Translation is the transporting of one language into another through a continuum of transformations. Translation passes through continua of transformations, not abstractions of identity and similarity. (325; quoted in Jacobson 106, with an edit of Jephcott's translation, replacing "removal from one language to another" with "the transporting of one language into another")

See also the commentaries to #13 and #17–18 for more speculation on the layering of linguistic unfoldings/emanations. As Jacobson adds: "If the language of creation is transformative, and God transferred at least a part of the creating word in the *nishmat chaim* ['breath of life'] of Adam, human language must also be transformative. Translation is thus the capturing of an element of this transformative aspect in language" (106).

*Other commentators*: Bartoloni (2004: np), Bellos (2010: 210), Benjamin (1989/2014: 90), Berman (2008/2018: 104–8), Bradbury (2006: 138), Britt (1996: 53), Derrida (1985: 187), Engel (2014: 5–6), Ferris (2008: 64), Gasché (1986: 78, 81), Gelley (2015: 23), Jacobs (1975: 757), Lacoue-Labarthe (2002: 11), Liska (2014: 232, 235), O'Keeffe (2015: 377–78), Pan (2017: 37–38), Pfau (1988: 1084), Rothwell (2009: 261), Smerick (2009: np), Steiner (2010: 48), Vermeer (1996: 167–68), Weber (2008: 69), Wurgaft (2002: 379).

## 20 The relationship between languages (2): how non-linguistic life signals that relatedness

| Denn dieses kennt | in Analogien und Zeichen andere Typen der |
|---|---|
| For this recognizes | in analogies and signs other types of the |

| Hindeutung, als die intensive, d.h. vorgreifende, andeutende |
|---|
| indication than the intensive, i.e. anticipatory, insinuatory |

Verwirklichung.
realization.

*Paraphrase*: For life outside of language tends to make things real in analogies and signs, suggestive indices other than "intensive" (anticipatory, insinuatory) ones.

*Commentary*: This is the second part of the unpacking of *keimhaft und intensiv* "germinally and intensively" in #19: here he defines *intensiv* as *vorgreifende, andeutende Verwirklichung*, which Zohn translates as an "anticipative, intimating realization"

(72), Hynd and Valk as "realizes by anticipation and allusion" (300), Rendall as an "anticipatory, intimating realization" (154), and Underwood as "anticipatory, allusive realization" (33). Werner Hamacher (2001/2012: 501) identifies this as an allusion to "Kant's formulation, in *The Critique of Pure Reason*, of the principle of the anticipations of perception and its founding concepts: intensity, anticipation, and reality," and notes that in a November 11, 1916 letter to Gershom Scholem Benjamin himself specifically linked it to "mathematical theories of intensive quantities."[22]

While Benjamin's argumentative trajectory here as elsewhere in the essay is toward pre-Kantian transcendentalism, here he is specifically addressing the earthly social-phenomenological layer (or emanation) of life, which does lend itself to understanding through Austinian performativity:[23] in "making things real in ... suggestive indices other than 'intensive' (anticipatory, insinuatory) ones," *anticipating* (expecting, adumbrating, foreshadowing) and *insinuating* (hinting, alluding, intimating) are speech acts that one might well regard as difficult to perform nonverbally. To read "intensive" in that sense would be to align it with the illocutionary *force* of speech acts. The intensity in question, in other words, would be a somatic—affective-becoming-conative—performativity.

By contrast, the "non-intensive" analogies and signs and other indices by which the social phenomenology of life outside of language makes things real would include events like my cat rubbing up against my leg, and, when I bend down to pick her up, dodging my hands in order to walk determinedly toward the kitchen with a come-hither look up at me over her shoulder. But then of course it would be silly to insist that she is not anticipating (expecting) or insinuating (hinting at) anything—that, in fact, she's not telling me nonverbally that it's dinner time and I should close my laptop and follow her, because she's *hungry*, dammit. And any cat's or dog's human will recognize the somatic/performative *intensity* of that communicative moment.

Arguably, of course, my cat walking suggestively toward the kitchen is an *analogue* of me following her in and feeding her. It's not exactly an *analogy*. The German for "analogue" is not *Analogie* but *Analog* or *Analogon*; Benjamin doesn't use either. I would say that my cat signals her desire for food by means of an embodied kinesthetic analogue, and *I* am the one who figures out the analogy.

In fact, of course, I am also the one who uses the word "analogue" for what she does. Arguably, in other words, both analogies and analogues are "kennings" operating *inside* the world of language, not outside it.

---

22 In neither the original German letter (Scholem and Adorno 1978: 128–30) nor its published English translation (Scholem and Adorno 1994: 81–83), however, is there a trace of either those five words or anything close to "intensive quantities"; the closest would be "Mathematik und Sprache, d. h. Mathematik und Denken, Mathematik und Zion" (128)/"mathematics and language, i.e. mathematics and thought, mathematics and Zion" (81).

23 I'm not in fact the only reader to hint at a speech-act reading of this passage: Engel (2014: 4n7), for example, suggests that "'intensiv' ist hier als Adjektiv von Intention, im Sinne von 'Versuch' oder 'Streben', zu verstehen"/"'Intensive' is to be understood here as an adjective of intention, in the sense of 'attempt' or 'striving'."

Also, since *Hindeutung* "suggestion" is morphologically a "pointing toward," I paraphrase it as "index," which derives from the Latin for the index/pointer finger and also means a pointing. I'm thinking especially of Charles Sanders Peirce's definition of the index, the Second type of sign (involving brute empirical reality) in which there is a factual correspondence between the sign and its object, like a weathervane pointing in the direction of the wind, or smoke pointing back to the fire that emits it. The First type of sign for Peirce, based in abstract potentiality, is an icon, a likeness, as in a diagram; the Third type, based in precepts or other established patterns, is a symbol, where the correspondence between sign and object is "imputed," as in traffic lights, or words like "cat," "walk," "kitchen," and "feed." Onomatopoeic words like "meow" would arguably be icons, emerging out of sound-likeness; but the fact that they emerge differently in different languages suggests also that they are hybrids, iconic symbols. Analogues like walking to the kitchen to signal a desire that your human walk there with you are also icons; but they depend for success not only on the agentive construction of an iconic *Bedeutete* or "*intendendum*"—the "intended object," as Zohn (73) and Rendall (160) have it in #19—but the agentive *interpretation* of that *intendendum*. My cat wants to lead me into the kitchen; my language-based (ana)logic (or again in Peircean terms "logical interpretant") constructs her walking as an analogue of that (presumed) desire.

There are, in other words, some problems in Benjamin's formulation here. One is that *Analogien* "analogies" are linguistic semioses that cannot be parsed outside the world of language. Another is that *Zeichen* "signs" is far too large a category to be used restrictively for non-linguistic semioses.

Most important, however, is the fact that signs are only signs if they are *interpreted* as signs. In Peircean terms, an object is construed as a sign by an interpretant. Translation as *die Darstellung eines Bedeuteten*, which I paraphrased in #19 as "the bodying forth of an *intendendum*," can be intended by the human translator (not, for example, by Google Translate), but it only has the activating effect on languages that Benjamin posits if it is interpreted as such. In the empirical earthly realm of human intentions and interpretations that Benjamin shuns, they would need to be interpreted by target readers; for Benjamin they are presumably interpreted by the languages themselves, as vitalistic Forms. But they do need to be interpreted.

This is especially obvious in the realm outside of language. A weathervane is only a sign—an index, a *Hindeutung* "pointing toward"—if it is interpreted as such. It cannot be intended as a sign by the weathervane. My cat can intend for me to follow her into the kitchen and feed her, but her intention does not thereby automatically become a sign (say an "analogue"). Walking toward the kitchen is only an anticipatory/insinuatory analogue of being fed if it is analogically constructed as such through a logical interpretant—mine, for example.[24] If I am oblivious to her *intendenda*, if it seems to me that she's just walking around

---

24 See Tomasello (2008) for the research showing that the only nonhuman animals capable of directing the attention of others by pointing at something—mobilizing "shared attention"—are those that have lived with humans.

on mysterious cat business, or if I am so busy writing this commentary that I don't even notice her perambulations, her rubbing and walking and looking do not constitute an analogue or any other kind of sign. (In fact she is relentless. She will keep at me until I pay attention and interpret her *intendenda* as she desires. For her, of course, the telltale indication that the Thirdness of my logical interpretant has constructed her *intendendum* accurately is the Secondness of my energetic interpretant: I stand up and follow her into the kitchen, where I give her some puréed chicken or fish. And that last movement from the Firstness of the emotional interpretant to the Secondness of the energetic interpretant would also be a Peircean mapping of intensity.)

More generally, a *Hindeutung* is only a "suggestion" if the "pointing toward" is interpreted as someone or something suggesting something. Benjamin uses some version of the verb *deuten* "to point, (and figuratively) to mean, to interpret" 33 times in the essay—usually in the form *bedeuten* "to bepoint, (and figuratively) to signify, to mean, to intend"—but here in #20 in two forms, *hindeuten* "to point toward, (and figuratively) to suggest, to indicate" and *andeuten* "to point on, (and figuratively) to hint, to insinuate, to intimate." In each case Benjamin seems to imply that the nonlinguistic sign doesn't just point but intends a meaning. That implication would of course problematically attribute agency to weathervanes and traffic lights. His foreclosure on the constitutive power of the reader, or more generally of the interpreter or interpretant of signs, creates a philosophical problem for him that he attempts locally to solve through his mystical Platonic vitalism, but only in the "big" cases, namely languages, originals, and translations. His vitalistic rethinking of nonhuman agency does not extend down as far as weathervanes, fires, plants—or even cats.

*Other commentators*: Gasché (1986: 81).

## 21 The relationship between languages (3): languages are *a priori* kin in what they want to say

Jenes gedachte, innerste Verhältnis der Sprachen ist aber das
That thought, innermost relationship of the languages is however that

einer eigentümlichen Konvergenz. Es besteht darin, daß die Sprachen
of a peculiar convergence. It stands therein that the languages

einander nicht fremd, sondern a priori und von allen historischen
one another not alien, rather *a priori* and from all historical

Beziehungen abgesehen einander in dem verwandt sind, was sie
relations seen one other in that kin are, what they

sagen wollen.
to say want.

*Paraphrase*: Languages are related—not exactly in the philological sense, but rather *a priori*, prior to every possible historical connection. Any two languages, even taken from two wildly different language families, are not alien (strangers) to each other but have a unique convergence, a kinship, specifically in what they want to say. This innermost relationship/relatedness is not observed empirically but *gedacht* "thought."[25]

*Commentary*: Benjamin's foreclosure on empirical language study is significant here. Beginning in #25 he does devote considerable attention to what might be called philology or historical linguistics; in #26, especially, we find a signal emphasis placed on the fruitful power of historical processes, and in #27 he draws that foundational binary distinction between his diachronic model of the organic propagation/growth/life of languages and the "dead theory of translation," which he describes as based on stop-frame synchrony. In #29 he admits that "etymological similarities cannot adequately account" for the affinities/kinship between languages, but nevertheless insists that "etymology will remain indispensable in thinking about the kinship of languages." The messianic growth toward pure language that he introduces in #35 is expressly thematized as an historical model. In a superficial reading it might seem as if his insistence on a mentally grasped (constructed? imagined?) kinship among all languages "prior to every possible historical connection" might be contradicted by this later insistence on historical processes, and indeed as if the stop-frame synchrony that he dismisses in #27 were methodologically akin to the apparent idealism of #21's *a priori* thought-experiment.

But in fact in #26 he splits *human* history off from what is "essential" in history, which appears to be a kind of transhuman, transcendental vitalism. And the kinship he describes here as residing in what languages "want to say" anticipates the notion he introduces in #30 that the messianic past and future history of languages is driven by the vitalistic "intentions" in languages.

*Other commentators*: Berman (2008/2018: 108–10), Britt (1996: 51), Engel (2014: 4–5), Fenves (2011: 149), Ferreira Duarte (1995: 275), Ferris (2008: 64), Gasché (1986: 78), Hamacher (2001/2012: 500, 507, 524), Jacobs (1975: 759–60), Johnston (1992: 44), Porter (1989: 1067), Rothwell (2009: 260), Smerick (2009: np), Vermeer (1996: 162).

---

25 Zohn and Wright have "posited," Hynd and Valk "presumed," Rendall "imagined," and Underwood "intentional."

## 22 The relationship between languages (4): not best proved through textual equivalence

> Mit diesem Erklärungsversuch scheint allerdings die Betrachtung auf
> With this explanation attempt seems though the reflection on
>
> vergeblichen Umwegen wieder in die herkömmliche Theorie der
> pointless digressions again into the conventional theory of the
>
> Übersetzung einzumünden. Wenn in den Übersetzungen die
> translation to flow in. If in the translations the
>
> Verwandtschaft der Sprachen sich zu bewähren hat, wie könnte sie
> affinity of the languages itself to prove has, how could it
>
> das anders als indem jene Form und Sinn des Originals
> that otherwise than in that that form and sense of the original
>
> möglichst genau übermitteln?
> most possibly accurately to transmit?

*Paraphrase*: It may now seem as if, after pointless digressions, our treatise flows through this attempted explanation back into the mainstream of the conventional theory of translation. After all, how else is one to mobilize translations to prove the affinity/kinship among languages but by conveying the form and sense of the source text as accurately as possible?

*Commentary*: This is Benjamin blocking the normative assumption conditioned by what he here calls "the conventional theory of translation," and in #27 will call the "dead theory of translation," namely that the task of the translator is to reproduce the source text in the target language as fully and accurately as possible. The line of argument he is pursuing is that translations test, reveal, and advance the kinship of languages, and his rhetorical question here is whether the obvious way to do that is not simply to do the expected and strive for equivalence. His implicit answer to his own question, of course, is *no*; and he begins to unpack that answer in #23.

*Other commentators*: Bellos (2010: 210), Berman (2008/2018: 110–11), Johnston (1992: 42).

## 23 The relationship between languages (5): not best proved through the similarity between two poems

| | | |
|---|---|---|
| Über den Begriff dieser Genauigkeit wüßte | | sich jene Theorie |
| On the concept of this accuracy | | would know itself that theory |

freilich nicht zu fassen, könnte also zuletzt doch keine Rechenschaft von
certainly not to grasp, could also finally though no reckoning of

dem geben, was an Übersetzungen wesentlich ist. In Wahrheit aber
that give, what in translations essential is. In truth however

bezeugt sich die Verwandtschaft der Sprachen in einer Übersetzung
testifies itself the affinity of the languages in a translation

weit tiefer und bestimmter als in der oberflächlichen und
far more deeply and specifically than in the superficial and

undefinierbaren Ähnlichkeit zweier Dichtungen.
indefinable similarity of two poems.

*Paraphrase*: Of course that mainstream theory would hardly know how to conceptualize this accuracy, and thus would be able to give no reckoning of the Essence of translation. But in fact what attests to the affinity/kinship among languages is far more profound and more sharply defined than any superficial and ineffable similarity between two poems.

*Commentary*: It is quite true that the mainstream equivalence-based theory of translation has proved utterly incapable of operationalizing what its proponents call translation quality assessment (TQA). Strikingly, like Benjamin, TQA mavens also radically foreclose on the judgment of the target reader, or even of the stereoscopic reader—but for very different reasons. For Benjamin, the reader is irrelevant because languages and texts are vitalistic agents that decide such things for themselves, and that judgment is all that matters; for TQA, lectorial assessments are problematic because they're varied and therefore difficult to aggregate reliably. TQ assessors' preferred alternative is of course not vitalism but scientism. The source text and target text must be mapped semantically, syntactically, and pragmatically as stable empirical objects that can be compared scientifically for exact and inexact matches, without the need for human interpretation. That approach, needless to say, would for Benjamin be no more able to give a reckoning of the transcendental Essence of translation than more commonsensical equivalentisms—because, as he puts it (#27), that scientizing approach "kills" the two texts in order to render them inert enough for empirical study.

The second sentence in this passage is a restatement of the basic divergence Benjamin plies between the mainstream equivalence theory ("similarity between two poems") and his own mystical model (the essential "affinity/kinship among languages").

*Other commentators*: Berman (2008/2018: 111–12), Engel (2014: 6n8), Weber (2008: 54).

## 24 The relationship between languages (6): the study of the authentic relationship between source text and translation likened to the epistemological devastation of objective representation

> Um      das echte     Verhältnis   zwischen Original und Übersetzung zu
> In order the authentic relationship between  original  and  translation   to
>
> erfassen, ist eine Erwägung     anzustellen, deren Absicht durchaus   den
> grasp    is an   investigation to conduct  whose aim      throughout of the
>
> Gedankengängen analog     ist, in denen die Erkenntniskritik     die
> thought paths     analogous is,  in which the knowledge critique the
>
> Unmöglichkeit einer Abbildtheorie zu erweisen     hat. Wird     dort
> impossibility  of an image theory to demonstrate has. Becomes there
>
> gezeigt, daß es    in der Erkenntnis keine Objektivität und sogar nicht
> shown,  that there in the knowledge no   objectivity  and even  not
>
> einmal den Anspruch darauf  geben könnte, wenn sie in Abbildern des
> once  the   claim      thereon give  could,  if   it   in images   of
>
> Wirklichen bestünde,    so ist hier erweisbar, daß keine Übersetzung
> the real     consisted,   so is here provable   that no   translation
>
> möglich wäre, wenn sie Ähnlichkeit mit  dem Original ihrem letzten
> possible were, if    it similarity  with the original to its last
>
> Wesen nach    anstreben würde.
> essence toward to strive    became.

*Paraphrase*: If we want to understand the authentic relationship between the source text and the translation, we must launch an investigation along thought-paths whose intent is exactly analogous to the epistemological refutation of the image theory of perception. Just as that critique demonstrates that if knowledge consists in images of the real there is no objectivity in knowledge, and that even giving adequate assurance of objectivity is impossible, so too would translation not be possible if in the end it were to take as its ultimate Essence the striving for similarity to the original.

*Commentary*: This is an intriguing analogical argument for the impossibility of equivalence-based (theories of) translation—but one that can easily backfire on Benjamin. If we accept the epistemological refutation of the image theory of perception that Kant lodged in *A Critique of Pure Reason*[26]—and most post-Kantian thinkers (what we nowadays call critical theorists) for the past two centuries have indeed accepted it—it can be taken analogically to dismiss equivalence-based translation (with some slippage, which we'll discuss in a moment). More directly, however, it undermines and ultimately undoes *any* objectivizing truth-claim, possibly even including almost everything Benjamin himself writes in this essay—especially, of course, *In völlig unmetaphorischer Sachlichkeit ist der Gedanke vom Leben und Fortleben der Kunstwerke zu erfassen* "when we speak of the life and ongoing life of an artwork, that manner of speaking should be understood as fully unmetaphorical objectivity/factuality" (#13) and *Wie weit eine Übersetzung dem Wesen dieser Form zu entsprechen vermag, wird objektiv durch die Übersetzbarkeit des Originals bestimmt* "How well a translation can assimilate itself to the Essence of this Form depends objectively on the source text's translatability" (#73).

One could argue, of course, that Benjamin uses different abstract nouns in the three passages—*die Sachlichkeit* in #13, *die Objektivität* in #24 and #73—and indeed Hynd and Valk translate that line in #13 as "And the life and continuing life of works of art must be understood not metaphorically but as simple matters of fact" (299). *Die Sache* can be translated as "the object," but it can also be "the fact" and more vaguely "the thing." It would, however, be difficult to make the case that objects, things, and facts were anything but the epistemological building-blocks of precisely the earthly empiricism that early Benjamin despised, or that the Platonic or Neoplatonist mysticism that he espoused throughout this essay—and explicitly objectified/reified in #13—was not susceptible to the same anti-objectivist refutation. I noted in the commentary to #13 that Benjamin would appear to be invoking a "higher" (Platonic-mystical cum proto-scientific)

---

26 Andrew Benjamin (1989/2014: 91) quotes the passage from "The Schematism of the Pure Concepts of the Understanding" in *The Critique of Pure Reason* according to which it is "schemata, not images of objects, which underlie our pure sensible concepts":

> the image is a product of the empirical faculty of reproductive imagination; the schema of sensible concepts, such as of figures in space, is a product and as it were, a monogram, of pure a priori imagination, through which, and in accordance with which, images themselves first became possible. (B181/A14214)

In other words, the Platonic copy theory on which traditional translation theory is based—the translation as a mimetic copy of the source text—is wrong. Mimetic reproductions of source-textual sense are not stable, scientifically measurable objects but the secondary and superficial byproducts of schemata, which in Benjamin are the affinities or "kinship" (*Verwandtschaft*) between languages.

kind of objectivity; but in the post-Kantian era that invocation too must yield to the Kantian critique. In precisely the same way as mimetic reproductions of source-textual sense are not stable scientifically measurable objects but the secondary and superficial byproducts of schemata, so too are metaphysical truth-claims like "Translation is a Form" the secondary and superficial byproducts of schemata (such as the phenomenologically derived conception of languages as possessing vitalistic "intentions").

And if the import of #24 is that translational equivalence is not just a belief but an illusion, a false belief, a gross error, by extension—at least under the aegis of the Kantian thought that Benjamin here invokes—the same charges might reasonably be brought against every other claim he makes.

The interpretation Thomas Pfau (1988: 1086) offers of this conundrum is that "an unbridgable hiatus thus separates the realm of ideas from the Messianic"—but of course, as he goes on to note, in Benjamin "translation affords an intensive and seed-like anticipation of that which man *speculates* to be the nature of an extensive Messianic revelation" (emphasis added), and that speculation partakes of a "realm of ideas" that is separated from the transcendental realm about which it makes absolute truth-claims. The upshot is that "Benjamin's essay makes it clear that any interpretive act will have to await its final validation by the disclosure of an ontology to which, as a purely historical 'task,' it continues to bear a strict and unbridgable non-relation."

A telling side-note: Stephen Palmquist (2000: chs. II and X) argues persuasively that Kant derived his Copernican Hypothesis—in this passage the epistemological devastation of objectivity in the claim that the schemata of the imagination *project* stable objects in space and time—from readings of Emanuel Swedenborg's mystical works. The implication of that linkage would be that our impression that we register empirical reality objectively and therefore reliably is what mystics call the Veil of Appearances. But where for mystics that makes "empirical reality" sheer illusion, Kant's transcendental idealism built a mediation between that view and science, explaining the apparent fact that we all seem "subjectively" to experience—and thus are able to study scientifically—the "same" reality by appeal to the uniformity of God's Creation. Because God created us with similar minds, we all project the same reality (this is what Kant called "universal subjectivism"). Later post-Kantian thought has rejected that recourse to God and explained the apparent similarity of our experience of the world culturally, as a social construct that varies slightly but significantly from culture to culture; Benjamin arguably moves in the opposite direction, *back* from Kant's recourse to God to Swedenborg's pre-Kantian mystical transcendentalism. In that reading, what makes Benjamin's objectivizing claims "true" is not earth-bound empiricism but *Offenbarung* "revelation."

The analogical sweep of Benjamin's critique (using the abbreviations SD for "source domain" and TD for "target domain") might be schematized like this:

| The Kantian impossibility of | (SD₁) knowing anything | (SD₂) objectively |
|---|---|---|
| *is analogous to* | | |
| The Benjaminian impossibility of | (TD₁) reproducing the source text's semantic content in the target language | (TD₂) accurately |

This is in fact a somewhat problematic analogy. The "investigation" that Benjamin imagines as proceeding "along thought-paths whose intent is *exactly analogous* to the epistemological refutation of the image theory of perception" is actually quite far from "exactly analogous" to that epistemological refutation, either in intent or in the thought-paths that it follows. There are, I suggest, four problems.

The first is structural: (SD₁) "knowing" is a simple element (I know X) and (TD₁) is a compound element (I read $X_1$ *and* I reproduce $X_1$ as $X_2$). Call "I read $X_1$" TD₁-a and "I reproduce $X_1$ as $X_2$" TD₁-b. As Benjamin sets it up, TD₁-b is one specific response to TD₁-a: TD₁-b as "establishing sense-for-sense equivalence between $X_1$ and $X_2$" makes $X_2$ not just "the target language" (TL) but a semantically and syntactically coherent TL rendering of the meanings of the sentences in $X_1$. Benjamin's preferred alternative would then be something like (TD₁-a) "I read $X_1$" and (TD₁-c) "I reproduce $X_1$ as $X_3$," where $X_3$ is a word-for-word translation that retains source-textual syntax in the target language and TD₁-c agitates the intentions in the source and target languages. Not only is there nothing like that articulated structure in (SD₁), the epistemological source domain, but it is precisely the effort to achieve TD₁ by means of TD₁-b that (according to the analogy) renders TD₁ impossible.

The second problem is directional: as Benjamin sets up the analogy, (SD₁) "knowing" entails the *internalization* of (SD₂) "images as ostensible truth," and (TD₁) "translating as reproducing the sense" entails the *internalization-and-externalization* of (TD₂) "images for ostensible accuracy." We could of course repair that problem by reframing (SD₁) "knowing" as "knowing and reporting"—by stipulating, for example, that the only way we know what someone else knows is that s/he reports that knowledge verbally. Benjamin does not suggest that repair, but of course that is no obstacle to making it mentally ourselves.

The third problem is probative: in the source domain, (SD₁) "knowledge" is tested for (SD₂) "objectivity" in the human perceptual system, and fails that test (leading to "Kantian impossibility") due to the distortive effects of the cerebral screening and interpretation of sense data; in the target domain, (TD₁) "translating as reproducing the meanings of whole source-textual sentences" is tested for (TD₂) "accuracy" by comparing the source and target texts linguistically, and arguably falls short in that test (leading to "approximate or pragmatic possibility") due to the structural differences between languages. The epistemological test was carried out by Kant as a thought-experiment, but nowadays neuropsychologists carry it out in the lab; the translational test is carried out textually by stereoscopic readers, who savor the semantic fields of words and phrases comparatively in the two texts, looking for matches and mismatches. It might be argued that this is not really a problem, because both the neurophilosophers and neuropsychologists in the source domain and the error analysts in the target domain tend to measure the possibility of knowing and translating against a transcendental yardstick: perfect godlike knowledge of objective reality in the source domain, perfect godlike reproduction of the source text in the target domain. But obviously "Kantian impossibility" is not analogous to "approximate or pragmatic possibility," and that points us to the final problem.

The fourth problem, finally, is evaluative: in the source domain, the impossibility of reliably knowing anything objectively is widely accepted as real but unfortunate; in the target domain, what is not only widely accepted as real but constitutes the prevailing professional norm for translation is "good enough" sense-for-sense equivalence. Those who, like Benjamin, seek to undermine and overturn that norm see sense-for-sense equivalence not as impossible but as undesirable—and undesirable only for a single fairly small subcategory ("fine writing") of one domain (literary works).

The net effect of those four problems is to showcase this passage as a rhetorical attempt to pass undesirability off as impossibility (problem 4) through a shoddily constructed analogy (problems 1–3). The questionable argumentative value of that attempt might make fans of Benjamin's essay wish #24 had been deleted in draft; but in fact the exact same questionable argumentative strategy is prominently on display in the essay's most illustrious predecessor, Friedrich Schleiermacher's "Über die verschiedenen Methoden des Übertsetzens"/"On the Different Methods of Translating." As I show at some length in the second chapter of Robinson (2013b), Schleiermacher not only tries to pass undesirability off as impossibility by mobilizing fatally wounded analogies, but does so with unbecoming hysteria. Benjamin at least never loses his cool.

*Other commentators*: Balfour (2018: 756), Benjamin (1989/2014: 91), Berman (2008/2018: 115–18), de Man (2000: 22), Ferreira Duarte (1995: 273), Gelley (2015: 20), Hamacher (2001/2012: 498–99), Jacobs (1975: 759), Pfau (1988: 1086), Smerick (2009: np), Vermeer (1996: 157–58).

## 25 After-ripening (1): the transformation and renewal of a living thing

Denn in seinem Fortleben, das     so nicht heißen    dürfte, wenn es nicht
For  in its      forthliving, which so not     be called might, if    it not

Wandlung      und Erneuerung des     Lebendigen wäre, ändert  sich das
transformation and renewal      of the living       were, changes itself the

Original. Es gibt eine Nachreife     auch der   festgelegten Worte. Was
original. It gives an    after-ripening also  of the established  words. What

| | | | | | | |
|---|---|---|---|---|---|---|
| zur | Zeit eines Autors Tendenz | seiner dichterischen Sprache | gewesen |
| in the time of an author tendency | of his poetic | language | been |

sein mag, kann später erledigt sein, immanente Tendenzen vermögen
have may, can later exhausted be, immanent tendencies to be able

neu aus dem Geformten sich zu erheben. Was damals jung, kann
new out of the formed itself to raise. What then young, can

später abgebraucht, was damals gebräuchlich, später archaisch klingen.
later worn out, what then current, later archaic sound.

*Paraphrase*: The source text is not a static (dead) thing that can be laid out on a table for vivisection—which is to say, for "scientific" comparison with a translation for translation quality assessment (TQA). The source text is a living organism that grows and changes over time: there is an after-ripening of the established word; the source text must be understood in terms of the transformation and renewal of the living. It's not just that what then was young can later be exhausted, and what then was commonplace can later sound archaic; it's also, more radically, that what in the author's time may have been the tendency of "his" poetic idiom can later be ruined, *in order* to be able to raise immanent tendencies anew out of the ("formed") source text/language. Old usages must die out in order to give birth to new ones—must decay in order to produce fertile soil for the new usages to grow in.

*Commentary*: This is the beginning of Benjamin's attempt to set up a polemical binary opposition between traditional theories of translational equivalence—which he explicitly thematizes in #28 as *die taube Gleichung* "the deaf equation/echoing" but implicitly attacks as static, synchronic, spatialized, or at least detemporalized—and the theory that he wants to advance, which is temporal. The quite accurate picture that he paints of the old equivalence theory in #27 is that it removes the languages of both the source text and the translation from historical time and treats them as dead (and therefore artificially stabilized) objects that can be compared analytically in search of errors; in his theory they are alive. See also the commentary to #24 for a discussion of the tensions between scientific and mystical "objectivity."

*Other commentators*: Baltrusch (2010: 121), Bannet (1993: 582), Bellos (2010: 211), Berman (2008/2018: 118–20), Biti (2019: 254), Chapman (2019: 40, 103), Derrida (1985: 183, 195), Gelley (2015: 21), Gold (2007: 616), Hamacher (2001/2012: 498–99), Johnston (1992: 43), Smerick (2009: np), Steiner (2010: 48), Uhl (2012: 456), Vermeer (1996: 79, 90, 148, 159, 168–69), Weber (2008: 43, 69).

## 26 After-ripening (2): linguistic change brought about by the ownmost life of language

> Das Wesentliche solcher Wandlungen       wie auch der       ebenso ständigen
> The essential     of such transformations as     also of the likewise continual
>
> des     Sinnes in der Subjektivität der       Nachgeborenen statt       im
> of the sense   in the subjectivity   of the later-born       instead   in the
>
> eigensten Leben der     Sprache und ihrer Werke zu suchen, hieße –
> ownmost life   of the language and its     works to seek,   would be called –
>
> zugestanden selbst den krudesten Psychologismus – Grund   und Wesen
> rightly       itself the crudest     psychologism   – ground and essence
>
> einer Sache verwechseln, Strenger       gesagt aber,       einen der
> of a   thing to exchange, more strongly said       however one   of the
>
> gewaltigsten     und fruchtbarsten historischen Prozesse aus     Unkraft
> most powerful and   fruitful       historical     processes out of impotence
>
> des     Denkens leugnen.
> of the thinking to deny.

*Paraphrase*: The temporal changes in a work over the centuries may be *grounded* in how readers read it, but that ground is not its Essence; its Essence is the ownmost life of language and its works. Confusing the lectorial ground with the transcendental Essence is the crudest psychologism, powered by an impotence of thought, and it leads to the denial of one of the most dynamic and fertile historical processes.

*Commentary*: The two explanatory models Benjamin adduces here are **Grund** *und* **Wesen** *einer Sache* "*ground* and *essence* of a thing"; for *Grund* Zohn has "root cause," Hynd and Valk have "basis," Rendall has "ground," Underwood has "reason," and Wright has "cause." The implication would appear to be that for Benjamin "the temporal changes in a work over the centuries" are indeed "*grounded* in how readers read it"—human cultural/historical reading practices are indeed the *root cause* of the temporal changes—but restricting our understanding of those historical processes to social and secular practices and mistaking those practices for what is most essential is "the crudest psychologism, powered by an impotence of thought."

Benjamin nowhere tackles the complex dynamics of the relationship between *Grund und Wesen* "ground/basis/root cause and Essence." Somehow human readers cause the changes in meaning and significance, but the humans themselves and the causal effects of their social practices have nothing to do with the Essence. The transcendent Platonic frame would seem to suggest that the vitalistic Essences of transcendental Forms wield the causal force and so drive the historical processes that Benjamin calls dynamic and fertile, and that the *Grund* "ground/root cause" effected by humans is actually a copy or an emanation of that transcendental agency that is the true efficient cause (see the commentary to #9). Presumably the metaphorics of *der Grund* "the ground" where the social causality of human reading and speaking practices is "rooted" implies that any emanation of the divine or transcendent putting down such roots would be very low indeed, plunging deep into the very dirt; but the Kabbalistic underpinnings of Benjamin's metaphysics in the essay (see the commentary to #57) do indeed predict that "roots" and other "grounded" causalities will still contain a spark of the divine wrapped in the protective Kelipot "shells" of evil.

*Other commentators*: Berman (2008/2018: 120–21), Chapman (2019: 30), Hamacher (2001/2012: 499), Jacobs (1975: 758), Kohlross (2009: 106), Smerick (2009: np), Vermeer (1996: 148).

## 27 After-ripening (3): the source and target languages both continue to change in the source text's continuing life

> Und wollte man auch des Autors letzten Federstrich zum Gnadenstoß
> And wanted one also the author's last quill-stroke to the *coup de grâce*
>
> des Werkes machen, es würde jene tote Theorie der Übersetzung doch
> of the work to make, it would that dead theory of the translation yet
>
> nicht retten. Denn wie Ton und Bedeutung der großen Dichtungen mit
> not save. For as tone and significance of the great poems with
>
> den Jahrhunderten sich völlig wandeln, so wandelt sich auch die
> the centuries themselves fully change, so changes itself also the
>
> Muttersprache des Übersetzers. Ja, während das Dichterwort in der
> mother tongue of the translator. Indeed, while the poet-word in the
>
> seinigen überdauert, ist auch die größte Übersetzung bestimmt in das
> its own outlasts, is even the greatest translation destined in the
>
> Wachstum ihrer Sprache ein-, in der erneuten unterzugehen.
> growth of its language to go in, in the renewed to go under.

*Paraphrase*: One might try to save the dead theory of translation by imagining a freezing of the source text through a magical transformation: the author's last quill-stroke as "his" work's *coup de grâce*. But that gambit won't save the dead theory, not only because the source language will continue to grow and develop after that quill-stroke, but because the source text's superlife is in translations, and the target language will continue to grow and change as well. And while the poet's word survives in the source language, ultimately even the greatest translation is destined to be subsumed into the growth of the target language and drown in its renewal.

*Commentary*: Since for Benjamin the "dead theory of translation" relies on the detemporalization of translation, he quite reasonably imagines the critical freeze-framing of the source text as that theory's necessary first step. The idea would be that even though the author's last quill-stroke is obviously only one event in a sequence of such events, if we imagine that event as encapsulating in a single blow all of *la gloire* "the glory" of the work, indeed even possibly of the author's entire oeuvre, it might subsume the entire history of "his" output into that single moment, frozen in time—chloroformed and pinned to the mat. Then it could be studied and interpreted and translated in (static) peace.

But of course, as Underwood reminds us in his translation, a *coup de grâce* is a "mercy killing" (34). This desperate attempt to redeem a dead theory magically transforms literature into a dead thing—kills it; puts it out of its misery. To stop time is to extinguish life. Life is growth; life is change. Benjamin's oppositional theory of translation is (at least metaphorically) genetic, germinational and maturational, based on vegetative growth (see Derrida 1985: 178[27]). In the tenor of that metaphor, it is teleological and eschatological, concerned with change as movement toward an end.

There is of course a simpler explanation of how proponents of the "dead theory of translation" seek to stop time: through abstraction, which is to say through idealization. Rather than needing to imagine a last stroke of the author's quill as a mercy killing, all one would have to do—and indeed all that traditional thinking about translation has ever done—is adopt what Ferdinand de Saussure would call a "synchronic" view of the source text and its translation. Imagine the source text as a freeze-frame instance of "the" source language and the translation as a freeze-frame instance of "the" target language; objectify each as a stable array of syntactic and semantic patterns; compare them analytically. Even if one freezes the source text in a specific historical era, there is no need to imagine the text *transitioning through* that era. The historical variant instantiated in the synchronic slice of the source language is what it is, period. There is no prehistory to specific phrasings; those phrasings are not "becomings" on their way to how native speakers of the source language would say or write them today. And really (so the traditional thinking goes), doesn't the introduction of an historical perspective only muddy the waters? Isn't it clearer all around if one simply idealizes each text all the way out of the historical time-line?

And—this is now my thinking, not the dead theory's—isn't this a far more realistic whipping boy than Benjamin's quill-stroke and *coup de grâce*?

Of course it is difficult to imagine diachronic changes not only in the semantics, syntax, and "tone" of the source text but also in the work's *Bedeutung* "significance" without changes in the social reading practices of the source and

---

27 And see de Man (1986, 2000) for the misreading that Benjamin too believed that translation invariably kills the source text. For Benjamin that murderous effect was only perpetrated in and by the "dead" mainstream theory.

target cultures; but, as we saw in #26, the transformative effect of those practices is precisely what early Benjamin refuses to identify as the "Essence" of the changes. The changes are motivated on a "higher" level, namely the transcendental level of the Platonic Realm of Forms and their Essences; human reading practices and any causal effect they may have on the growth of languages are just imperfect earth-bound copies of those vitalistic forces.

Note also that here the old traditional theory of equivalence is *tot* "dead," but in #28 Benjamin presents the source and target languages not as "dead" but as *erstorben* "having-died." He doesn't elaborate on this, but the idea would appear to be that the ostensible deadness of the two languages is an artifact of bad theory: in actual fact, he seems to be suggesting, even so-called dead languages like Sanskrit and Latin have repeatedly been reborn through translation, and translation *merkt* "marks or notices" the birth pangs of that rebirth.

Antoine Berman (2008/2018: 122–23) draws our attention to Benjamin's association of *eingehen* (lit. "to go in") with *das Wachstum* "growth" and of *untergehen* (lit. "to go under") with *Erneuerung* "renewal." He writes: "When a publication *geht ein*, this means that it will cease to appear. Here, therefore, *eingehen* means a certain kind of disappearance, but in the sense of entering into the growth of the language, shrinking within it, dissolving in it and, consequently, ceasing to appear" (122). "When the language to which a translation belongs is renewed," by contrast, "translation fades, goes under. *Eingehen* and *untergehen* therefore indicate two modes of disappearance" (123).

*Other commentators*: Chapman (2019: 39), Rendall (1997b: 185), Smerick (2009: np), Vermeer (1996: 156–57).

## 28 After-ripening (4): translation tracks the changes in the source language and triggers the birth pangs of new usage in the target language

So weit ist sie entfernt, von zwei erstorbenen Sprachen die taube
So far is it removed, of two dead languages the deaf

Gleichung zu sein, daß gerade unter allen Formen ihr als Eigenstes es
equation to be, that directly among all forms its as ownmost it

zufällt, auf jene Nachreife des fremden Wortes, auf die Wehen des
falls, upon that after-ripening of the foreign word, upon the woes of

eigenen zu merken.
the own to mark.

*Paraphrase*: One might think of translation as the deaf echoing of one dead language in another, but so far from being that, of all literary Forms it is the one entrusted with two critical tasks: tracking both the changes in the source language in the source text's after-ripening and the birth pangs of the target language in the translational superlife of the original.

*Commentary*: The temporal dynamic of Benjamin's theory sets a translation up not as a passive dead object for analysis but as an active living driver and indicator of language change, both in the source text/language and in the target language. The indications that a certain word or phrase in the translation is more modern than its counterpart in the source text, rather than being counted an error in an abstract TQA machine, are signs of the passage of time from the genesis of the source text to the genesis of the translation. But also the very attempt to translate a text from an earlier era uncovers semantic shifts within the source text/language ("the source language will continue to grow and develop after that quill-stroke"), and retranslation uncovers the ways in which "the target language will continue to grow and change as well" (#27).

As I render those two tasks—tracking changes in both the source and the target languages—Benjamin seems to be mixing his metaphors: the source text is *ripe* at publication and afterwards just keeps getting riper, perhaps overripe (like a fruit); the target language is constantly *being born* in and through the writing and publishing and reading of the translation (like a human baby). Apparently the target language is perpetually in the linguistic birth canal—that is, if we read Benjamin's *Wehen* "woes" as birth pangs, as I follow Zohn, Rendall, and Wright in doing. As Paul de Man (2000: 25) reminds us, of course, those *Wehen* aren't necessarily birth pangs; but given that fruit doesn't moan in pain as it ripens, probably the mixed metaphor is unavoidable. Underwood tries to move to a higher level of metaphorical generality with the phrasing "noting the further maturing of the foreign language at the same time as the throes of its own" (34); but of course maturing doesn't necessarily occasion "throes" either. Hynd and Valk write of "the ripening process in a foreign language and the pulse of changing life in its own" (301), which seems to avoid the mixed metaphor somewhat better—at least if we assume that fruit pulses as it ripens.

*Other commentators*: Berman (2008/2018: 123–25), Chapman (2019: 103), de Man (2000: 24–25), Gelley (2015: 21–22), Johnston (1992: 43–44), Smerick (2009: np), Vermeer (1996: 157).

## 29 After-ripening (5): the kinship of language is not brought about by equivalent translations

| Wenn | in der Übersetzung | die Verwandtschaft | der | Sprachen | sich |
|---|---|---|---|---|---|
| If | in the translation | the kinship | | of the languages | itself |

| bekundet, | so geschieht es | anders | als durch | die vage | Ähnlichkeit |
|---|---|---|---|---|---|
| manifests, | so happens it | otherwise | than through | the vague | similarity |

> von Nachbildung und Original. Wie es denn überhaupt einleuchtet, daß
> of   reproduction and original. As   it   then in general   is evident     that
>
> Ähnlichkeit nicht notwendig bei Verwandtschaft sich   einfinden muß. Und
> similarity   not   necessary   by   kinship                itself present   must. And
>
> auch insofern ist der Begriff   der     letzten in diesem Zusammenhang mit
> also insofar   is the concept of the last     in this       together-hang   with
>
> seinem engern   Gebrauch einstimmig, als er durch   Gleichheit der
> its       narrower usage     univocal,     as it through likeness     of the
>
> Abstammung in beiden Fällen nicht ausreichend definiert werden   kann,
> descent        in both   cases not   sufficiently defined   become can,
>
> wiewohl freilich     für die Bestimmung jenes engern   Gebrauchs
> although admittedly for the determination of that narrower usage
>
> der     Abstammungsbegriff unentbehrlich bleiben wird.
> of the descent-concept       indispensable remain will.

*Paraphrase*: The affinity/kinship between languages as manifested in translations has nothing to do with that similarity between source text and translation that we have come to call "equivalence." Indeed it has generally become clear that similarity is not necessary for affinity/kinship. And while the concept of affinity/kinship in this connection is compatible with its narrower usage, to the extent that etymological similarities cannot adequately account for relatedness, still etymology will remain indispensable in thinking about the kinship of languages.

*Commentary*: In #25 and #28 the source text is alive, like a fruit tree; that aliveness is contrasted in #27 with dead theory and in #28 with the dead theory's imagination of the source and target languages as having died. In #27 the binary opposition between life and death is reframed as an opposition between space and time, or between stop-frame synchrony and the diachrony of organic growth (and note that Saussure too used a plant metaphor to explain the opposition between synchrony and diachrony). #26 was focused on the fertile dynamism of historical processes, and thus implicitly life, organic growth, and time rather than death, ideality, and space, but in terms of a binary opposition between "the subjectivity of later generations" and a vitalistic Essence. Here in #29 the life vs. death binary is mobilized as competing explanations of the light translation can shed on the "kinship between languages": either translation creates a static similarity between the source and target languages (death, ideality, space) or, as in #28, translation opens a critical perspective on the "after-ripening" of words, phrases, and texts (life, change, time).

*Die Abstammung* is rendered differently by the various translators. For Zohn, Hynd and Valk, and Rendall it is "origin"; for Underwood (and for the dictionary, and my interlinear) it is "descent"—indeed back in #16 Benjamin himself called it *Deszendenz*. It could also be translated "ancestry." In language studies, however, it should probably be "derivation" or "etymology"—hence, for example, the importance of Hölderlin tracking Greek words back to their etymological origins and translating the latter. I have been translating *die Verwandtschaft* as both "affinity" and "kinship," and this passage demonstrates the importance of maintaining both: what makes "derivation" or "etymology" partially inadequate as a translation of *die Verwandtschaft* is that the philological/etymological relatedness of two languages cannot account for the essential affinity between them. Effectively what Benjamin is saying here is that despite the fact that etymological kinship is too narrow a concept to account for the full affinity of languages, he's going to use it here anyway—possibly because of the overwhelming prototypicality that he assigns in #76 to Hölderlin's translations of Sophocles and Pindar.

*Other commentators*: Bartoloni (2004: np), Berman (2008/2018: 127), Smerick (2009: np), Vermeer (1996: 89).

## 30 The supplementation of intentions (1): the transhistorical processing leading to pure language

> Worin      kann die Verwandtschaft zweier Sprachen,  abgesehen von  einer
> Wherein can   the kinship         of two languages, viewed       from a
>
> historischen, gesucht werden? In der Ähnlichkeit von Dichtungen jedenfalls
> historical,  sought become? In the similarity  of   poems       anyway
>
> ebensowenig wie in derjenigen ihrer    Worte. Vielmehr beruht   alle
> just as little   as  in that      of their words. Rather  is based all
>
> überhistorische Verwandtschaft der    Sprachen  darin,  daß in ihrer jeder
> suprahistorical  kinship           of the languages therein, that in their every
>
> als ganzer jeweils eines und zwar   dasselbe gemeint ist, das dennoch
> as whole each    one and in fact the same meant    is,  that nevertheless
>
> keiner einzelnen von ihnen, sondern nur  der Allheit ihrer    einander
> no   single   of  them, rather  only the totality of their one another
>
> ergänzenden  Intentionen erreichbar ist: die reine Sprache.
> supplemented intentions    reachable is:  the pure language.

*Paraphrase*: The affinity/kinship between any two languages is not historical but suprahistorical (the history of superlife), and consists not in the kinds of structural similarity traditionally explored in contrastive linguistics, but in the fact that the same thing is meant in each, namely that which can be attained by no single one of them on its own, but only by the collectivity of their mutually supplemented intentions: pure language.

*Commentary*: Werner Hamacher (2001/2012: 511) offers this gloss:

> For translation is not the synthesis of already given languages. In its translation of the language of the original into its own, it transforms this language and its relation to the former, and projects a relation between languages in general that works toward their integral totality. Translation between two languages is thus always also the translation of languages into the one language as such that is not yet given and never given at all. As such, translation is protosynthesis, from which languages can first emerge at all as languages and, indeed, as languages of the one language. Translation is as little a belated connection between two given languages as history is the relation between two already completed times, epochs, or stages of history. Like translation, history is the leap that leads from one instant to another that is not given and that only emerges from this leap in the first place.

The kinship of languages, in other words, is like the kinship of humans: just as one human is related to another by dint of both being human, so too is any one language related to another language because both are languages. But a better word for that, as I've suggested in the commentary to #29, would be "affinity": we humans are not all kin, not all related by blood, but our shared humanity generates at least a protoaffinity for each other. The search launched by contrastive linguists (especially the Chomskyans) for the presence in all languages of the same syntactic structures, proving the existence of Universal Grammar, is thematized by UG's proponents as a scientific quest for kinship; Benjamin would prefer to think of it as an affinity that transcends likenesses among specific linguistic structures. (Strikingly, Hynd and Valk translate *die reine Sprache* "pure language," which for Benjamin is ultimately the basis of the kinship of all languages, as "pure, universal language" [301].[28] Indeed 1968, when they published their translation, was the heyday of Chomskyan TG grammar, which seemed to promise a transformational-generative explanation not only of all languages but of all human cognition.)

Antoine Berman (2008/2018) has an interesting secularizing reading of pure language: that it isn't anything messianic or mystical; it's just natural language *imagined* in terms of purity. According to Berman that imagination was fueled in Benjamin by reading Hölderlin, who writes obsessively about *das Reine* "purity," so the finest example of "pure language" would be the language of poetry (and

---

28 George Steiner (1975/1998: 66) too, somewhat surprisingly, assimilated Benjamin's "pure language" to "the concept of 'universal language'." David Bellos (2010: 211) makes a similar leap: to the question "Wherein lies the kinship between all languages?", he writes, "Benjamin comes up with an answer you might expect from machine translation specialists: 'pure language', otherwise known as Interlingua, the 'invariant core' which expressions in any language encode." As is typical in mystical discourse, Benjamin defines pure language negatively, making it impossible to know what it is positively; but to the negatives he lists in #48, I would add "it's not universal language and it's not Interlingua."

translation) like his. Given that Hölderlin typically uses *das Reine* as a kenning for "the Spirit," of course, even in a Hölderlinian purview "pure language" would be the language of the Spirit, not of Hölderlinian poetry. But Berman is determined to secularize Benjamin on this point: "In other words, pure language is not some vague ideal, is not a universal *logos*, but *language itself*—what Benjamin [in a letter to Martin Buber, July 1916] calls the 'dignity of its essence,'[29] bearing in mind that all dignity and purity can only exist within the infinite medium of language" (130). This is utterly at odds with the Edenic past context (in "On Language as Such") and the messianic future context (in the "Task") in which Benjamin always presents pure language; but Berman shies away from the mystical and the messianic in Benjamin's thought,[30] and so keeps repeating his secularization, in the hope that repetition will convince: "Pure language is language itself and in itself" (137); "Pure language is the *unsaid* [the *non-dit*] par excellence of 'natural' languages" (137; Wright's insertion); "What also remains obscure is *how* this pure language which, for Benjamin, is language itself—this pure language which is non-transitive, non-communicative and non-signifying—is proclaimed in translation" (137). The answer is that it is *not* "proclaimed in translation." Presumably Berman is alluding to #19, where Benjamin's verb is not *verkünden* or *verkündigen* "proclaim" but *darstellen*, which I translate as "body forth" and Jacobs (1975: 758–59) and Berman (2008/2018: 99–100) both translate as "perform." That use of *darstellen* in fact is there followed by *keimhaft oder intensiv verwirklichen*, which I translate as "to make it real germinally or intensively" and Berman doesn't discuss or translate—but is also clearly not a proclamation. What translation does according to Benjamin is not to proclaim but largely unconsciously to *activate* and *fuel* the messianic movement toward pure language—to help "bring the seed of pure language to ripeness" (#36, #51), and "to keep probing the holy growth of languages, testing how far removed what is sequestered inside them is from revelation, and how present it might become through knowledge of the removal" (#35). Berman, however, wants that not to be true. In the service of that desire, he neglects to translate and comment on the passages that are most clearly messianic and mystical, and keeps working to provide circumstantial evidence for his claims from Romantic and post-Romantic writers like Hölderlin and Paul Valéry. For example: "Benjamin's Messianic announcement of 'pure language' might secretly correspond

---

29 The Jacobsons' English translation in Scholem and Adorno (1994: 80) is "its dignity and its nature"; Chantal Wright (2018: 133n14) explains that Berman misquotes the French translation of *ihrer Würde und ihres Wesen* (Scholem and Adorno 1978: 127) "of its dignity and its essence."

30 Note, however, that Berman (2008/2018: 102) does mention, in connection with #15, that for Benjamin "all the purposefulness inherent in human beings points towards an 'end' which is not immanent in them but has to be sought outside life, *beyond* life and even above it. The purpose of life is *über* life." This would seem to contradict Berman's insistence that for Benjamin "pure language," the greater purpose that encompasses and fulfills all lesser linguistic purposivenesses (#18), is not transcendent but immanent in all natural human language.

to Hölderlin's prophetic *Bald sind wir Gesang* [Soon we shall be song]" (129). "Secretly" there implies that the "Messianic announcement" *might be*—but actually can only be *read as*—a cover for a hidden and therefore truer Romantic celebration of song. And:

> This is what we find in Valéry when he says that poetry is the translation of the language of men into the language of the gods. Pure language is not the language of the gods, it is a particular language that was created by a process of purification, it is a language that one can also define by traits that have much in common with Benjamin's pure language, which are the absence of content, non-communicability, emptiness—a series of predicates that appear to be the same. (Berman 2008/2018: 133n16)

There's the circumstantial evidence: "*one can also define* by traits that have *much in common* with Benjamin's pure language." If the two definitions are that similar, they can plausibly be construed as referring to basically the same thing.

Samuel Weber (2008: 70) reads pure language along lines similar to Berman's:

> The notion of "pure language" is at first a negative notion: "pure" means purged of elements that are external. What are such elements and where do we find them? Paradoxically, we find them in the original works of poetry, insofar as these are determined by their relation to extra-linguistic "contents" and "contexts." The original can only singularize itself as a work inasmuch as it is determined by its relation to nonlinguistic entities.

The fact that translation by definition severs those relations with (the source) culture is for Benjamin precisely what makes it untranslatable.

What Benjamin elsewhere (#19, #36, #50–51) calls the "seed" of pure language would of course include the preparatory facts that each language *meint* "means or intends" (or possibly also "says or thinks") the same things as all the others and that the intentions of each are supplemented, which is to say mixed and mingled, interlingually through translation. As he explains in #31–33, this does not mean that individual words and sentences in any two languages have the exact same semantic content, let alone the same syntactic form: the "meanings" or "intentions" in languages are transcendental forces, vitalistic agents that feed off translations in order to grow toward pure language.

*Other commentators*: Bartoloni (2004: np), Benjamin (1989/2014: 92), Britt (1996: 53), Chapman (2019: 76–78), Engel (2014: 5), Ferreira Duarte (1995: 278), Ferris (2008: 64), Gasché (1986: 78–79), Jacobs (1975: 757, 760), Johnston (1992: 44), Pan (2017: 40), Pfau (1988: 1083), Rothwell (2009: 260), Smerick (2009: np), Steiner (2010: 48), Vermeer (1996: 18, 42–59, 70–79, 88–92, 158–70).

## 31 The supplementation of intentions (2): distinguishing the *intendendum* from the manner of intending

> Während nämlich alle einzelnen Elemente, die Wörter, Sätze,
> While namely all single elements, the words, sentences,
>
> Zusammenhänge von fremden Sprachen sich ausschließen,
> contexts of foreign languages themselves exclude,
>
> ergänzen diese Sprachen sich in ihren Intentionen selbst.
> supplement these languages themselves in their intentions themselves.
>
> Dieses Gesetz, eines der grundlegenden der Sprachphilosophie
> This law, one of the fundamental of the language philosophy
>
> genau zu fassen, ist in der Intention vom Gemeinten die Art des
> precisely to grasp, is in the intention from the meant the art of the
>
> Meinens zu unterscheiden.
> meaning to distinguish.

*Paraphrase*: Obviously the words, sentences, contexts—all the individual elements—in two languages are mutually exclusive. There is no reason to think that these would ever match up in a translation. But in their intentions—(#21) "what they want to say"—languages supplement each other. This is one of the most fundamental laws in the philosophy of language. To grasp it fully, one must distinguish between what is intended (the *intendendum*) and the manner in which it is intended (the *modus significandi*).

*Commentary*: Benjamin conceives the intentions of each language as structuring agents; and while the specific structures that they organize in speakers' and writers' phenomenological orientations to communication—namely, the *Gemeinte*, the *intendendum* or "what is intended," which Zohn and Rendall translate as "the intended object"—are divergent, the manner in which they intend those things interacts with other languages in the act of translating. Benjamin calls this a fundamental law in the philosophy of language; I would say specifically that it is an insightful phenomenological observation that Benjamin himself must have made while translating.[31] He tends to externalize the phenomenology—to project it onto "the languages themselves"—while I would situate the "supplementation" (or partial alignment) of those intentions in the translator's experience of translating. But it does ring experientially true that one translates not words or sentences

---

31 Johnston (1992: 43) too suggests that "Benjamin means this in the Husserlian, phenomenological sense."

or contexts but that feeling that "the language" "wants" one to read or translate a certain way, and that one does so by bringing the intentions of the source and target languages mentally, perhaps affectively, perhaps even kinesthetically, into partial alignment or overlap.

Samuel Weber (2008: 71–72) follows up on Rodolphe Gasché's (1986: 79) observation that in Benjamin's essay *die Art des Meinens* or "way of meaning/intending"

> is an almost literal translation of the scholastic concept known, in Latin, as the *modus significandi*. Whereas the scholastics, for instance Thomas of Erfurt in his famous treatise on the modes of signification, interpreted the *modus significandi* as the expression of a conscious intention, Benjamin gives the notion a different spin. He considers it not as a framework for producing meaning—this was the interest of the scholastics—but rather, in a more Saussurean manner, as a movement of language that is prior to the communication or constitution of meaning. In thus separating the "way of meaning" from "the meant" (that is, from meaning as concept, object, or referent), Benjamin develops an argumentation that had already been explored in a book that Benjamin had read, although with very mixed feelings.

That book that Benjamin read in 1920 was the *Habilitation* dissertation of Martin Heidegger, defended in 1915: *Die kategorien- und Bedeutungslehre des Duns Scotus/The Doctrine of the Categories and of Signification of Duns Scotus* (1916). Weber explains that before finding that book, which he disliked intensely, Benjamin had been planning to write his own *Habilitation* dissertation on the same subject, and had to change course; but the relationship between the *modus significandi* and syntax that Heidegger outlines there arguably did form the core of Benjamin's thinking of translation in the "Task." It's also tempting to speculate that Benjamin had a more recent model as well: in his translator's preface to his 1778 Homer, Johann Jakob Bodmer (1698–1783) refers in passing to translators who render literally because they honor "die Weisen, wie ein Urheber die Sachen vorgetragen" (quoted in Louth 1998: 17): how authors *put* things. See also Fenves (2011: 57–58) for discussion.

In Benjamin's brief list of linguistic constructs in the first sentence—*Wörter, Sätze, Zusammenhänge* "words, sentences, contexts"—Zohn and Rendall translate *Zusammenhänge* as "structures." This is quite misleading, as words and sentences are typically structuralized in linguistics as well: morphological, semantic, and syntactic structures. See the commentary to #13 for a full discussion of the Diltheyan term *Zusammenhang* and its use in the essay.

*Other commentators*: Benjamin (1989/2014: 92), Berman (2008/2018: 139–40), Chapman (2019: 77), Gelley (2015: 23), Menke (2002: 90), Mosés (1995: 140–42), Rendall (1997b: 175), Rothwell (2009: 260), Smerick (2009: np), Vermeer (1996: 86), Weber (2005: 74).

## 32 The supplementation of intentions (3): an example of the distinction between what is intended and the manner of intention

> In »Brot« und »pain« ist das Gemeinte zwar    dasselbe, die Art, es zu
> In *Brot*   and   *pain*  is  the meant    in fact the same, the art  it  to
>
> meinen, dagegen    nicht. In der Art des    Meinens nämlich liegt es,
> mean     in contrast not.   In the art of the meaning namely lies    it,
>
> daß beide Worte dem   Deutschen und Franzosen je      etwas
> that both  words to the German    and Frenchman always something
>
> Verschiedenes bedeuten, daß sie  für beide nicht vertauschbar sind,
> different      mean,    that they for both  not   exchangeable are,
>
> ja   sich         letzten Endes auszuschließen streben; am    Gemeinten
> indeed themselves of last  end   to exclude      strive;  on the meant
>
> aber,    daß sie,   absolut    genommen, das Selbe und Identische
> however, that they, absolutely named,     the same and identical
>
> bedeuten.
> mean.

*Paraphrase*: In the German and French words for "bread," *Brot* and *pain*, what is "meant" or "intended" (the *intendendum*) is the same; but in the *modus significandi* or way of intending they mean different things to Germans and French people, so they are not mutually exchangeable; their usage tendencies in the two languages are toward mutual exclusion. In an absolute sense, however, in terms of the *intendendum*, they mean exactly the same thing.

*Commentary*: This is a very simple and perhaps rather bland and pedestrian example that doesn't yet illustrate the language-philosophical "law" that Benjamin formulated in #30 and #31, namely that the translator while translating can feel the divergence of the intentions in the source and target languages, but can also bring them mentally into a mutually supplementing relation. (He moves on to that in #33.)

Anthony Pym (2009) has commented usefully on this passage. On the one hand,

> we are all now daydreaming about different kinds of bread, comparing bubbling warm baguettes with heavy nourishing rye, fondly remembering *patisseries* and quick breakfasts in the early morning of wet train stations. How true, how true, we surmise: our cultures are so different in even the most basic of things (well, especially in the basics). The citations at this

point might pair up with Eva Hoffman's story about Polish milk, which she remembers she had to boil before drinking, and so could never translate as English milk (Hoffman 1989). Such memories are certainly not interchangeable. Bread is never just bread; milk is not simply milk; cultures differentiate everything. (29–30)

But now on the other hand,

> Benjamin's text was written as the preface to his renditions of Baudelaire's *Tableaux parisiens* (a section of *Les Fleurs du mal*). Now, in this case, the text is so firmly set in Paris that the French *pain* might fairly be rendered as *baguette* (as an English word), allowing few glimpses of any pure meaning of bread. However, as it happens, the only bread in Baudelaire's *Les fleurs du mal* comes from explicitly Christian tradition ("bread and wine" in the poem *La Bénédiction* and "to earn your daily bread" in *La Muse vénale*), and that common Christian heritage or imposition gives French and German shared expressions (yes, equivalents) at both those points. At one very important level, the French and German Baudelaires are parts of the same common culture, and in the practices of the here-and-now. (30–31)

In other words, in Baudelaire's source text—the French text to whose German translation Benjamin's essay is attached as a kind of translator's preface—the transnational culture of Christianity, of Christian ritual practices like the Eucharist and the Lord's Prayer ("Donne-nous aujourd'hui notre pain de ce jour," "Unser tägliches Brot gib uns heute," "Give us this day our daily bread"), trumps national cultural differences between baguettes and rye bread. As Benjamin puts it in this passage, the *Art des Meinens* or "*modus significandi*" differentiates French baguettes from German rye bread, but in terms of the *Gemeinte* or "*intendendum*"—bread—they mean exactly the same thing. The difference, of course, is that in Benjamin the two *intendenda* are united by some transcendental entity, while in the ritual practices of Christianity they are united by the socioideological forces of a universalized religion.

Pym's article is titled "On Empiricism and Bad Philosophy in Translation Studies," his idea being to show that hard-headed empirical pragmatism can save our discussions of translation from a lot of philosophical hot air.[32] The hot air

---

32 Strikingly, Pym's section on Benjamin begins with a list of Benjamin's critics who are to his mind guilty of this kind of "bad philosophy" through a lack of empiricism, and one of them is Vermeer (1996)—though Vermeer's book is a thoughtfully and meticulously argued empirical testing ground for Benjamin's metaphysical claims, leading to very much the same kinds of counterarguments as are lodged by Pym. Indeed Pym's decision to go to Benjamin's translation of Baudelaire to test Benjamin's theory might be read as a brief reprise of Vermeer's longer, more detailed, and far more devastating critique in his fourteenth chapter, which begins with a study of the Proust translations Benjamin did with Franz Hessel (204–7) and concludes with a study

that exercises him in this case is the poststructuralist focus on difference: the constant reminders from theorists that translations, rather than simply reproducing the source text, create difference. And that's true, of course, he admits; but why is it bad form to insist that translations are expected to stand in *some* kind of derivative and imitative relation to the source text? He also seems to be marshalling Benjamin's *Brot*-and-*pain* example as more evidence that too many theorists stress difference over sameness.

"Translational dialectics can surely continue to the end of the world," he adds, "but various institutional churches have solved the problem in the meantime. One only has to go and see, in the texts, in the translations, or in the churches" (Pym 2009: 31). But of course "solved the problem" is doubly misleading: for Benjamin, obviously, for whom there is no problem, but also for more globally minded scholars, who would take the solution imposed by transnational Christianity to be a form of colonial privilege and therefore ultimately a kind of supercharged localism. For Benjamin, the differences between the French and German manners of intending are not a problem but an opportunity: they illustrate the all-important clash of languages that drives the sacred history toward pure language. (For him the fact that Christianity imposes a symbolic unity on bread would be simply an irrelevancy.) And globally minded scholars would note that the cross-cultural identity of bread-*intendenda* can't be assumed when translating Baudelaire into (say) Asian or African languages: because that supposed "solution" would rest on Eurocentric assumptions about Christian universalism, it would ultimately leave target readers in the dark.

*Other commentators*: Bartoloni (2004: np), Bellos (2010: 211), Benjamin (1989/2014: 92, 162), Berman (2008/2018: 140), Britt (1996: 51–52), Chapman (2019: 77), de Man (2000: 28), Engel (2014: 4), Ferreira Duarte (1995: 274–75), Ferris (2008: 63), Jacobs (1975: 760–61), Johnston (1992: 43, 55n4), Kohlross (2009: 102, 104), Pan (2017: 37), Porter (1989: 1067), Rendall (1997b: 176), Sandbank (2015: 216, 218–19), Smerick (2009: np).

---

of his solo translation of Baudelaire's *Tableaux parisiens* (207–10). Having not only compared a passage from Proust in French and German but quoted from Benjamin's printed remarks on the translations—documenting his frustrated attempt to imitate Proust's periodic and "asthmatic" style—Vermeer offers a rather blunt assessment of the Baudelaire:

Den Baudelaire-Gedichtübertsetzungen Benjamins fehlt es an Poesie. Benjamin war nicht der Mann für Poetik … Hier hatte er sich an das falsche Objekt gewagt. … Benjamin bleibt einfach hinter seinen eigenen Aussprüchen zurück. Er hätte bei der Theorie haltmachen sollen. (207, 209)

Benjamin's translations of Baudelaire's poems lack poetry. Benjamin wasn't the man for poetics … Here he had ventured on the wrong object. … Benjamin simply falls short of his own remarks. He should have stopped at theory.

## 33 The supplementation of intentions (4): entering into mutual supplementation

> Während dergestalt   die  Art  des     Meinens in diesen beiden Wörtern
> While      in that form the way of the meaning in these  both     words
>
> einander     widerstrebt,   ergänzt      sie sich in den beiden Sprachen,
> one another against-strives, supplements it   itself in the both    languages
>
> denen       sie   entstammen. Und zwar   ergänzt       sich in ihnen die
> from which they derive.         And in fact supplements itself in them the
>
> Art des    Meinens zum  Gemeinten.
> way of the meaning to the meant.

*Paraphrase*: While the *modus significandi* or manner of intending is in conflict in the two words, the conflicting manners of intending also enter into a relation of mutual supplementation in the two languages from which they stem. And indeed in this case the manner of intending enters into a relation of mutual supplementation with the *intendendum*.

*Commentary*: Benjamin would appear to be describing the phenomenology of translation, here—just not explicitly. He theorizes the entering into relations of mutual supplementation as if it were something that the intentions of the two languages did on their own, as vitalistic agents thirsting for pure language. I suggest, however, that his theory is a projection onto transcendental agents of his own phenomenological—kinesthetic-becoming-affective-becoming-conative—experience of translating. (See Robinson 2017b: 108–10 for discussion.) If my guess is right, of course, Benjamin would want to turn that around: the translatorial phenomenology of translating—the *feeling* of working to bring what seem like the intentions of the source and target languages into rough alignment—is an earthly copy of the transcendental/vitalistic supplementation of the intentions of ideal Forms and their Essences. Or, perhaps, the feeling is not so much a copy as it is an emanation, or perhaps an *Andeutung* "intimation" or *Offenbarung* "revelation": Benjamin is "given" the transcendental truth in phenomenological form. (For Benjamin's mobilization of Romantic theories of *Gefühl* "feeling," see #41–42, #54.)

*Other commentators*: Berman (2008/2018: 141–43), Pan (2017: 37).

## 34 The supplementation of intentions (5): what languages intend remains buried and in constant transformation until it emerges as pure language

> Bei den einzelnen, den unergänzten   Sprachen nämlich ist ihr
> In  the single,   the unsupplemented languages namely is their
>
> Gemeintes niemals in relativer Selbständigkeit anzutreffen, wie bei den
> meant     never   in relative independence to meet,   as in the
>
> einzelnen Wörtern oder Sätzen,    sondern vielmehr in stetem
> single   words  or  sentences, rather  far more in constant
>
> Wandel       begriffen, bis  es aus der  Harmonie all jener    Arten
> transformation understood, until it out of the harmony all of those ways
>
> des   Meinens als die reine Sprache  herauszutreten vermag. So lange
> of the meaning as the pure language to step out     could.  So long
>
> bleibt  es in den Sprachen verborgen.
> remains it in the languages hidden.

*Paraphrase*: In each individual—which is to say unsupplemented—language we never find what is intended in relative independence, in individual words or sentences; rather, it is constantly churning and changing, until it manages to emerge from the harmony of all the manners of intending as pure language. Until then it remains hidden in the languages.

*Commentary*: On the surface this passage seems mired in unarticulated contradiction. On the one hand, the individual languages are unsupplemented, which sounds like they have never been brought into contact with other languages, through translation or other channels of interlingual interaction. On the other hand, apparently even without supplementation, what is intended is somehow being transformed, and eventually, through the clash and ultimately the harmonizing of different manners of intending, emerging as pure language.

Rather than contradiction, however, what seems to have happened is that Benjamin neglected to articulate a crucial argumentative step. I suggest that what he means by "individual—which is to say unsupplemented—languages" is something like "languages as (mis)understood by mainstream linguistics and 'the dead theory of translation'": stable sign systems built out of static blocks of various sizes (words, clauses, sentences, etc.). From his perspective, these would not be real languages *before* supplementation, but imaginaries conjured up by bad theory *without* the "law" of supplementation. What he arguably meant to say, then, would be that languages are never stand-alone structures: they are always in the toil and turmoil of interlingual supplementation. As a result, the reason we don't find what is intended in "relative independence, in individual words or sentences," is that such stable independence is again an artifact of bad theory. What is intended in languages is *always* interdependent, always being churned up by interlingual clashes and tensions. It is out of that churning that languages move toward the messianic goal of pure language.

We will be seeing more detailed hints at what *die reine Sprache* "pure language" might be like as we proceed; but let us pause here to note what Benjamin wrote about it at the ripe age of 24, in "Über Sprache überhaupt und über die Sprache des Menschen"/"On Language as Such and on the Language of Man":

> Der Inbegriff dieser intensiven Totalität der Sprache als des geistigen Wesens des Menschen ist der Name. Der Mensch ist der Nennende, daran erkennen wir, daß aus ihm die reine Sprache spricht. Alle Natur, sofern sie sich mitteilt, teilt sich in der Sprache mit, also letzten Endes im Menschen. Darum ist er der Herr der Natur und kann die Dinge benennen. (Benjamin 1916/1977: 144)

> The quintessence of this intensive totality of language as the mental being of man is naming. Man is the namer, by this we recognize that through him pure language speaks. All nature, insofar as it communicates itself, communicates itself in language, and so finally in man. Hence he is the lord of nature and can give names to things. (Benjamin 1978/1986: 318–19)

In Eden, because the Lord of Hosts breathed a few whiffs of that pure paradisal language into Adam, pure language speaks through him, making him "the lord of nature [who] can give names to things." Nature, which supposedly speaks "the language of things," actually has no language, and in Eden speaks only in and through Adam.

Since the *Sündenfall* "fall into sin," however, that ability to channel pure language is lost:

> Der Sündenfall ist die Geburtsstunde des menschlichen Wortes, in dem der Name nicht mehr unverletzt lebte, das aus der Namensprache, der erkennenden, man sagen darf: der immanenten eigenen Magie heraustrat, um ausdrücklich, von außen gleichsam, magisch zu werden. (153; quoted in Jacobson 275n107)

> The fall from grace marks the birth of the human word, in which the name no longer remains intact, stepping out of naming language, the language of knowledge—from what we may call its own immanent magic—in order to become expressly and, indeed, over time, externally magical. (327; quoted in Jacobson 108)

It is thus only after the fall that translation becomes both necessary and mystically enabling:

> Die Sprache der Dinge kann in die Sprache der Erkenntnis und des Namens nur in der Übersetzung eingehen—soviel Übersetzungen, soviel Sprachen, sobald nämlich der Menschen einmal aus dem paradiesischen Zustand, der nur eine Sprache kannte, gefallen ist. (152; quoted in Jacobson 274n103)

> The language of things can pass into the language of knowledge and name only through translation—as many translations, so many languages—once humanity fell from the paradisiac state that knew only one language. (326; quoted in Jacobson 108)

In other words, as Jacobson paraphrases, "Language's damaged immediacy gave birth to a multiplicity of languages and served as the impetus for translation, generating its imperative in the profane" (112). Or, more fully:

> Exile is the point at which Benjamin marks the transition from the creating word to a language that is no longer able to express creation. The magic of this expression, in which linguistic creation was also immanent revelation communicable, was at once lost with the expulsion from paradise. In this the nature of revelatory language was to change along with its magic. If language was once used to express the unfolding of God's divine plan, it was now the mere appearance of the knowledge of how this plan works, a mimicking that is reduced to mere imitation of the creating word. Now that the word must express something outside itself, it typifies "the fall of linguistic spirit" (327) ["Der Sündenfall des Sprachgeistes" (153; quoted in Jacobson 275n108)]. No longer is the spirit of the word capable of being expressed in its name, as all things are to turn faceless with regard to their proper names. The word expresses outwardly as a condition of lost identity. (Jacobson 109)

*Other commentators*: Bartoloni (2004: np), Britt (1996: 52), Engel (2014: 4–6), Hamacher (2001/2012: 512), Johnston (1992: 44), Liska (2014: 235), Smerick (2009: np).

## 35 Translation's mystical task (1): probing languages to see how close they are to the messianic end of their history

Wenn aber     diese derart   bis   ans     messianische Ende ihrer
If       however these like this until on the messianic    end of their

Geschichte wachsen, so ist es die Übersetzung, welche am      ewigen
history     grow,    so is it  the translation   which on the eternal

Fortleben der    Werke und am     unendlichen Aufleben der    Sprachen
forthliving of the works and on the unending   upliving  of the languages

```
sich  entzündet, immer von   neuem die Probe auf   jenes heilige Wachstum
itself enkindles,  ever     from new    the probe into that  holy    growth

der    Sprachen zu machen: wie  weit ihr   Verborgenes von  der
of the languages to make:     how far   their hoard      from the

Offenbarung entfernt  sei, wie  gegenwärtig es im      Wissen    um diese
revelation   removed be, how present        it in the knowledge of  this

Entfernung werden  mag.
removal    become may.
```

*Paraphrase*: But if the languages keep growing like this until the messianic end of their history, the eternal ongoing life of literary works and the unending "up-living" or uprising (*Aufleben*) of languages enkindle translation to keep probing the holy growth of languages, testing how far removed what is sequestered inside them is from revelation, and how present it might become through knowledge of the removal.

*Commentary*: In most of Benjamin's essay the Jewish mysticism is implicit; in this sentence it becomes explicit. "Messianic," "eternal," "holy," and "revelation" make the mystical subtext that has been running like a *verborgener* "hidden" scarlet thread through the essay *gegenwärtig* "present." Harry Zohn seems to have been decently embarrassed about that explicitness: he dropped "messianic" from the first line entirely, making it "If, however, these languages continue to grow in this manner until the end of their time" (74), and translated *heilige* as "hallowed," which sounds rather more poetically secular than the cognate "holy." (The other three translations all write of "the messianic end" and "holy/sacred growth.")

In my interlinear *das unendliche Aufleben* becomes "the unending upliving," and I liked the cognate "upliving" so much that I dragged it down into the paraphrase as well, in scare quotes: the languages keep living it up. And indeed the verb *aufleben* can be used for the "livening up" of a party. The other translators have mostly rendered it "renewal"—only Rendall has "revival"—and those are accurate translations. They just seem a bit abstract to me, for a process that has "life" and "up" in it. The verb *aufleben* can also be "to perk up" or "to buck up," and when it's "to revive" or "to revivify," it implies that the entity was dying or declining and has been brought back to full life. An endless coming back to life; a continuous resurgence of life. "Uprising" is another possible translation of the noun, usually implying an insurgency; I like the image of endlessly rising up, higher and higher, driven by an agitation, a turbulent churning and convulsing as the intentions of the languages keep crashing into each other. Much more kinesthetic a process than some bland "renewal" or "revival."

This passage and the five that follow it (#36–40) also formulate one definition, arguably the primary definition, of the translator's task: to activate that probing into the holy growth of languages. As Benjamin will hint in #36, the translator is incapable of acting directly on that growth: it is, after all, holy, and the translator is no Messiah. But Benjamin's vision brings the translator into the messianic history at second hand—by remote control, as it were, and at three removes, as I suggest in the commentary to #18. The translator's task in this light is not to reproduce the meaning of the source text accurately in the target language, but to bring the source and target languages into interrelation, to intermesh them in humanly flawed ways that nevertheless stir up the intentions of both languages to engage and grow. And, as we will see increasingly toward the end of the essay (#55–56, #61–62, #77–78), the less the translator seeks to transmit the meanings of whole sentences—i.e., the more literally s/he translates—the more transformative the stirring and intermeshing becomes.

*Other commentators*: Balfour (2018: 758–62), Benjamin (1989/2014: 97), Berman (2008/2018: 144), Britt (1996: 52), Derrida (1985: 183, 202), Engel (2014: 6), Ferreira Duarte (1995: 276), Hamacher (2001/2012: 512), Johnston (1992: 55n5), Liska (2014: 240), Mosés (1995: 142), Pan (2017: 42), Pfau (1988: 1085), Smerick (2009: np), Steiner (1975/1998: 67), Steiner (2010: 49).

## 36 Translation's mystical task (2): ripening the seed

> Damit      ist allerdings zugestanden, daß alle Übersetzung nur eine
> Therewith is  though    right           that all   translation   only a
>
> irgendwie            vorläufige Art ist, sich  mit der Fremdheit  der
> somehow or other tentative way is  itself with the foreignness of the
>
> Sprachen auseinanderzusetzen. Eine andere als  zeitliche und vorläufige
> languages to come to terms.      An other    than passing and tentative
>
> Lösung dieser Fremdheit, eine augenblickliche und endgültige, bleibt
> solution of this foreignness, an   instantaneous    and definitive,  remains
>
> den    Menschen versagt oder ist jedenfalls unmittelbar nicht anzustreben.
> to the humans     denied or   is at least   immediate  not to pursue.
>
> Mittelbar aber    ist es das Wachstum der   Religionen, welches in den
> Mediable however is it the growth      of the religions   which   in the
>
> Sprachen den verhüllten Samen einer höhern reift.
> languages the veiled      seed  of a  higher ripens.

*Paraphrase*: Human translation is, however, only a tentative, makeshift, hit-or-miss way of (re-/dis)solving the foreignness of foreign languages: the ability to resolve or dissolve the problem of that foreignness instantly or conclusively is denied to humans, or at least cannot be pursued immediably (without the possibility of mediation). The necessary mediability (capacity for mediation) can be found in the growth of religions, which ripens the seed that is hidden in the languages and raises it to a higher level.

*Commentary*: Here Benjamin makes it very clear that he is *not* making it the translator's task to resolve or dissolve that foreignness (see the Novalis quote in the commentaries to #0 and #51) and ripen that seed—to act directly ("immediably") on languages so as to accelerate their holy growth toward their messianic goal, pure language. What previous hints (especially in #35) lead one to expect him to say next is that, while the human translator can't do it, translation can: translations bring languages into contact and conflict, and that activates a mystical vitalism resident in both the source and target languages that accelerates the holy growth toward pure language. But that is not what he says here. Rather, the growth of *religions* "mediably" accelerates the holy growth of *languages*. Since this is the only mention of religion in the essay, we are left guessing at precisely how religions grow, and by what medium their growth ripens that seed.

Perhaps religions grow through dissemination of their sacred writings to new target cultures via translation? That was certainly part of the official theology of Christianity (rather less, until the late sixteenth century, part of the social practices tolerated by the Roman Catholic Church), but not so much of Judaism, where the Bible was written in Hebrew by God in his own hand, and the shape of every letter and every stray ink dot contained a mystery, and translations into other languages, beginning with the Septuagint in the third century BCE, were tolerated as cribs but not validated as sacred writ. (See the commentary to #78 for elaboration.)

More likely, perhaps, is the possibility that by "religions" Benjamin means not official ecclesiastical institutions but rather the kinds of religious perspectives that he seems to be evoking with his talk of messianic ends, holy growth, and so on. See the commentary on #57 for the influence on Benjamin's essay of his friend Gershom Scholem's expertise on Kabbalah; certainly if we read "The Task of the Translator" as a veiled mystical treatise in the Kabbalist vein, this cryptic phrase "the growth of religions" might be read as a hint at the mystical key to all the other cryptic phrases that elude and frustrate the interpretive efforts of secular readers.

Antoine Berman (2008/2018: 147) offers a different explanation of this "growth of religions" as basically ecstatic Jena Romanticism:

> All the great Western translations have a religious foundation, are religious texts; and this goes far beyond translations of the Bible. Hölderlin's translations

of Pindar and Sophocles are religious. So too is the French translation of Milton's *Paradise Lost* by Chateaubriand, or George's translation of Baudelaire. Religion has to be understood in a very broad sense here, as anything that links man to the world as a whole. In the sense that every great text, sacred or profane, expresses and establishes this link, in the sense that every great text is "religious," the act of translating such a text is religious too.

The reader might be forgiven for complaining that Berman's definition of "religious" is a bit grandiose here.

Dominik Zechner (2020: 320), who is interested in the directionality of translation in Benjamin—forward-translation and back-translation—notes that *vorläufig* "tentative, makeshift, hit-or-miss" comes from the verb *vorlaufen* "to run ahead," and that harks back to *vorgreifende* "anticipatory" or (lit.) "fore-gripping" in #20. All six of the human animal's senses are attuned to the future—to what is coming.

*Other commentators*: Britt (1996: 54), Chapman (2019: 77–78, 104–5), Engel (2014: 6), Ferris (2008: 63, 66), Gasché (1986: 81), Gelley (2015: 23), Hamacher (2001/2012: 538), Smerick (2009: np), Vermeer (1996: 167).

## 37 Translation's mystical task (3): pointing the way to pure language

Übersetzung also,     wiewohl sie auf Dauer     ihrer Gebilde nicht
Translation   therefore, although it   on duration of its products not

Anspruch erheben kann und hierin unähnlich der Kunst, verleugnet nicht
claim     make     can   and herein unlike     the art,   denies   not

ihre Richtung auf  ein letztes, endgültiges und entscheidendes Stadium
its   direction onto a   last,   entelechial and decisive        stage

aller Sprachfügung.     In ihr wächst das Original in    einen gleichsam
of all linguistic providence. In it  grows  the original into an    as it were

höheren und reineren Luftkreis der    Sprache  hinauf, in welchem es
higher   and purer   air circle of the language up,   in which   it

freilich      nicht auf die Dauer    zu leben vermag, wie es ihn auch bei
admittedly not   on the duration to live    could,   as   it it  also by

weitem nicht in allen Teilen seiner Gestalt erreicht, auf den   es aber
far    not   in all   parts of its   form   reaches, on which it however

dennoch in einer wunderbar   eindringlichen Weise wenigstens hindeutet als
even so   in a      wonderfully haunting        way   at least    points     as

> auf    den vorbestimmten, versagten Versöhnungs- und Erfüllungsbereich
> toward the predestined,    denied    reconciliation and fulfillment realm
>
> der    Sprachen.
> of the languages.

*Paraphrase*: Unlike art, translation can never lay claim to the long-term endurance of its products, but it nevertheless keeps striving to attain a last definitive entelechial stage of linguistic providence. In the translation the source text grows as it were into a higher and purer realm of language—and even though it can't live there forever, because it never attains that realm in every aspect, it still points in a wonderfully haunting way toward the predestined yet inaccessible kingdom of linguistic reconciliation and fulfillment.

*Commentary*: Throughout this section (#35–38) Benjamin alternates between seeing translation's cup as half-full and seeing it as half-empty—specifically, presenting human translators' inability to operate on the highest mystical level alternately as a striving and a falling short. In #35 he presents translation as the test of languages' holy growth; in #36 as a makeshift and hit-or-miss way of resolving and dissolving the foreignness of foreign languages; and, here in #37, as an impressive, urgent, haunting (for *eindringlich* Rendall has "penetrating," Hynd and Valk and Underwood "insistent") striving and pointing toward pure language, in the course of which it propels the source text, even if only temporarily, into "a higher and purer realm of language."

Only hinted at here and developed more fully in #38–40 is Benjamin's notion that originals endure but translations don't, and therefore that originals are infinitely retranslatable but translations are not.

I take "haunting" from Ira Allen's translation of Werner Hamacher's (2001/2012: 538) gloss on this passage:

> That translation, in Benjamin's words, "suggests in a wonderfully haunting manner [...] the predetermined, withheld realm of the reconciliation and fulfillment of languages" (15) makes of it a sort of negative mysticism of pure language, a wonderfully haunting—i.e., once again intensive—anticipation of that which is accessible to no anticipation, an intention toward that which refuses to be intended. Thus the intentionless moves into intention and makes intensity—piercing, pressure, increase, escalation—which is bound together with every intention, into an intensity of the intentionless.

Talk about "wonderfully haunting": Hamacher is far and away the most philosophically poetic and the most poetically philosophical reader of Benjamin I know.

Antoine Berman (2008/2018: 152–58) is quite eloquent on this passage. His overall point is borrowed from his 1986 article on the Platonism of translation; for commentary see Lee and Yun (2011). Obviously Plato never wrote about translation; Berman is extrapolating from Plato's metaphysical hierarchy between the sensual and the nonsensual, which entails also the hierarchies between the individual and the universal and between the body and the soul, the nonsensual and the universal occupying a higher ontological status than the sensual and the individual. Berman extends the implications of that metaphysics to language first by identifying the sensual in language with sounds and letters and the nonsensual with signification and sense, then by suggesting that the "Platonic" translator discards the source-language (SL) signifiers as sensual and individual and therefore disposable, and replaces them with target-language signifiers that refer to the most universal signifieds. Because (as Benjamin would insist) in the source text signifiers and signifieds are inextricably welded together, access to that deep metaphysical level of universality is more difficult to achieve in the translation. Based on the resulting image of the "Platonic" translator splitting the source-textual signifiers off from their signifieds and throwing them away, thus giving the disembodied signifieds pride of place, and the most universal signifieds the greatest prominence, we can postulate a "Platonic" theory of translation as entailing the nonsensual enhancement of meaning: the "Platonic" translator as the Ciceronian, Hieronymian sense-for-sense translator that Benjamin rejects.

And yet, Berman notes, even within a Platonic purview "translation, because it liberates meaning, produces a different relationship between signifiers and signifieds in the translating [target] language, a relationship where the *ideality* of meaning is allowed to dominate" (2008/2018: 154; emphasis added). As a result, "the [Platonic] essence of translation [can be understood to be] clarifying, illuminating, enriching and embellishing" (154).

So does that mean that Benjamin is "simply reformulating, in his own fashion, the Platonic conviction that the language of translation is superior to (purer, higher, more aerial, more luminous than) the language of the original, which is mired in the depths of its natural language" (154)? Berman says that the answer is both yes and no.

On the one hand, *Yes*, due to Benjamin's Platonism—a characterization on which I have insisted here as well, though in my reading Benjamin's Platonism is mystical and vitalist, based on the transcendental Forms and the possibility (in Jewish Neoplatonism) that those Forms are mobilized by a divine agent called the Logos, while in Berman's it is rational and static. Berman adds that "pure language could *also* be the Platonic *logos*" (154)—but he doesn't go so far as to offer up the Philonian Neoplatonist Logos (#59). Little as Berman liked Plato, he would have liked Philo's Plato even less.

On the other hand, however, *No*, in that Benjamin insists that the translation cannot sustain the "higher" language to which it raises the source text, and that it only raises it to that level piecemeal. "In the Platonic tradition," Berman notes—meaning by "the Platonic tradition" nothing that Plato or his followers ever wrote, but his own speculative extrapolation—"it is the *totality* of the text that is liberated by translation. For Benjamin, the original text only reaches a purer language in covert and fragmentary fashion" (154). Therefore, Berman concludes, we "cannot interpret Benjamin's thought within the framework of the traditional Platonic theory of translation" (154). This for Berman is a very good thing.

I would insert a corrective at this point: as I read the intertextuality on this point, the intersection between Plato and Benjamin is not at the liberation of *meaning*, as it is for Berman, but at the liberation of *Form*, which is to say of the ideal structure of the source text. For Berman's Plato that would have meant the liberation of the signifieds, which is to say of *der Sinn* "the sense or meaning," from the signifiers (which are discarded); for Benjamin's Plato it would have meant the liberation of the ideal (vitalistic) Form of the source-textual syntax, as *paced off* by the signifiers. For Berman's Plato what is left of the source text once the SL signifiers have been discarded is meaning; for Benjamin's Plato it is syntax. Both are disembodied Forms; both partake of the nonsensuous and therefore the universal. For Benjamin, however, that transcendental Form is only the foundation on which the translator builds, and the building s/he erects on that foundation is multiply embodied, which is to say embodied in metaphysical layers: first through literalism; then in the prototypicality of Hölderlin's Sophocles and Pindar (#76) through radical etymologism; then through the "protosynthetic" clashing and churning of the intentions in the two languages.

What is interesting is that at this point Berman begins listing examples of cases where influential readers have claimed that a translation is superior to its source text: Nietzsche on Schopenhauer in French; Novalis on Shakespeare in A.W. Schlegel's German; various scholars on Hölderlin's Sophocles in German; George Steiner on Jules Supervielle in Paul Celan's German. In each case, however, he reads the "superiority" of the translation(s) as *local*: "the languages have only entered into harmony at this *one* point" (157); "the harmony of the two languages that are brought together in translation can only be sporadic" (157).

Berman does not notice a possible contradiction between Benjamin insisting here that translations raise a text to a higher language and elsewhere that translations age and originals do not, and so he defends both (arguably conflicting) stances passionately. (See the commentary to #40 for discussion of the argument that translations are mortal and originals immortal.) Berman would himself have almost certainly rejected the notion that these two passages conflict, on the grounds that while "in the translation the source text grows as it were into a higher and purer realm of language, ... it can't live there forever, because it never attains that realm in every aspect." Any perceived superiority that might be attributed to a translation is necessarily short-lived. But more about that in #38 and #40.

*Other commentators*: Bellos (2010: 211), Chapman (2019: 39), Ferreira Duarte (1995: 275), Ferris (2008: 63–64), Gold (2007: 616), Liska (2014: 237), O'Keeffe (2015: 376), Pfau (1988: 1084), Roberts (1982: 120), Smerick (2009: np), Vermeer (1996: 160), Weber (2008: 70), Zechner (2020: 320).

## 38 Translation's mystical task (4): elevating the source text by transmitting its semantic content as little as possible / Translating vs. the writing of an original work (1): the essential kernel as the part of the original that is not translatable (1): stump and stalk

> Den erreicht es nicht mit Stumpf und Stiel, aber in ihm steht
> That reaches it not with stump and stalk, however in it stands
>
> dasjenige, was an einer Übersetzung mehr ist als Mitteilung.
> that which in a translation more is than with-sharing.
>
> Genauer läßt sich dieser wesenhafte Kern als dasjenige bestimmen,
> More precisely lets itself this essential kernel as that thing to determine
>
> was an ihr selbst nicht wiederum übersetzbar ist.
> what in it self not again translatable is.

*Paraphrase*: Through translation the original does not reach the predestined yet inaccessible empire of linguistic reconciliation and fulfillment "stump and stalk"—completely, in every way or every aspect—but it does contain that aspect of the translation that does not transmit a message. More precisely, that essential aspect is the kernel of un(re)translatability in any translation.

*Commentary*: The rather complex idea here is that (a) translation should not transmit a message (accurately reproduce sentential meanings) but (b) should bring the intentions of the source and target languages into interactive contact by rendering word for word; (c) the more a translation fulfills the b-task, the higher and purer the air into which it raises the source text; because (d) a translation is always inferior to the source text, (e) its elevating effect is both incomplete and short-lived, but (f) to the extent that it has fulfilled the b-task, whatever elevating e-effect it has contains that which exceeds the a-task; and, due to the d-inferiority and the e-effect, (g) the f-result can be defined as the part of the translation that makes its own translatability impossible.

The underlying image seems to be the purification of a metal and the sloughing off of the dross. The less dross that needs to be discarded, the nobler (both more ennobled and more ennobling) the purification process is to be considered. Even the greatest translation, however—namely, the radically literal translation that seeks hardly at all to transmit the semantic content of the source text into the target language, and thus elevates the source text into the highest possible realm while the effect lasts—is ultimately discarded in its entirety as dross, and must be succeeded by a new attempt to elevate the original. And because translations are fundamentally dross, impure waste matter, they cannot themselves be translated.

Two notes:

1 The idea of the translation chain, where each translation becomes the source text of a new translation event, would have been anathema to Benjamin—a frivolous game that has nothing to do with the holy growth of languages, or even with translation.
2 Benjamin was always dissatisfied with his own German translations—of Baudelaire and Proust, especially—presumably because they ended up being oriented to reproducing the French source text as accurately as possible, and thus seemed ultimately like a waste of time and effort.[33]

*Other commentators*: Bellos (2010: 211), Berman (2008/2018: 159–61), Felman (1999: 202), Gasché (1986: 77), Hamacher (2001/2012: 531), Jacobs (1975: 757), Pfau (1988: 1084), Smerick (2009: np), Weber (2008: 70), Zechner (2020: 321).

## 39 Translating vs. the writing of an original work (2): the essential kernel as the part of the original that is not translatable (2): the fruit and its skin, the folds of a royal mantle

| Mag man nämlich an Mitteilung aus ihr entnehmen, soviel man kann
| May one namely on with-sharing out of it remove, as much one can
|
| und dies übersetzen, so bleibt dennoch dasjenige unberührbar zurück,
| and this translate, so remains even so that very untouchable back,
|
| worauf die Arbeit des wahren Übersetzers sich richtete. Es ist nicht
| toward which the work of the true translator itself directed. It is not
|
| übertragbar wie das Dichterwort des Originals, weil das Verhältnis
| transposable like the poetic word of the original, because the relationship
|
| des Gehalts zur Sprache völlig verschieden ist in Original und
| of the tenor to the language fully different is in original and
|
| Übersetzung. Bilden nämlich diese im ersten eine gewisse Einheit
| translation. Compose namely these in the first a certain unity

---

33 See Vermeer (1996: 203–10) and Berman (2008/2018: 36–39) for useful accounts of the radical divergence of Benjamin-the-translation-theorist from Benjamin-the-translator: the fact that he was passionate about translation in theory but found it boring in practice; the fact that he despised the reproduction of meaning in theory but kept trying and failing to achieve it in practice, and so on.

| | | | |
|---|---|---|---|
| wie Frucht und Schale, so umgibt | | die Sprache der | Übersetzung ihren |
| like fruit and shell, so surrounds | | the language of the translation | its |
| Gehalt wie ein Königsmantel in weiten Falten. | | | |
| tenor like a royal mantle in wide folds. | | | |

*Paraphrase*: The semantic payload of any source text can indeed be translated; but no matter how much of it the translator seeks to extract from the source text and transmit in the translation, this effort will leave untouched the element toward which the true translator's work is stirred. Like the source text's poet-word, that element is untranslatable, because the relation between the tenor and the language is different in the source text and the translation. In the source text, tenor and language are joined together with a certain unity, like a fruit and its skin, while in the translation the language is wrapped loosely around the tenor, like the commodious folds of a royal mantle.

*Commentary*: The first thing to note here is that in this passage Benjamin makes it very clear that he is not claiming that translations cannot be translated. He is claiming that translations can't be translated *properly*. If all you want out of a translation is the meanings of the sentences, no problem: that kind of sense-for-sense translation can always be achieved, either directly from the source text or indirectly from a translation. Above and beyond that pedestrian purpose, however, there is in every great source text, he says, an element that is grounded in the close relationship between the source language and the source culture, and every true translator seeks (and invariably partly fails) to translate that; and it is the translated version of that "kernel" that Benjamin says is untranslatable, because the relationship between the target culture and the target language that supports it is shakier than it was in the source text. This is not a trivial claim—nothing to dismiss as aggressively as David Bellos (2010: 212) does: "This is rubbish." What Benjamin describes is indeed a resistance that great translators work very hard to overcome. They can *feel* the resistance even as they fight it—and often send the result off to the publisher with a sense of their own partial failure gnawing at them. That they sometimes arguably succeed, and that a second great translator is arguably capable of overcoming that same resistance left in a translation by a first, might stand as empirical evidence against Benjamin's claim; but it is also quite easy to contest that evidence. The kind of success that Benjamin declares impossible doesn't happen often; and when it does, it is inevitably a judgment call.

Two notes:

1 Translation chains work best when the translators are great poets accustomed to using their own poetic imaginations transformatively to overcome the resistance all human experience puts up to poeming.

2 If, with David Bellos, you're inclined to scoff at all this, you're either not operating at the high level Benjamin is describing (you're translating the sense and not worrying too much about the literary quality of the result) or you're not paying attention.[34]

In her introduction to Cahier 7 in Berman's *The Age of Translation*, Chantal Wright (2018: 151) notes Berman's translation of Benjamin's *Gehalt* as *teneur* "tenor," from the Latin verb *teneō* "I hold." (Actually, Berman simply follows Maurice de Gandillac's 1959/1971 lead in this.) The tenor voice in music is the one that "holds" the melody. The tenor of a discourse is the chain of thought that "holds on" throughout—the general drift. Since Benjamin himself makes a clear distinction between the *Inhalt* (lit. "in-held") "content" of a source text, which communicates to the reader and therefore should *not* be translated, and the *Gehalt* of a source text, which exceeds or avoids communication and *should* be translated—and, in a translation, remains unretranslatable—it is essential to make some sort of semantic differentiation between the two in English as well. *Gehalt* derives from Middle High German *gehalt* "custody, prison, inner value," from the verb form *gehalten* "to keep still, to hold or preserve, to imprison"; its current sense of "content or constituent" developed in the fifteenth century, for the gold content ("inner value") of a coin. For that sense Wright chooses "substance"; but to my mind that is too much caught up in medieval theology—as *substantia*, the Latin translation of the Greek ὑπόστασις/*hypostasis*, for the three "persons" of the Trinity—so I have instead followed Berman's and Gandillac's French lead and rendered *Gehalt* "tenor."

Jacques Derrida (1985) has a famous deconstruction of #38–39, based on Gandillac's (1959/1971) French translation, in which *der Kern* "kernel" from #38 is translated "le noyau" (cited in Derrida 236), which in turn is translated by Joseph F. Graham into English as "core."[35] Now *un noyau* in French can indeed be "a core," but only in geology, not in botany, where it is generally translated as the "pit/pip/stone" (of a fruit)—which in certain fruits, such as peaches and plums, can also be called a "kernel." A *Kern* in German, like a kernel in English, can also be a nucleus in physics and a single seed or grain in botany; both are also used for various functions and devices in mathematics and computing. A kernel

---

34 This is not idle snark. I spent three decades translating technical, commercial, legal, and medical texts in the professional translation marketplace, and in all of those jobs I valued the accurate transmission of sense. It was while immersed in that work that I published my first (dismissive) take on Benjamin, in Robinson (1996: 209); the tagline of that squib was "Find someone else, Walter; I'm too busy translating chain saw manuals." This past decade-plus I have been translating increasingly experimental literary works, and that has prepared me for a more sympathetic understanding of Benjamin's "Task."
35 Since he is translating Derrida's Benjamin quotes from Gandillac's French rather than German, Graham too, like Chantal Wright translating Berman and Gandillac, translates *Gehalt* as "tenor."

in English can be the edible meat of a nut, which is not something that Germans describe as *ein Kern* or that the French describe as *un noyau*; *un noyau* in French is also a "group" (of artists) or a "cell" (of terrorists), which is not something that is ever described as *ein Kern* in German or a kernel in English. I would venture to say that *le noyau* was a slightly problematic translation of *Kern*, because though it can be a "stone" in a fruit, it can't be a "seed or grain" (*la graine, la semence*), and it refers to many semantic fields that are not referents of *Kern*. "Core," however, was in every way a misleading translation of *le noyau*, as it cannot mean a stone/pip/pit, a seed, or a grain.

So let's read Derrida in Joseph F. Graham's English translation:

> It is not certain that the essential "core" and the "fruit" designate the same thing. The essential core, that which in the translation is not translatable again, is not the tenor, but this adherence between the tenor and the language, between the fruit and the skin. This may seem strange or incoherent (how can a core be situated between the fruit and the skin?). It is necessary no doubt to think that the core is first the hard and central unity that holds the fruit to the skin, the fruit to itself as well; and above all that, at the heart of the fruit, the core is "untouchable," beyond reach and invisible. (193)

Right: *der Kern* "the kernel" in #38 is not necessarily part of the fruit that Benjamin mentions in #39. It could be a seed or a grain—though seeds, grains, and stones are all *propagative*, and Benjamin specifically refers to the "kernel of un(re)translatability in any translation," which is to say, a translation's *non*-propagative aspect. So perhaps I am wrong to insist that it be a seed, grain, or stone. Perhaps the vagueness of "core" is better suited to Benjamin's purpose after all. Derrida identifies the kernel as "this adherence between the tenor [*der Gehalt*] and the language, between the fruit and the skin" (Derrida's insertion), presumably because its untranslatability has something to do with the difference in relation between tenor ("fruit") and language ("skin") in the source text and translation. This is a speculative reading, of course: in the pomological vehicle of this metaphor there might be hormonal chains by which the adherence of skin to fruit renders a stone infertile without requiring that the stone be positioned between the fruit and the skin.

Derrida infers that the *noyau* must be "'untouchable,' beyond reach and invisible," presumably because "no matter how much of the meaning the translator seeks to extract from the source text and transmit in the translation, this effort will leave untouched the element toward which the true translator's work is stirred"—though nothing in Benjamin's wording would seem to require that the kernel be *invisible*. It could be a stone that the "bad" translator sees but discards as inedible. That would mean touching the stone; but of course we could still imagine the stone as untouched in a figurative sense: touching it and discarding it doesn't diminish its mystical power. Imagine eating a peach: the sweet fruit might be the meaning that the "bad" translator reproduces in the translation, and the rough stone is the precious mystical payload that the "true" translator translates. But how can it be translated if it is infertile? In Benjamin's conceit, it is only infertile in the translation. The stone (or seed or grain) is the mystical payload in the source text, "the element toward which the true translator's work is stirred." It can be retranslated an infinite number of times, but only from the source text. Each translation propagated from that stone, however, is infertile.

Noting that "the core [kernel as stone/seed/grain] would be the first metaphor of what makes for the unity of the two terms in the second metaphor"—the fruit and the skin—Derrida moves on to the third metaphor, that of the royal mantle:

> What in fact is it that Benjamin notes, as if in passing, for rhetorical or pedagogical convenience? That "the language of the translation envelops its tenor like a royal cape with large folds. For [and here we move on to #40] it is the signifier of a language superior to itself and so remains, in relation to its own tenor, inadequate, forced, foreign." That is quite beautiful, a beautiful translation: white ermine, crowning, scepter, and majestic bearing. The king has indeed a body (and it is not here the original text but that which constitutes the tenor of the translated text), but this body is only promised, announced and dissimulated by the translation. The clothes fit but do not cling strictly enough to the royal person. This is not a weakness: the best translation resembles this royal cape. It remains separate from the body to which it is nevertheless conjoined, wedding it, not wedded to it. One can of course embroider on this cape, on the necessity of this Übertragung, of this metaphoric translation of translation. For example, one can oppose this metaphor to that of the shell and the core just as one would oppose technology to nature. An article of clothing is not natural; it is a fabric and even—another metaphor of metaphor—a text, and this text of artifice appears precisely on the side of the symbolic contract. (194)

Three metaphors: the kernel, the fruit-and-skin, and the royal mantle. The first two are natural metaphors, apparently troping the fecundity of nature (the stone, seed, or grain in the source text is fertile), the third artificial and symbolic, apparently troping the sterility of technology, including text(iles) (the translated text cannot propagate a new translation). Of course, as Derrida points out, "The king has indeed a body": the third metaphor is not the royal mantle but the royal mantle *on the king's body*. It is a human–textile hybrid; and while not all hybrids are infertile, and robed kings—the vehicle of this third metaphor—are certainly not necessarily infertile, Benjamin is using this one to trope the infertility of translations.

> Now, if the original text is demand for translation, then the fruit, unless it be the core, insists upon becoming the king or the emperor who will wear

new clothes: under its large folds, *in weiten Falten*, one will imagine him naked. No doubt the cape and the folds protect the king against the cold or natural aggressions; but first, above all, it is, like his scepter, the eminent visibility of the law. It is the index of his power and of the power to lay down the law. But one infers that what counts is what comes to pass under the cape, to wit, the body of the king, do not immediately say the phallus, around which a translation busies its tongue, makes pleats, molds forms, sews hems, quilts, and embroiders. But always amply floating at some distance from the tenor. (194)

Derrida goes on to write of the royal couple, "this couple of spouses (the body of the king and his gown, the tenor and the tongue, the king and the queen)" (194), hinting at foreplay and then intercourse and thus procreation, fertility despite the artifice of royalty and royal power: if under his mantle the king is naked, and the mantle fits him loosely, obviously he can take it off and *be* naked, be a naked natural nonhybrid procreator as a metaphor for (perhaps) the retranslatability of translations. If the mantle that he removes is figuratively language, the naked king presumably becomes a prelinguistic primate or other nonhuman animal, no longer a talker, no longer a king, no longer a purveyor of symbolic power: a translation, then, as gestural communication? Haptic translation as biosemiosis? (See Marais 2019.)

Derrida is more interested, however, in the symbolic trappings of power and the law:

> Truth is apparently beyond every Übertragung and every possible Übersetzung. It is not the representational correspondence between the original and the translation, nor even the primary adequation between the original and some object or signification exterior to it. Truth would be rather the *pure language* in which the meaning and the letter no longer dissociate. If such a place, the taking place of such an event, remained undiscoverable, one could no longer, even by right, distinguish between an original and a translation. In maintaining this distinction at all cost, as the original given of every translation contract …, Benjamin repeats the foundation of the law. (194–95)

The law this time, though, for Derrida is not the transcendental law of translation as a Form, but copyright law. And perhaps that's enough of that.

*Other commentators*: Berman (2008/2018: 159–62), Biti (2019: 255), Cohen (2002: 103–4), de Man (2000: 30), Ferris (2008: 64), Flèche (1999: 101–2), Gasché (1986: 77–78), Gelley (2015: 21), Hamacher (2001/2012: 531), Jacobs (1975: 757–58), Liska (2014: 238), O'Keeffe (2015: 376, 380, and *passim*), Pfau (1988: 1085), Sandbank (2015: 220–21), Smerick (2009: np), St. André (2011: 110), Weber (2008: 70), Wurgaft (2002: 381).

## 40 Translating vs. the writing of an original work (3): the essential kernel as the part of the original that is not translatable (3): the rupture

> Denn sie bedeutet eine höhere Sprache als sie ist und bleibt dadurch
> For it betokens a higher language than it is and remains thereby
>
> ihrem eigenen Gehalt gegenüber unangemessen, gewaltig und fremd.
> to its own tenor across from ill-suited, violent, and alien.
>
> Diese Gebrochenheit verhindert jede Übertragung, wie sie sie zugleich
> This brokenness prevents every transposition, as it it likewise
>
> erübrigt. Denn jede Übersetzung eines Werkes aus einem
> superfluidizes. For every translation of a work out of one
>
> bestimmten Zeitpunkt der Sprachgeschichte repräsentiert hinsichtlich
> specific time-point of the language history represents with regard to
>
> einer bestimmten Seite seines Gehaltes diejenigen in allen übrigen
> one specific side of its tenor those in all remaining
>
> Sprachen. Übersetzung verpflanzt also das Original in einen
> languages. Translation transplants therefore the original into an
>
> wenigstens insofern – ironisch – endgültigeren Sprachbereich,
> at least in this respect – ironically – more entelechial language realm,
>
> als es aus diesem durch keinerlei Übertragung mehr zu versetzen ist,
> as it out of this through no kind of transposition more to transfer is,
>
> sondern in ihn nur immer von neuem und an andern Teilen erhoben zu
> rather in it only ever from new and in other parts elevated to
>
> werden vermag.
> become could.

*Paraphrase*: For a translation betokens a language higher than its own, and as a result remains at violent odds with and alienated from its own tenor. This rupture renders the translation itself untranslatable, and at the same time makes it superfluous. For every translation of a work at a specific point in the history of the language represents, with regard to a given side of its tenor, translation into all other languages. Thus translation transplants the source text into what in this respect is ironically one more entelechial realm of language, for it (the source text) cannot be moved out of that realm by a new translation; it can only be elevated to it ever anew and in other parts.

*Commentary*: On a superficial reading, the "higher language" that a translation "betokens" (*bedeutet*, translated "signifies" by most translators, "indicates" by Rendall [158]) would be the source language; if that were true, this claim would also betoken the age-old assumption of the translation's de facto inferiority to the source text. But this passage makes it clear that the higher language is actually the "more entelechial realm of language" to which the translator "transplants" or "elevates" the source text, even implying perhaps that the translation is by definition *superior* to the source text! But it's more complicated than that too: betokening that higher language is the undoing of the translation. The very fact that the translation has that elevating effect on the source text puts it "at violent odds with and alienated from its own tenor"—from that mystical kernel or "poet-word" that the poet engages in the source language. That tenor is described in #39 as the mystical kernel "toward which the true translator's work is stirred," but that stirring ruptures the unity between the kernel-tenor and language, and leaves the latter floating at a distance from the former, "like the commodious folds of a royal mantle." Where in the source text the kernel/tenor/poet-word and the source language fit together snugly, in the translation the king's mantle (target language) becomes a kind of royal smallpox blanket.

What I paraphrase as "rupture" Benjamin calls a *Gebrochenheit* "brokenness"; Zohn has "disjunction"; Hynd and Valk have "incongruity"; Rendall "fracture"; Underwood "fragmentation." Charlie Louth (1998: 148) notes that in writing of the *Gebrochenheit* of the language of translation Benjamin "has Hölderlin's Pindar in mind," but what is true of Hölderlin's Pindar is "inherent in all translation of the Vossian type: ... it is estranged from itself, 'eigenen Gehalt gegenüber unangemessen, gewaltig und fremd' [at violent odds with and alienated from its own tenor]."

Benjamin's German verb for "to make superfluous" is *erübrigt*; in that rendering I follow all four previous full translations. *Übrig*, an adjective derived from *über* "over," is something like "left over," as in removed from use, decommissioned, derailed, shunted aside, discarded, junked in the attic. This verb thus participates in the proliferation of *übers* in the essay: *übersetzen* "to translate," obviously—"to overset" as "to superset"—but also (#39–40, #62, #72, #75–76) *übertragen* "to overdrag" or "to overcarry" as "to translate" or "to transpose," (#13) *das Überleben* "overlife" as "superlife," (#6, #22) *übermitteln* "to overmiddle" or "to overshare" as "to convey too much," (#27) *überdauern* "to overdure" as "to endure too long," (#30) *überhistorisch* "overhistorical" as "suprahistorical," and (#47) *übereinkommen* "to over-in-come" as "to cross over into unison." In this same passage (#40) Benjamin claims that the translation of any one work represents "with regard to a given side of its tenor" translation *in allen übrigen Sprachen* "in all (left)over languages," or what I've paraphrased as "in all other languages." There are also such ordinary "grammatical" conjunctions and prepositions as *überdies* "over-this" as "in addition," *gegenüber* "over-against" as "across from" or "in comparison with," and *überhaupt* "overhead" as "in general." In some contexts for Benjamin the "overage" or "superfluity" (from the Latin for "overflow") is a bad thing: *übermitteln* is one of his derogatory verbs for sense-for-sense translation (conveying the sense as conveying too much), and *erübrigen* here consigns the translation to superfluity. Mostly, however, the "overage" signals participation in *das Überleben* "the superlife" that the translation brings to the source text. Arguably, in fact, the "superfluidization" (*die Erübrigung*) of the translation and the "superdurance" or survival (*die Überdauer*) of the source text in and through the translation register the unfortunate side-effects of a good thing: precisely because the translation "superizes" the source text, it also decays and is ultimately discarded.

"Entelechial" is my paraphrase here of *endgültig*, which Hynd and Valk and Underwood render "final" and Zohn and Rendall render "ultimate"; *endgültig* is usually defined in German as *von letzter abschließender Gültigkeit, unumstößlich* "of final validity, irrevocable," with such synonyms as *ausgemacht* "agreed," *beschlossen* "decided," and *besiegelt* "sealed"—signed, sealed, delivered. With semantic associations like those, it is obvious why Benjamin calls this translational "elevation" or "transplantation" ironic, since the elevating effects of a translation on a source text are for him temporary, transitory, short-lived, and no retranslation can elevate it further, raise it to an even higher level. The ongoing life of the source text in translation is a series of such transitory elevations, always to the same level. But that very state of affairs that makes the elevation ironic also makes "final" and "ultimate" translations problematic (and is it even possible for something to be *more* final or *more* ultimate?). Hence my suggestion of "entelechial" as an alternative translation. In a looser morphological translation *endgültig* would be something like "end-validated"; "entelechy" is Aristotle's coinage ἐντελέχεια/ *entelékheia*, from ἐν/*en* "in" + τέλος/*télos* "end" + ἔχω/*ékhō* "to have," or "having an end within." That would make the "ironic" *Endgültigkeit* of which Benjamin writes here not a finality but an intrinsic *orientation* to finality, one that is never actually finalized, never finally accomplished, never brought to full fruition in a gloriously triumphant end. The triumphant end would presumably be pure language, but no source text ever achieves that end, because no translation has the power to usher it into that glorious final state; but through translations literary works are nevertheless more or less strongly *oriented* toward that end.

Antoine Berman (2008/2018) likes Benjamin on this point a lot. Noting that great original works endure, "even if their tone and their meaning have changed completely" (124), he insists that "this is not the same for translation":

> The growth and becoming of its language brings aging and decline. It is well known that translations are mortal and texts (virtually) immortal. We still read Homer, Plato, Shakespeare—but not the translations of their texts from two centuries ago. Why do we find translations from the Renaissance or the classical age "old" but not the original texts that were their contemporaries? If Homer or Virgil were [sic] well-translated in the sixteenth century, why don't we leave it at that, why do we persist in re-translating them or—at best—in "adapting" existing translations of texts as Cassou did with translations of *Don Quixote*? (124)

Counterexamples do seem in order here. When John Keats wrote "On First Looking into Chapman's Homer" in 1816, exactly two centuries had passed since the 1616 publication of both Homeric epics in Chapman's translation. Why then do we ask rhetorical questions like "[Why do] we still read Homer, Plato, Shakespeare—but not the translations of their texts from two centuries ago"? Keats did. When in the 1750s and 1760s Laurence Sterne drew inspiration for *Tristram Shandy* from Sir Thomas Urquhart's 1653 translation of Rabelais, only a century had passed; but Urquhart's Rabelais is still today, nearly four centuries after its publication, considered one of the greatest English translations ever created. Yes, both source texts have been retranslated many times since; but connoisseurs of those two seventeenth-century translations still read them, enjoy them, even publish on them, today, just as they do with the source texts. The blanket statement that "It is well known that translations are mortal and texts (virtually) immortal" is ideology, not empirical fact.

What makes some (perhaps even most) translations date quickly, I would argue, is the translator's timidity—the self-abnegating belief that any translation is inevitably going to be inferior to the source text—and the resulting ideological governor that is (self-)placed on the translator's verbal creativity. George Steiner (1975/1998) is eloquent on the crushing effect brilliant translations have on hohum source texts: everyone remembers the translations rather than the originals.[36] In the case of Chapman's Homer and Urquhart's Rabelais, the translation *matches* (and even in some places outdoes) the source author's verbal creativity, with the result that both source text and target text are "(virtually) immortal."

*Other commentators*: Bellos (2010: 212), Bradbury (2006: 138), Britt (1996: 68n49), Derrida (1985: 195), Ferris (2008: 64), Gasché (1986: 77), Hamacher (2001/2012: 509, 537–38), Jacobs (1975: 758, 764), Liska (2014: 231), Pan (2017: 44–45), Pfau (1988: 1084), Smerick (2009: np), Zechner (2020: 321–22).

## 41 Translating vs. the writing of an original work (4): the Romantics as translators and on poetry and translation

> Nicht umsonst mag hier  das Wort ›ironisch‹ an Gedankengänge der
> Not  in vain   may here the word "ironic"  of thought-paths   of the
>
> Romantiker erinnern. Diese haben vor      andern Einsicht in    das Leben
> Romantics  remind.  These have   before others  insight into the life

---

36 For example, Steiner (1975/1998: 405) reads Paul Celan's German translation of Jules Supervielle's "Chanson," and remarks: "After this it is almost impossible to go back to Supervielle; translation of this order being, in one sense, the cruellest of homages." But see Robinson (1991: 20–21) for a series of challenges to this claim: doesn't Steiner mean that it's almost impossible *for him* to go back? Isn't he pontifically universalizing his own somatic response? What about readers who compare Celan's translation with the French original and prefer Supervielle? What about monolingual French readers who love Supervielle and have no way of experiencing Celan?

| | | | | | |
|---|---|---|---|---|---|
| der | Werke besessen, | von welchem die | Übersetzung | eine | höchste |
| of the | Works possessed, | of which | the translation | a | highest |

| | | | | |
|---|---|---|---|---|
| Bezeugung ist. | Freilich | haben sie | diese als solche kaum | erkannt, |
| attestation is. | Admittedly | have they | these as such hardly | recognized, |

| | | | | |
|---|---|---|---|---|
| vielmehr ihre | ganze Aufmerksamkeit der | Kritik | zugewendet, | die |
| rather their | whole attention | to the criticism | turned, | which |

| | | | | |
|---|---|---|---|---|
| ebenfalls ein wenn auch geringeres Moment im | Fortleben | der | Werke |
| as well one if also trivialer | moment in the forthliving of the works |

| | | | |
|---|---|---|---|
| darstellt. | Doch wenn auch ihre Theorie auf | Übersetzung kaum | sich |
| represents. | Though if also their theory upon | translation hardly | self |

| | | | |
|---|---|---|---|
| richten mochte, so ging doch | ihr | großes Übersetzungswerk selbst mit |
| to steer liked, so came though their great | translation work itself with |

| | |
|---|---|
| einem Gefühl von dem Wesen und der Würde dieser Form zusammen. |
| a feel for the essence and the worth of this form together. |

*Paraphrase*: Not coincidentally, the word "ironically" reminds us of the Romantics, whose insight into the life of artworks was unparalleled—and to that life translation attests most eloquently. To be sure the Romantics didn't exactly recognize translation as that kind of testimony; their attention was directed much more toward criticism, which of course is also a factor, if a more trivial one, in the ongoing life of literary works. But even if they scarcely steered their theorizing toward translation at all, the great work they did as translators was informed by a feeling for the Essence and worth of translation as a Form.

*Commentary*: It strikes us now as quite ungenerous for Benjamin to dismiss Romantic theorizations of translation as insignificant ("didn't exactly recognize translation," "scarcely steered their theorizing toward translation at all"); but that may be simply because as translation scholars we tend to *know* the Romantics' writing on translation better than we do their copious literary criticism. Their remarks on translation—especially of course Friedrich Schleiermacher's 1813 Academy address "Über die verschiedenen Methoden des Übersetzens"/"On the Different Methods of Translating," which Benjamin never mentions and may not have known, but also the incisive aphorisms of Herder and Novalis and the detailed literary-critical discussions of precisely that "great work they did as translators" by the Schlegel brothers (Robinson 1997/2014: 207–8, 212–38 in English)—were not exactly negligible, and should not be so casually written off. And the Pannwitz quotation in #72, which Benjamin touts in #71 as one of the finest things ever written on translation in German, is really just a tired rehash of the translation theory pioneered by the early Romantics.

On the parallels Benjamin mentions between Romantic criticism and Romantic translation, Charlie Louth (1998: 36n69) observes in passing that Benjamin was the first to notice this—that "Criticism, as a vital part of the Romantics' achievement, was seen as a creative act, contributing to the life of a work and heightening it as a translation could" (37). For Friedrich Schlegel and Novalis in particular, criticism and translation were parallel not only in the *account* both provided of a work but in the *enhancement* of the work. Both criticism and translation inserted themselves into the work's perfectability and stretched their limbs there. Benjamin suggests that the Jena Romantics seemed to favor criticism or criticizability more intensely than they did translation or translatability, at least in their critical writings—but in their practical work of translating they surpassed their achievements in criticism and showed that translation actually has the upper hand, specifically because it is better able to jettison the material encumbrances that drag the work down. Criticism too seeks to bring the work to greater perfection by sloughing off the work's full materiality, but for Benjamin translation far more transformatively liberates the work from the discursive transmission of meaning.[37]

As Rodolphe Gasché (1992/2002) shows in his detailed investigation of this matter, Benjamin dealt with this issue at far greater length, with far greater influence in the field of art criticism—even today—in his 1919 doctoral dissertation *Der Begriff der Kunstkritik in der deutschen Romantik* (1920/1980)/"The Concept of Art Criticism in German Romanticism" (Lachterman 1996; see also Lacoue-Labarthe 2002).

It is also perhaps no coincidence that what Benjamin finds in the Romantics is not exactly the Platonic mysticism that he himself embraces but a *feeling* for that mysticism, since *Gefühl* "feeling" was so close to the heart of the Romantic vision. But it is also arguably an ironic coincidence, since a feeling is a phenomenology, and Benjamin's vitalism is so determinedly anti- or transphenomenological.

But then that too is appropriate for this passage, since in it Benjamin specifically associates irony with the Romantics (no doubt because of Friedrich Schlegel's early theorization of Socratic irony).

*Other commentators*: Bellos (2010: 213), Berman (2008/2018: 170), Hanssen and Benjamin (2002a, 2002b: 4), Liska (2014: 234), O'Keeffe (2015: 376), Rendall (1997b: 170).

---

37 I would like to thank Theo Hermans for directing my attention back to this parallel between criticism and translation in Jena Romanticism, after I had prematurely decided that it wasn't important enough to include here.

## 42 Translating vs. the writing of an original work (5): the relation between great poets and great translators

| | | | |
|---|---|---|---|
| Dieses Gefühl – darauf deutet alles hin | | – braucht nicht notwendig im | |
| This feeling – to that points all | | toward – needs not necessarily in the | |
| Dichter am stärksten zu sein; ja | | es hat in ihm als Dichter vielleicht | |
| poet at the strongest to be; indeed it | | has in him as poet perhaps | |
| am wenigsten Raum. Nicht einmal die Geschichte legt das | | | |
| at the least room. Not once the history backs the | | | |
| konventionelle Vorurteil nahe, demzufolge die bedeutenden Übersetzer | | | |
| conventional judgment up, that the significant translators | | | |
| Dichter und unbedeutende Dichter geringe Übersetzer wären. | | | |
| poets and insignificant poets mediocre translators were. | | | |

*Paraphrase*: All indications are that the Romantic feeling for the Essence and worth of translation as a Form need not be strongest in the poet; there may in fact be in the poet the least room for it. The conventional wisdom is that poets make the best translators and a mediocre poet will be a mediocre translator; but history does not back that assumption up. Not once.

*Commentary*: Not once? Again, George Steiner (1975/1998) would disagree; his celebration of Paul Celan as a brilliant poet and brilliant translator whose German translations of Jules Supervielle supersede the French source texts (cited in the commentary to #40) gives us the single counterexample that overturns that "not once." True, Celan was still a baby at the writing of "Die Aufgabe des Übersetzers"; Benjamin could not have known his poems, original or translated. But Benjamin himself gives us two counterexamples in #43, Friedrich Hölderlin and Stefan George, saying somewhat lamely that they "cannot justifiably be acclaimed as poets alone if the full scope of their output, in particular their work as translators, is taken into consideration." No, but the claim here in #42 wasn't about "acclaim as poets alone"; it was about whether a poet has *ever* been a great translator. A few counterexamples do not flip Benjamin's judgment over to the opposite pole, of course—it is certainly not a universal *rule* that poets invariably make the best translators—but they do niftily undo a blanket judgment like *nicht einmal* "not once." Benjamin's universalizing remarks fare about as well here as Schleiermacher's similar remarks in the 1813 Academy address "On the Different Methods of Translating," especially perhaps his claim that no one ever wrote brilliantly in a foreign language (see Robinson 2013b: 159 for counterexamples). Benjamin's more cautious claims in the first sentence—"need not be," "may in fact be"—fare considerably better. He would have been wiser, perhaps, to use the same caution in the second sentence as well: "poets don't always make the best translators, and not all mediocre poets are mediocre translators."

*Other commentators*: Berman (2008/2018: 170–71), Smerick (2009: np).

## 43 Translating vs. the writing of an original work (6): the translator's task (1): different from the poet's: Hölderlin (1): examples of great translators who were not great poets

> Eine Reihe der größeren wie Luther, Voß, Schlegel sind als Übersetzer
> One row of the greater like Luther, Voß, Schlegel are as translators
>
> ungleich bedeutender denn als Dichter, andere unter den
> far more significant than as poets, others among the
>
> größten, wie Hölderlin und George, nach dem ganzen Umfang
> greatest, like Hölderlin and George, according to the whole scope
>
> ihres Schaffens unter den Begriff des Dichters allein nicht zu fassen.
> of their creations under the concept of the poet alone not to grasp.
>
> Zumal nicht als Übersetzer. Wie nämlich die Übersetzung eine eigene
> Especially not as translator. As namely the translation an own
>
> Form ist, so läßt sich auch die Aufgabe des Übersetzers als eine eigene
> form is, so lets itself also the task of the translator as an own
>
> fassen und genau von der des Dichters unterscheiden.
> to grasp and precisely from that of the poet to distinguish.

*Paraphrase*: A whole row of the greatest German writers, including Martin Luther (1483–1546), Johann Heinrich Voß (1751–1826), and August Wilhelm Schlegel (1767–1845), are immeasurably weightier as translators than as poets, and others, including Friedrich Hölderlin (1770–1843) and Stefan George (1868–1933), cannot justifiably be acclaimed as poets alone if the full scope of their output, in particular their work as translators, is taken into consideration. After all, given that translation is a Form in its own right, so too is the translator's task its own Form, which must be distinguished from that of the poet.

*Commentary*: Notable translations by that "row of greats":

- Luther's German Bible translation (New Testament 1522, whole Bible 1534) was of course formative for German as a "national" literary language (scare quotes around "national" because Germany was not unified as a nation until 1871).

- Voß was a renowned translator of both Homeric epics (*Odyssey* 1781, *Iliad* 1793), Ovid (1798), the complete works of Virgil (1799, rev. 1821), Hesiod (1806), Horace (1806), Theocritus (1808), and the complete works of Shakespeare (1818–1829). Not only was he venerated by the Romantics for that astonishing achievement; the brilliant literalism of his Homeric translations fueled the Romantic preference for literalism.
- A.W. Schlegel (older brother of Friedrich, also a renowned translator and fellow leading light of Jena Romanticism) is best known for his translation of the complete works of Shakespeare (1797–1810) 20 years before Voß, and his translations are generally considered superior to Voß's (and everyone else's), though they are also criticized as so saturated in Romantic thought that—as Voß himself claimed—they are more Schlegel than Shakespeare. He also translated Horace Walpole from the English (1800), Calderón from the Spanish (1803–1809), assorted poems from the Italian, Spanish, and Portuguese (1804), Albertine Necker de Saussure (Ferdinand's great-aunt) and Madame de Staël from the French (1820), and the *Bhagavad-Gita* (1823) and the *Ramayana* (1829) from the Sanskrit—of which he was professor and the premier scholar in Europe at the time.
- Hölderlin's radically literal translations of Pindar (1800) and Sophocles (1804) were read with derision in his lifetime, especially after he was declared incurably insane (in 1806); they were championed by German thinkers like Benjamin, Heidegger, and the Stefan George circle.
- Stefan George published transcreations (what he called *Umdichtungen* and *Übertragungen*) of poems by several famous poets—Baudelaire's *Les fleurs du mal* (1891 and 1901), Mallarmé's *Herodias* (1905), "places" from Dante's *Divine Comedy* (1909, 1912), Shakespeare's sonnets (1909)—and poems by many lesser-known poets (1904–1905) as well.

So "the translator's task [is] its own Form, which must be distinguished from that of the poet": what is the difference between those two Forms? Benjamin begins to limn in this distinction next, in #44: the translator's task is to "[find] that target-language intention that awakens the echo of the source text," and in #45, more specifically, it is to "[stand] outside the wood and [call] into it without ever setting foot in it, seeking that one sweet spot where the source-language echo will reverb the source text in the target language." So perhaps that last line of #43 should actually be moved to #44? Perhaps. The advantage of leaving it in #43, however, is that as a tag to the list of great German translators it implicitly defines the Form of the translator's task by example: think of what those translators achieved, think of how they achieved it, and begin to imagine *that* as the Form of the translator's task. In #55, in fact, he begins a series of disquisitions on the translator's task as rendering word for word by noting that Hölderlin stood as a "monstrous" exemplar of literalism to the nineteenth century. And in #69, he returns to the list of exemplary German translators, saying explicitly that "it is the translator's task to transcreate the source text in which pure language is imprisoned, in order to unleash in the target language that pure language that is spellbound in the source language. For pure language's sake the translator smashes through the target language's rotten barricades: Luther, Voß, Hölderlin, and George all pushed back the boundaries of the German language."

Readers often complain that Benjamin's argumentation is too metaphysically abstract to offer much practical assistance to translators, and there is considerable truth to that complaint; but along the way he does insert these names of exemplary translators, and there is indirect guidance to be gleaned from them.

*Other commentators*: Bellos (2010: 213), Berman (2008/2018: 171–72), de Man (2000: 16, 21), Rendall (1997b: 178), Rose (1982: 167n8).

## 44 The translator's task (2): finding the intentions in the target language that produce an echo of the source text

> Sie besteht darin, diejenige Intention auf die Sprache, in die
> It consists therein, that intention upon the language into which
>
> übersetzt wird, zu finden, von der aus in ihr das Echo des Originals
> translated will be, to find from which out in it the echo of the original
>
> erweckt wird. Hierin liegt ein vom Dichtwerk durchaus
> awakened will be. Herein lies one of the poem-work thoroughly
>
> unterscheidender Zug der Übersetzung, weil dessen Intention niemals
> differentiating feature of the translation, since this's intention never
>
> auf die Sprache als solche, ihre Totalität, geht, sondern allein
> upon the language as such, its totality, acts, rather alone
>
> unmittelbar auf bestimmte sprachliche Gehalts-zusammenhänge.
> immediately upon specific linguistic tenor together-hangs.

*Paraphrase*: The task of the translator lies in finding that target-language intention that awakens the echo of the source text. This is an aspect of translation that radically distinguishes it from the work of the poet, whose intention is never trained on (the) language as such, on its totality, but only and without mediation on specific tenor-intertwinings.

*Commentary*: This is how Benjamin reframes the traditional reproductivity of translation: the translator should not simply reproduce the source text's semantic content, but neither may s/he invent an entirely new literary work with no subordinacy to the source text; rather, the translator's task is to *awaken an echo* of the source text in the target language. Or, specifically here, to *find the target-language intention* that awakens that echo: the active agent is first the "intention" of the target language—what the language *wants to say* (#21)—and then the intention of the source language, which is stirred into action by the echo awakened by the target-language intention.

Menke (2002) is a brilliant and extremely useful exploration of Benjamin's use of the echo trope in the larger context of German Romanticism:

> Echoes—in the Romantic—function as an answer of (or from) nature, as a voice of the (dead) past, or as an answer to that question which grows lost amidst the broken monuments, pertaining to the endurance of all great things that have been. Accordingly, in that hallucinatory sharing of a common space of understanding, an end is put to (and a strong hold taken against) all the nonsensical reverberations and the indeterminable and uncontrollable multiplication of "voices" (in reverberations and their repetitions). In the case of Benjamin's echoes, however, it is to be stressed that the echo is not the *voice* from (beyond) the ruins, but rather that echoes *ruin* words and voices. (95)

The translator sets that interaction into motion by "finding the target-language intention," but this conception restricts the translator's task to a triggering role. The primary translatorial action (*das translatorische Handeln*, as attributed to the *human* translator by Justa Holz-Mänttäri in 1984[38]), is performed not by the translator but by the intentions in the two languages, as an event in the holy growth of those languages toward the messianic end of pure language.

The notion that the poet's "intention is never trained on (the) language as such, on its totality, but only and without mediation on specific tenor-intertwinings" is interesting. The parenthetical "(the)" reflects the fact that *die Sprache* can be translated into English either as "the [specific] language [that we're talking about]" (as Zohn has it, 76) or as "language [in general]" (as the other three translations have it). As Zohn reads the passage, the translator's intention is trained on the intentional totality of the target language, and the poet's intention is trained only on specific intertwinings of the tenor or poet-word in the source language, without stirring the source language's intentions into messianic action. As the others read it, the translator's intention is trained on language in general, "language as such"—a much larger entity, and thus a much weightier task. Zohn's interpretation would seem to fit the quite severe restrictions that Benjamin imposes on the translator's task throughout most of the essay—the purely instrumental triggering role—while the other translators' interpretation fits the more grandiose messianic mysticism of the essay as a whole.

As for the poet's intention being trained "only and without mediation on specific tenor-intertwinings," the idea is apparently that poets (and generally

---

38 And see Vermeer (1996: 1n2, 6n7, 10, 44, 86, 155, 164n1, 166, 242, and 253) for repeated recurrence to Holz-Mänttäri's theory of translatorial action as a corrective to Benjamin. My thanks also go to Holz-Mänttäri, my colleague in the Department of Translation Studies at the University of Tampere in 1987–1989, for long discussions about *skopos* theory, and for introducing me to Hans Vermeer.

literary writers) work with small bits of language at a time; but surely that's what translators do as well. The source text's *Unmittelbarkeit* "immediability" is a lack of access to the mediation of religion in #36 and sense in #77, but in the commentary to #46 we will see Werner Hamacher reading immediability as a lack of access to human subjects (readers), and in #2, #4, and #6 Benjamin insists that that kind of immediability is by necessity true of translators as well. And if Benjamin's mystical vision is that the work of the translator with those small bits *has that mystical intention* trained on (the) language as such in a higher, more transcendental sense—after all, the intertwined *Gehalt* "tenor" that the poet engages in the source language is described in #39 as the mystical kernel "toward which the true translator's work is stirred"—surely the same might be said of poets as well.

*Other commentators*: Berman (2008/2018: 172–75), Chapman (2019: 76), Gasché (1986: 77–78), Kohlross (2009: 99, 103), Pan (2017: 38), Rendall (1997b: 184), Smerick (2009: np), Szondi (1986: 164), Vermeer (1996: 160), Wright (2018: 167–68).

## 45 Translating vs. the writing of an original work (7): the translator's task (3): calling into the forest of the source language to awaken the source text's echo in the target language

> Die Übersetzung aber     sieht sich  nicht wie die Dichtung gleichsam
> The translation     however sees  itself not  like the poem      as it were
>
> im     innern Bergwald      der   Sprache  selbst, sondern außerhalb
> in the inner   mountain forest of the language itself, rather   outside
>
> desselben,  ihm gegenüber und ohne    ihn zu betreten ruft sie das
> of the same, it   across from and without it   to enter    calls it  the
>
> Original hinein, an demjenigen einzigen Orte hinein, wo    jeweils   das
> original into,   on that very    single    place in,  where each time the
>
> Echo in der eigenen den   Widerhall      eines Werkes der    fremden
> echo in the own      of the reverberation of a   work    of the foreign
>
> Sprache  zu geben vermag.
> language to give     could.

*Paraphrase*: Unlike the literary source text, however, which penetrates deep into the source language's inner mountain forest, the translation stands outside the wood and calls into it without ever setting foot in it, seeking that one sweet spot where the source-language echo will reverb the source text in the target language.

*Commentary*: "Echo" here, as in #44, is obviously a metaphor, but Benjamin manifestly does not mean it to signal the creation of a rough likeness: the *Bergwald* "mountain forest" conceit in this passage tropes the source text not as a dead text with specific semantic patterns that are to be imitated, but as a living thing, a singing or ringing or other sonorous entity/activity that vibrates and resonates in the source language in response to the target-language singing or yoo-hooing of the translator, and creates a reverberation in the target language.

Carol Jacobs (1975: 764) usefully contextualizes this passage in German proverbial territory:

> There is an unmistakable echo here of a German saying that both amplifies and clarifies the predicament: "Wie man in den Wald hineinruft, so schallt's heraus ['As one calls into the forest, so it will resound']." Translation's call into the forest of language is not a repetition of the original but the awakening of an echo of itself. This signifies its disregard for coherence of content, for the sound that returns is its own tongue become foreign. Just as the vase of translation built unlike fragment on unlike fragment only to achieve a final fragmentation, so the echo of translation elicits only fragments of language, distorted into a disquieting foreignness. (Jacobs' insertion)

The obsolete English verb "to reverb" in my paraphrase happily suggests that the reverberation is also a reverbalization. This is actually a lucky accident of Latinate derivations in English: the convergence of the Latin *verbum* "word" and *verber* "lash, whip, rod, scourge." "To reverberate" is etymologically not to reword but to rewhip. It doesn't work in German, where Benjamin's term for reverberation is *Widerhall*, literally "against-resonance": the sound bounces off a surface and returns. The new English noun "reverb," recovered from the obsolete verb to describe the echo-like effects produced electronically in a sound system, suggests the same kind of *active* production of an echo or reverberation: for Benjamin the point is that the source text is the living sound-producing actor in the translation process. In #43 and #44 it is the *translator's* task to awaken that echo by calling into the wood; in #45 the *translation* is the one doing the calling.

One is tempted to liken Benjamin's animation/agentization of the source text to the Aeolian harp, which in Romantic poetry is typically played by a god or other spirit, whose breath is manifested as a wind; and indeed Benjamin will himself invoke the mystical/Romantic image of the Aeolian harp in #75, in connection with Hölderlin's translations of Sophocles.

*Other commentators*: Gasché (1986: 77), Liska (2014: 234), Menke (2002), Smerick (2009: np), Wright (2018: 168–69).

## 46 Translating vs. the writing of an original work (8): the translator's vs. the poet's intentions

> Ihre Intention geht nicht allein auf etwas anderes als die der
> Its intention acts not alone upon something other than that of the
>
> Dichtung, nämlich auf eine Sprache im ganzen von einem einzelnen
> poem, namely upon a language in the whole from a single
>
> Kunstwerk in einer fremden aus, sondern sie ist auch selbst eine andere: die
> artwork in a foreign out, rather it is also itself an other: that
>
> des Dichters ist naive, erste, anschauliche, die des Übersetzers
> of the poet is naïve, first, expressive, that of the translator
>
> abgeleitete, letzte, ideenhafte Intention.
> guided, last, mindful intention.

*Paraphrase*: Not only is translation's intention trained upon something other than that of the poem (literary work)—namely, upon a language taken in its totality, entered through a single artwork in a foreign language—but it is itself something other. The poet's intention is naïve, leading, and colorful, while the translator's is guided, following, and mindful.

*Commentary*: The six adjectives in that second sentence—*naive, erste, anschauliche*, and *abgeleitete, letzte, ideenhafte*—have proved difficult to understand and translate. Zohn has "spontaneous, primary, graphic [and] derivative, ultimate, ideational" (76–77); Hynd and Valk have "naïve, primary, concrete [and] derivative, final, conceptual" (303); Rendall has "spontaneous, primary, concrete [and] derivative, final, ideal" (159); Underwood has "naive, initial, concrete [and] derivative, ultimate, abstract" (38); and Wright has "naïve, immediate, expressive [and] derived, current, conceptual" (175).

*Naive/abgeleitete*: Zohn and Rendall clearly balk at the negative modern connotations of "naïve" as ignorant and inept, but seem to have no problem with the negative connotations of "derivative." Hynd and Valk, Underwood, and Wright keep "naïve" for Benjamin's *naive*—and Benjamin in fact may be thinking more along the lines of Friedrich Schiller's distinction between "naïve" and "sentimental" poetry: the former the stance that creates art for its own sake, the latter the one that is cognizant of larger connectivities. Translations are, of course, by definition "derivative" or "derived"—rewritings of source texts in a target language—but it's useful to keep Schiller's notion in mind as well, because the translational rewriting of the source text is typically (or preferably) accompanied by the translator's broader awareness of the source text's place and significance in source-cultural (and perhaps world) literary history, the tensions between source-cultural and target-cultural literary and linguistic histories, and so on. (I was tempted to follow Schiller and make the third characteristic of the translator's intention "sentimental"; given the idiomatic associations of that word with "mushy, sappy, corny," however, I backed off and made it "mindful" [see below].)

Note also, however, that while Benjamin's German participle *abgeleitete* is usually translated "derived" or "derivative," morphologically it is "led away" or "guided away," and that construction actually seems to align more strongly with Benjamin's mystical vitalism: it's not just that the translation comes later, is "belated," or that the translation lacks the original's "originality," but that there is a vitalistic force *guiding* the translator *away* from the (meaning of) the source text.[39] Traditionally we think of the translator as guided by the source author and the source text, and that works as well; but Benjamin would insist that the translator is guided at the very least by the target language, and indeed by the compulsion to find in the target language the sweet spot that triggers in it an echo of the source language (#45). Above and beyond that guidance, too, the translator is guided by the holy messianic growth of languages *away* from the communication of meaning *toward* pure language (#34–35), and on an even higher level by the Platonic Forms (#7, #28, #41, #43) channeled by the Logos (#59). Compared with that, the source author's "naivete" is a kind of pure simplicity: the poet does not trigger or activate that holy growth, not just because s/he engages with a single language, but because that engagement is not with the *whole* language, only specific tenor-intertwinings between the source culture and the source language (#44).

*Erste/letzte*: In German these are simply "first" and "last." Zohn, Hynd and Valk, and Rendall all elevate those to the more Latinate/philosophical terms "primary" and "final," and Underwood elevates them even further to "initial" and "ultimate." As Chantal Wright points out, however,

> "final" is problematic, because *letzte* in German can also mean "most recent" and the entire sense of translation that we gain from "The Task of the Translator" is that translation is provisional, multiple, that it can and should be superseded by further translations, that its language gestures toward pure language, performing it rather than producing it. None of this is "final." And all translators know that there is nothing final about the texts they produce. (169)

(See also the commentary to #40 for the problems in translating *endgültig* as "final" or "ultimate.")

Wright herself chooses "immediate" for *erste* "first," because "Benjamin upholds the value of the derived and the conceptual against an idealization of the immediate: it is translation that gestures toward pure language, not the first act of

---

39 The Latin verb *dērīvō* from which the English verb "to derive" derives also means "to lead or turn away," but specifically of a stream (*rivus*) or other liquid, as in "to draw off." German *leiten* can also be the diverting of a stream, but is more strongly associated with a physical guiding of another person, or, metaphorically, guiding as ruling or governing (or chairing a committee).

inspired creation" (170)—but of course what Benjamin mentions is the firstness not of the poet's creative *act* but of the poet's intention. "Immediate" also seems to gesture toward *die Unmittelbarkeit* "immediability," which in #44 was specifically assigned to the poet, "whose intention is never trained on (the) language as such [as the translator's is], on its totality, but only and without mediation on specific tenor-intertwinings" (see also #36 and #77). Based presumably on the fact that *vermitteln* is "to convey or communicate" in the specific sense of mediating a message from one person to another, Werner Hamacher (2001/2012) suggests that the mediality that the poet's intention lacks is mediation by human subjects; but Benjamin's foreclosure on readers in #2, #4, and #6 would make that kind of immediability (the inability to convey a meaning to a reader) typical of translations as well as source texts. And in any case immediability has no apparent link to firstness. So that doesn't really work here.

It's also not clear, *pace* Wright, how the *Letztheit* "lastness" of the translator's intention makes it "current." My guess would be that the translator experiences it as current while translating; but describing the *Essence* of that intention as current seems problematic, and indeed surely the source author too experiences his or her intention as current while writing. (And, for that matter, isn't the currency of an experience also immediate, and the immediacy of an experience also current?) Based on my paraphrase of *abgeleitete* as "guided," I took a chance and paraphrased the two as "leading" and "following." In fact the opposite of *ableiten* in German would be *anleiten*, morphologically "to lead on," usually translated as "to guide or train," sometimes as "to incite": the implications of that opposition for translation would obviously be that the poet leads or guides (or trains or incites) on and the translator submits to being led or guided (or trained or incited) away. The poet's intention is to lead; the translator's is to follow.

*Anschauliche/ideenhafte*: Zohn has "graphic" (76)/"ideational" (77); Hynd and Valk have "concrete/conceptual" (303); Rendall has "concrete/ideal" (159); Underwood has "concrete/abstract" (38); and Wright has "expressive/conceptual" (175). The verb behind *anschaulich* is *anschauen* "to look at," making the obvious translation of the adjective something visual; Zohn leans toward troping literary art as graphic art, the other three possibly as "concrete poetry," poetry arranged typographically on the page so as visually to represent the desired idea or image. Both seem somewhat unfortunate: graphic art is more commonly associated with advertisements and other forms of publicity, all of which Benjamin despised, and concrete poetry is an extremely minor subgenre of poetry that seems ill-suited to represent all literary expression (not to mention that "concrete" evokes images of sidewalks and cinderblocks). Chantal Wright notes that "something *anschaulich* can be rich in images, pictorial; it can be lively, expressive, descriptive. Paired with *naiv*, it suggests that the poet works with images, intuition and instinct, rather than with the intellect, and indeed Berman and Gandillac have opted for *intuitive*" (169), and "*ideenhaft* literally means 'like ideas, of ideas'—the more usual adjective *ideenreich* means 'rich in ideas,' but Benjamin does not use this" (169). She gives us "expressive" and "conceptual." Hearing as I do echoes of Schiller's distinction between naïve and sentimental poetry in this list, I paraphrased *ideenhafte* as "mindful"; and since thinking along those lines also makes translation seem more complex a literary activity than writing "original" works, I decided to introduce a slight diminishment into the poet's *anschauliche Intention* by calling it "colorful."

*Other commentators*: Bellos (2010: 213), Berman (2008/2018: 175–76), Liska (2014: 238), Pence (1996: 87–88), Pfau (1988: 1083), Roberts (1982: 121), Smerick (2009: np), Uhl (2012: 456), Weber (2008: 71).

## 47 Translation's mystical task (5): pure language at translation's beck and call

| | | | | |
|---|---|---|---|---|
| Denn das große Motiv | einer Integration der | | vielen Sprachen | zur |
| For the great motive of an integration of the many languages to the | | | | |
| einen wahren erfüllt | seine Arbeit. Dies ist aber | | jene, in welcher zwar | |
| one true performs its work. This is however that in which in fact | | | | |
| die einzelnen Sätze, | Dichtungen, Urteile | sich | | nie |
| the single sentences, poems, judgments themselves never | | | | |
| verständigen – wie sie | denn auch auf Übersetzung angewiesen bleiben –, | | | |
| correspond – as they then also on translation dependent remain –, | | | | |
| in welcher jedoch | die Sprachen selbst | | miteinander, | |
| in which however the languages themselves with one another, | | | | |
| ergänzt | und versöhnt in der Art ihres | | Meinens, übereinkommen. | |
| supplemented and reconciled in the way of their intention, agree. | | | | |

*Paraphrase*: For the great motivating force of the integration of many languages into one true one is on the job. That integrative force, however, is the one in which individual sentences, lines of poetry, and judgments never correspond, for they remain at the beck and call of translation. But in that true language the individual languages of which it is comprised, mutually supplemented and reconciled in the modes of their intention, cross over into unison.

*Commentary*: The vitalistic agent in this passage is not pure language (as Zohn has it, 77) but the *movement toward* pure language. It is in the turmoil of that movement, the churning, the clashing of intentions, that "individual sentences, lines of poetry, and judgments never correspond, for they remain at the beck and call of translation." What I've paraphrased there as "never correspond" is not entirely clear: *sich nie verständigen* would usually be translated "never communicate," and that is how Zohn translates it; but communicate with whom? With the reader?

Foreclosing on that kind of communication would be supererogatory at this point. The verb *verständigen* comes from the adjective *verständig* "understanding," as in an understanding person, or bending an understanding (i.e., sympathetic) ear; *das Verständnis* can mean "the understanding" but also "sympathy." Whatever communicating is not going on would presumably involve sympathetic listening as well as talking. Underwood, in fact, says that they "never talk to one another" (38); the other two translations seem to imply that (lack of) talking as the preparatory step to what hasn't happened: in Hynd and Valk they "never concur" (303), and in Rendall they "never arrive at agreement" (159). If you don't talk, you can't concur/agree. All four translations seem to me to work, but each only partially. How might we aggregate them? I offer "never correspond" in a dual sense: never match up ("agree" in the textual sense) and never write letters to each other. Writing letters is a bit silly, perhaps; but to the extent that "individual sentences, lines of poetry, and judgments" are linguistic constructs, they are made up of letters. (Okay, that's even sillier.)

Remaining "at the beck and call of translation"—or, as the other translators all have it, "dependent on translation"—emphatically does not mean that those linguistic constructs are silenced. Rather, translation beckons and calls them to engage, to disagree, perhaps, to bicker, but overall to remain in a kind of verbal tension that might be troped as a long-term personal relationship. The phrase *sich nie verständigen* might be overtranslated as "they never relate *themselves*": they don't engage on their own, but they do engage at the beck and call of translation.

*Other commentators*: Bellos (2010: 213), Engel (2014: 6), Gasché (1986: 81), Liska (2014: 240), Sandbank (2015: 217), Smerick (2009: np), Szondi (1986: 164), Vermeer (1996: 167).

## 48 Translation's mystical task (6): the true language, hidden in translations

Wenn anders es aber eine Sprache der Wahrheit gibt, in
If otherwise it however a language of the truth gives, in

welcher die letzten Geheimnisse, um die alles Denken sich müht,
which the last mysteries about which all thinking itself labors,

spannungslos und selbst schweigend aufbewahrt sind, so ist diese
tensionless and themselves silent preserved are, so is this

Sprache der Wahrheit – die wahre Sprache. Und eben diese, in deren
language of the truth the true language. And even this, in whose

Ahnung und Beschreibung die einzige Vollkommenheit liegt, welche der
divining and describing the single perfection lies, which the

| Philosoph | sich | | erhoffen kann, | sie ist intensiv | | in den |
|---|---|---|---|---|---|---|
| philosopher | him/herself | hope for can, | it is | intensively | in the |

Übersetzungen verborgen.
translations   concealed.

*Paraphrase*: But if, contrary to all common sense, there actually is a language of truth, in which, without suspense or even the spoken word, the ultimate mysteries that all thought labors to reveal are kept, then that language of truth is the true language. The only perfection philosophers can hope to achieve is to divine and describe that language, which is intensively concealed in translations.

*Commentary*: That paraphrase "contrary to all common sense" is my tentative unpacking of a single adverb, *anders* "otherwise." A closer rendition of that first clause would be "But if (it is) otherwise (and) there is (indeed) a language of truth …" Rendall took a stab at that "otherwise" with "If there is *nevertheless* a language of truth" (159), Underwood similarly with "If *on the other hand* there is a language of truth" (38); but the whole adverb is problematic, because in the previous passage Benjamin does not even hint at the possibility that no such language of truth exists. Zohn and Hynd and Valk, therefore, omit it altogether: "If there is such a thing as a language of truth" (Zohn 77) and "If there is a language of truth" (Hynd and Valk 303). For sheer argumentative continuity, it seems to me, Zohn and Hynd and Valk are right. I have, however, tried to imagine what might have led Benjamin to add that *anders* to the sentence, and come to the conclusion that he must have been considering a commonsensical retort, an implicit statement of "sensible" empirical resistance to his claims, and responded to that imagined dismissal with *anders*. It's also possible, of course, that in an earlier draft he anticipated that retort, saying something like "Now you may protest that …" and then wrote *anders* as an adverbial return to his main claim—but, editing the retort out of that draft, neglected to edit the adverbial response out as well.

The image of the ultimate mysteries being stored or kept in the true language "without suspense or even the spoken word" is one of the few hints Benjamin gives us of the nature of pure language: there will be in it no suspense, which is to say no time, no striving, no uncertainty, no fear of failure or incomplete action; and there will be no spoken words, which is to say that pure language will no longer be the rude medium of marketplace communication that Benjamin begins the essay by despising.[40] "Art," including great literature, *anticipates* that future

---

[40] It should go without saying, too, contra Berman (2008/2018: 209), that there will be in it no *Mundart* "dialect," lit. "mouth-kind." *Spannungslos und schweigend* "unstrained and silent" in Benjamin's German does not specify the cessation of orality, only the cessation of all sound; but it should be clear that one cannot have dialect or any other form of oral communication without sound.

state of perfect noncommunication—and to be true to Benjamin's eschatological vision, translations of that literature must adhere to the same anticipatory prescription. Hawkers in the market shout out their sales pitches, but in that future messianic end of time, when pure language reigns, there will be no more hawking, no more selling, no more huckstering. Indeed there will be no more noises of any kind: Benjamin specifically says *schweigend* "staying silent." The promised lack of *Spannung*—tension or suspense—also suggests that pure language will not be used to write plotted novels, either. All time and all noise stop. See also the commentaries to #47 and #76 for a comparison of the apparently opposite takes on silence in the essay: pure language may be silent, but (#47) the movement toward it is not, and (#76) the "most appalling peril" of the kind of great translation that Benjamin touts is that it will trap the translator in silence.

Benjamin's claim that "The only perfection philosophers can hope to achieve is to divine and describe that language" is surreptitiously self-referential: that is the perfection *he* hopes to achieve in his essay on the translator's task. He is the philosopher who has divined it, and now it is his task to describe it. But of course that is an exceedingly difficult task, precisely because pure language is *concealed* in translations. It isn't there for everyone to see. In fact it would be more accurate to say that it isn't there at all: what is there to be divined is the future *prospect* of pure language, its *Andeutungen* "intimations." And that prospect is anything but simple or direct: translations stir up the intentions in the source and target languages, and in so doing bring those two languages into conflict, into tension (*Spannung*), creating a sense of suspense (*Spannung* again) as to whether the tension will ever be resolved in the reconciliation of all languages in the "true" or "pure" language. What may be divined and described in translations is not pure language but the working of a mystical engine (*ingenium*, #49) that powers the holy growth of languages toward their messianic end and may or may not eventually help them reach that end.

What exactly, then, is *intensive* about the concealment of all that in translations?[41] Hamacher (2001/2012) is a long and brilliantly dense answer to this question, in his engagements with this specific passage (500, 528, 539–40) but especially with #19–20, where what intensifies the performance of translation's reach in and through the affinity or kinship or relatedness of languages is the anticipation of the advent of pure language.

*Other commentators*: Bellos (2010: 213), Berman (2008/2018: 177), Gasché (1986: 81), Mosés (1995: 142), Ruin (1999: 150), Smerick (2009: np), Steiner (1975/1998: 67–68), Steiner (2010: 48).

---

41 Zohn has "concealed in *concentrated* fashion in translations" (77; emphasis added), and Underwood has "is *thoroughly* concealed in translations" (39; emphasis added). Hynd and Valk (303) and Rendall (159) stick with "intensively."

## 49 Translation's mystical task (7): the yearning for the language manifested in translations

| | | | | |
|---|---|---|---|---|
| Es gibt keine Muse der | | Philosophie, es gibt auch keine Muse der | | |
| It gives no muse of the philosophy, | | it gives also no | | muse of the |
| Übersetzung. Banausisch aber, | | wie sentimentale Artisten sie | | wissen |
| translation. Banausic | however, as | sentimental artistes | | them to know |
| wollen, sind sie nicht. Denn es gibt ein philosophisches Ingenium, dessen | | | | |
| want, are they not. For | | it gives a philosophical | genius | whose |
| eigenstes die Sehnsucht nach jener Sprache ist, welche in der Übersetzung | | | | |
| ownmost the yearning for | | that language is, which | in the | translation |
| sich bekundet. | | | | |
| itself manifests. | | | | |

*Paraphrase*: There is no muse of philosophy, and there isn't one of translation either. But despite what maudlin artistes would want to tell you, that doesn't make philosophy and translation banausic. There is, after all, a kind of philosophical genius that is possessed of a yearning for that language that is manifested in translation.

*Commentary*: "Banausic" is a word you don't see every day. It means "mechanismic," in the sense of pedestrian, uncultured, unrefined. It comes from the Greek word for mechanismic, βαναυσικός/*banausikós*, from the word for ironsmith, βάναυσος/*bánausos*, from the word for forge or furnace, βαύνος/*baúnos*. (Hynd and Valk [303], Rendall [160], and Underwood [39] all translate *banausisch* "philistine"; Zohn leaves it as "banausic" [77].) The idea is that for those "maudlin artistes" the only true arts are the ones that have muses; those that lack a muse, like philosophy and translation, also lack art. If you're a philosopher or a translator, cut off from the filmy realms of artistic creation, you might as well be an ironsmith. If your *métier* is not ποίησις/*poíēsis* (creating original art/poetry) but ἐπιστήμη/*epistēmē* (organized and habitualized knowing), a mere τέχνη/*tékhnē* (craft, skill, trade, artisanry), why, you hardly belong in the polis at all. Your rightful place is out in the villages with the horses and the peasants.

What is interesting about Benjamin's disparaging remarks about those maudlin artistes, however, is that he defends philosophy and translation not by defending the τέχνη/*tekhnē*-as-ἐπιστήμη/*epistēmē* in them but by finding the divinatory, the vatic, the mantic spark in them: *das philosophisches Ingenium* "the philosophical genius" that doesn't need a muse to sniff out the Delphic vapors. (Ironically, of course, an *ingenium* in Latin is also a machine, an engine; the English word "engineer" derives from it.)

The "language that is evinced in translation" is not the target language, or even the specific articulation of the target language given in every translation. It is the "pure language" that for Benjamin is the messianic end of the holy growth of languages. That is the eschatological language-of-the-future that neither the philosopher as epistemologist (through ἐπιστήμη/*epistēmē*) nor the translator as technician (through τέχνη/*tekhnē*) can see; but then apparently it is invisible or unavailable to the poet (through ποίησις/*poíēsis*) as well. It can only be seen through the philosophical *ingenium* "genius" that is an engine only in the mystagogic sense of conjuring up occult epiphanies.

*Other commentators*: Berman (2008/2018: 177–79), Bradbury (2006: 142), Gasché (1986: 81), Liska (2014: 238), Smerick (2009: np).

## 50 Translation's mystical task (8): standing, with its germ of the language that speaks that truth, midway between poetry and teaching

> »Les langues    imparfaites en cela que  plusieurs, manque la  suprême:
> "The languages imperfect  in this that plural     lack      the supreme:
>
> penser étant écrire sans     accessoires, ni  chuchotement mais tacite
> to think being to write without accessories, not whispering    but   tacit
>
> encore l'immortelle  parole, la  diversité, sur terre, des     idiomes
> still    the immortal  speech, the diversity on earth  of the idioms
>
> empêche personne de    proférer   les mots qui, sinon    se
> prevents anyone      from proffering the words that otherwise themselves
>
> trouveraient, par une frappe unique, elle-même matériellement la vérité.«
> would find   by a     stroke single,  itself      materially      the truth."
>
> Wenn, was  in diesen Worten Mallarmé gedenkt, dem    Philosophen
> If     what in these   words   Mallarmé thinks    to the philosopher
>
> streng    ermeßbar ist, so steht   mit  ihren Keimen solcher Sprache die
> strongly estimable is, so stands with their  germ    of such language the
>
> Übersetzung mitten  zwischen Dichtung und der Lehre.     Ihr Werk steht
> translation    midway between poetry      and the teaching. Its  work comes
>
> an Ausprägung diesen  nach, doch   es prägt  sich  nicht weniger tief
> on stamping     of these after, though it stamps itself not     less    deeply
>
> ein in die Geschichte.
> in  in the history.

*Paraphrase*: "Languages, imperfect in their plurality, lack the supreme thing: thinking being writing without accessories, without even whispers, the immortal word is still unspoken; the diversity of languages on earth makes it impossible to speak the words that would otherwise, in a single stroke, assume material form as truth." If Mallarmé's idea here is philosophically coherent, translation with its germ of the language that speaks that truth stands midway between ποίησις/ *poíēsis* "poetic creation" and διδαχή/*didakhē* "teaching." Its work is less marked than both, but the mark it leaves on history is just as deep.

*Commentary*: The standard critical response to the Mallarmé quotation in this passage is: "why is this not translated?" After all, it appears in a prologue to a German translation from the French (of Baudelaire); why leave it in French? Presumably the target readers of Benjamin's translation are reading it in German because they can't read it in the original French.

But then remember that in #2 Benjamin hinted that those target readers of a translation who can't read the source language have no value, worth, or force for the translation either: his theory would suggest that his translation was not written for readers with no French. He doesn't want us to give any thought at all to the target reader; but perhaps tacitly he is thinking about readers who are capable of comparing his German translation to Baudelaire's source text.

Ian Balfour (2018: 749) articulates the obvious Babelian resonances of the Mallarmé quotation:

> The passage evokes, via the ideal of the diversity of tongues from the Tower of Babel story, the utterly far-reaching event in which God, in Derrida's [1985: 170] phrase, "*at the same [à la fois] time* imposes and forbids translation," the moment when God instituted for all time the simultaneous necessity and impossibility of translation, whose most immediate purpose was to prevent any communication that might result in the building of a tower rising up to God and the heavens. All of a sudden one passed from one and only one language to a multiplicity of tongues requiring but not allowing full communication, much less translation. Every text operates in the shadow and aftermath of this mythic, fictional event. (the first bracketed insertion is mine, the second Balfour's)

Noting that Mallarmé's post-Babelian foreclosure on the materialization of words as truth also manifests as a (negative) truth, Balfour also offers a pertinent quotation from Derrida in "Freud and the Scene of Writing": "The materiality of a word cannot be translated or carried over into another language. Materiality is precisely that which translation relinquishes. To relinquish materiality: such is the driving force of translation. And when that materiality is reinstated, translation becomes poetry" (Derrida 1978: 210; quoted in Balfour 2018: 750). For a discussion of Jewish and Christian attitudes toward translation's inability to render the material "body" of the source text, see the commentary to #78;

Mallarmé's idea that a pre-Babelian and thus pre-translational truth would have been material, materializable, seems to suggest also that a post-Babelian return to "pure language" might restore that state.

Zohn (77) and Rendall (160) both translate *mitten zwischen Dichtung und der Lehre* as "midway/half-way between poetry and doctrine"; for Hynd and Valk it is "midway between creative writing and teaching" (303); for Underwood it is "midway between literature and theory" (39); and for Wright it is "right in the middle of poetry and teaching" (184). To stand there on that middle ground, "midway between ποίησις/*poíēsis* 'poetic creation' and διδαχή/*didakhē* 'teaching,'" as I somewhat ostentatiously have it, is to have some of the qualities of each. The root of ποίησις/*poíēsis* is ποιεςν/*poiein* "to make," so that *poíēsis* is the activity of making something new, creating a thing that never existed before. And certainly translations are newly made things—but for Benjamin they are inferior to *Dichtungen* "poems" in that they "follow" or derive from source texts (#46). In some sense, of course, the translation did "exist" before, as the Essence of the source text; but that belatedness (#13) and secondariness of translations also gives them the larger and broader perspective on the source text and its place and significance in literary history that raises them above the poet's "naivete" into the Schillerian realm of "mindful" "sentimentality" that we saw in #46, and that perspective is akin to *die Lehre* "teaching," especially in the doctrinal sense of expounding sacred scripture. For Benjamin, however, they are nevertheless inferior to teaching/doctrine in that they only contain a *Keim* "germ" of the eschatological language of truth. Given that it requires a special philosophical genius to see and appreciate that germ at all (#49), one is tempted to identify Benjamin's essay about translating as itself *die Lehre* or the διδαχή/*didakhē* "teaching" that is superior to translating. Certainly, as Antoine Berman (2008/2018: 36–39) rightly points out, Benjamin cared passionately about the former and found the latter boring and frustrating.

Still, though translating is less "marked" an activity than writing poetry or teaching—less obviously conscious of its desired impact, which is thus easier to miss (requires a Benjaminian philosophical genius to spot and cherish)—it does nevertheless have a significant impact on history. By "history," of course, Benjamin means specifically *Heilsgeschichte*, the sacred messianic history of languages' growth toward pure language. Translation triggers baby steps in that history; however minutely, it powers the eschatological movement.

Mallarmé's remark is useful for Benjamin, of course, in the notion that the diversity of languages prevents the speaking and thus materializing of the immortal word of truth; all that is lacking in Mallarmé's formulation for Benjamin's purposes is the follow-up notion that it is translation that *engages* the "imperfect" diversity of languages and in so doing provides fuel for the mystical *ingenium* "engine" driving from imperfection to perfection, from thought to its linguistic materialization as truth.

*Other commentators*: Bellos (2010: 213–14), Berman (2008/2018: 184–85), Bradbury (2006: 142), Britt (1996: 55), Cohen (2002: 103), Derrida (1985:

177–78), Hamacher (2001/2012: 508), Johnston (1992: 44), Kohlross (2009: 99), Liska (2014: 240), Rendall (1997b: 178–80), Roberts (1982: 121), Smerick (2009: np), Vermeer (1996: 88), Weber (2008: 75–78).

## 51 The translator's task (4): seemingly impossible

| Erscheint die Aufgabe des | Übersetzers in solchem Licht, so drohen die |
| Appears the task | of the translator in such light, so threaten the |

Wege ihrer Lösung    sich um so    undurchdringlicher zu verfinstern.
ways of its resolution itself the more impenetrable    to darken.

Ja,     diese Aufgabe: in der Übersetzung den Samen reiner    Sprache
Indeed, this   task:    in the translation   the seed   of pure language

zur    Reife    zu bringen, scheint niemals lösbar,  in keiner Lösung
to the ripening to bring,   seems   never   soluble, in no    solution

bestimmbar.  Denn wird einer   solchen nicht der Boden entzogen,
determinable. For  will  of one such   not  the floor  be pulled out,

wenn die Wiedergabe des    Sinnes aufhört, maßgebend zu sein? Und
if    the reproduction of the sense  ceases   definitive  to be? And

nichts   anderes ist ja    – negativ    gewendet – die Meinung alles
nothing other   is indeed – negatively turned   – the meaning of all

Vorstehenden.
the above.

*Paraphrase*: If the translator's task is viewed in this light, the pathways to solving it seem threatened with an all the more impenetrable darkness. Indeed that task, of translating so as to bring the seed of pure language to ripeness, seems insoluble, unclarifiable in any solution. For if we stop talking about the reproduction of source-textual meaning in the target language as the measure of good translation, doesn't that pull the rug out from under the translator's whole task? And indeed, in a negative sense, that is exactly the implication of everything we've been discussing.

*Commentary*: As we saw in the commentary to the title (#0), Antoine Berman (2008/2018: 42–44) argues that in the word "Aufgabe" Benjamin is alluding to a German Romantic tradition going back to Novalis linking *die Aufgabe* "the task" with *die Auflösung* "the resolution or the dissolution." I mentioned there that one of Novalis's fragments seems to establish the link; even with the Novalis fragment, however, it all seemed somewhat speculative, back then. But if the pairing of *die Aufgabe* and *die Auflösung* seemed far-fetched to you, #51 should banish all skepticism. In this passage, in fact, what is in need of being (re-/dis)solved is not the foreign (as in #36) but the translator's task itself. The *fremdes Daseyn* "foreign being/presence/existence" that needs to be dissolved is Benjamin's metaphysics of translation: "that task, of translating so as to bring the seed of pure language to ripeness." If as Berman (2008/2018: 43) says "the 'task' is therefore confronted with a problem (to solve), with a hostile materiality (to dissolve), or with dissonance (to resolve musically)," the problem (task) for the conventional translator to (dis-)solve is not so much a hostile materiality as a hostile transcendentality—hostile in the sense of being utterly alien to, and therefore dissonant with, everyday pragmatic empiricism.

If any further evidence is needed, consider also this passage from Benjamin's essay on Hölderlin:

> [Diese andere Funktionseinheit ist nun die Idee der Aufgabe,] entsprechend der Idee der Lösung, als welche das Gedicht ist. (Denn Aufgabe und Lösung sind nur in abstracto trennbar.) Diese Idee der Aufgabe ist für den Schöpfer immer das Leben. In ihm liegt die andere extreme Funktionseinheit. Das Gedichtete erweist sich also als Funktionseinheit des Lebens zu der des Gedichts. In ihm bestimmt das Leben durch das Gedicht, die Aufgabe durch die Lösung. (Benjamin 1914–15/1991: 107; quoted in Berman 2008/2018: 48n43; bracketed text not cited by Berman)

> [This other functional unity is now the idea of the task, which] corresponds to the idea of resolution, which is the poem. (For task and resolution are only separable in the abstract.) The idea of the task, for the creator, is always life. The other extreme functional unity lies within it. The poetic composition therefore proves itself to be the transition from the functional unity of life to the functional unity of the poem. Within the poetic composition life determines itself through the poem, the task through the resolution. (translation Wright 2008/2018: 44; bracketed text translated by DR)

Note also that in #51 Benjamin mingles the (re-/dis)solution trope with the imagery of light and darkness: *Erscheint die Aufgabe des Übersetzers in solchem Licht, so drohen die Wege ihrer Lösung sich um so undurchdringlicher zu verfinstern* "If the translator's task is viewed in this light, the pathways to solving it seem threatened with an all the more impenetrable darkness." The idea there would seem to be that the *light* of Benjamin's transcendental Platonist/Neoplatonist metaphysics is so alien to and dissonant with everyday empiricism that it *seems* like an impenetrable darkness, which therefore seems to threaten the pathways to (re-/dis)solving it. The resolution to this imagined quandary, it seems clear—a clarified solution, into which the alien darkness has been dissolved—is to relax, to relinquish all loyalties to everyday experiential pragmatism, and accept the transcendental metaphysics, like the initiate to a mystical religion seeing the light in the darkness with eyes wide shut. And yes, from a pragmatic point of view, that does "pull the rug [literally *den Boden* 'the floor'] out from under the translator's whole task," and that, Benjamin adds with a triumphant gleam in his eye, is the whole point.

As long as you are standing calmly, confidently, empirically on a rug (or a floor), you are going to reject as absurd all talk of the Essence of translation-as-a-Form and "bringing the seed of pure language to ripeness." Pulling the rug out from under that confident stance is the metaphysical countermeasure of choice.[42]

*Other commentators*: Bellos (2010: 214), Berman (2008/2018: 188–86), Britt (1996: 55, 63), Ferreira Duarte (1995: 273), Gelley (2015: 21), Jacobs (1975: 757), Smerick (2009: np), Vermeer (1996: 88), Weber (2008: 73).

## 52 Translational fidelity (1): the traditional take

> Treue und Freiheit – Freiheit der sinngemäßen Wiedergabe und
> Fidelity and freedom – freedom of the sense-measured reproduction and
>
> in ihrem Dienst Treue gegen das Wort – sind die althergebrachten
> in its service fidelity against the word – are the traditional
>
> Begriffe in jeder Diskussion von Übersetzungen. Einer Theorie, die
> concepts in every discussion of the translations. To a theory that
>
> anderes in der Übersetzung sucht als Sinnwiedergabe, scheinen sie
> other in the translation seeks than sense-reproduction, seem they
>
> nicht mehr dienen zu können.
> not more to serve to be able.

*Paraphrase*: Fidelity and freedom, the freedom to reproduce the sense of whole sentences and, in its service, fidelity against the word, are the old chestnuts inevitably brought to bear on translation in every discussion. To a theory that seeks something other than the reproduction of sense they would seem to be no longer of service.

*Commentary*: This passage is a pretty straightforward statement of Benjamin's rejection of what in #27 he calls "the dead theory of translation." The one even marginally problematic phrase is *in ihrem Dienst Treue gegen das Wort*, literally "in its service fidelity against the word"—which is also, of course, how I paraphrase it. In that I follow Rendall, who has "in its service, fidelity in opposition to the

---

42 Compare J.L. Austin's (1962) use of the same trope at Harvard in 1955: "So far then we have merely felt the firm ground of prejudice slide away beneath our feet" (12), and "to feel the firm ground of prejudice slipping away is exhilarating, but brings its revenges" (61). For Austin, stepping off the firm ground of prejudice onto the ice and there slipping and falling leads to an intuitive encounter with ordinary language; for Benjamin, it leads to a revelatory encounter with extraordinary (transcendental) language. But the human phenomenology of both transformative/transitional exhilarations is the same. (See also the commentary to #55 for a similar exhilaration.)

word" (160).⁴³ But that is a minority reading: Zohn (78) and Hynd and Valk (304) both have "in its service, fidelity to the word," and Underwood has "in thrall to it, fidelity to the text" (39). The German preposition *gegen* does mean "against," in every possible sense; I assume Zohn and Hynd and Valk must have decided that "fidelity against the word" is not an *althergebrachter Begriff* "old chestnut" of translation studies, and adjusted it to fit their assumption about what is. In colloquial English too, of course, we say "faithful *to*," not "faithful *against*." But then *Freiheit der sinngemäßen Wiedergabe*, which I've paraphrased as "the freedom to reproduce the sense of whole sentences," is sense-for-sense translation, and the kind of fidelity that would be "in its service" would be precisely "fidelity against the word." "Fidelity *to* the word" would be word-for-word translation, and that would not be in the service of sense-for-sense translation.

Most likely, in fact, "fidelity against the word" is Benjamin's rhetorical *reversal* of the expected "fidelity to the word" (which of course, as we'll see in #55–56, #61–62, and #77, he emphatically supports), and indeed a skewing of the conventional ("old chestnut") opposition of freedom versus fidelity. The freedom and fidelity that he is attacking here are the freedom to render the sense of sentences and fidelity not *to* the word but *against* it.

Underwood's "in thrall to it, fidelity to the text" is a whole other kettle of fish. He has avoided the dilemma sketched out in the previous three paragraphs by replacing "word" with "text"—but that basically devastates the whole sentence. *Everyone*, including Benjamin, claims fidelity to the text! They just define "text" differently. Even if we imagine "text" as restricted to what discourse analysts mean by it, so that these traditional translators and translation theorists that Benjamin is ridiculing here might be read as faithful to sentence-sense and in the service of that fidelity faithful to text-sense, "text-sense" for the old text-linguists and more recent discourse analysts is just a larger chunk of

---

43 Rendall (1997b) also quotes the blurb Benjamin sent his publisher to promote the Baudelaire translation, with a specific link between the translation and the "preface," namely "Die Aufgabe des Übersetzers"/"The Task of the Translator":

> Was dieser Übertragung ihren Platz sichern wird, ist, daß in ihr einerseits das Gebot der Treue, welches der Übersetzer in seiner Vorrede unwiderleglich begründet, gewissenhaft erfüllt, andrerseits aber das Poetische überzeugend erfaßt wird. (183n24)

> What will guarantee this translation its place is that on the one hand it conscientiously fulfills the requirement of fidelity, which the translator in his preface irrefutably establishes, and on the other it also convincingly catches the poetic element. (183)

"Fidelity" there of course refers to word-for-word translation, "fidelity *to* the word," not sense-for-sense translation, or "fidelity *against* the word"—although, as Rendall goes on to observe, the translation is actually sense-for-sense with distortions caused not by literalism but by Benjamin's attempts to "[catch] the poetic element," i.e., to reproduce the rhyme. Rendall's conclusion is that "fidelity to the word" for Benjamin also included fidelity to rhyme. Given that Hölderlin's translations of Pindar and Sophocles were for Benjamin the prototypes of all literary translating and both relentlessly sacrificed rhyme and meter to expansive literalism, Rendall's suggestion seems unlikely.

communicable/mediable sense, organized pragmatically through cohesive structures of relevance and so on. "The text" to which Benjamin declares fealty is source-textual syntax stripped of all or almost all communicable/mediable sense. At a deeper level of course he finds the true translator stirred by the nontextual (or perhaps pretextual) and therefore untranslatable *Kern* "kernel" of the source text (#39); but at the textual level fidelity *to* the word entails fidelity to the syntactic skeleton of the source text. (And isn't "thrall" a little extreme for *Dienst* "service"?)

*Other commentators*: Bellos (2010: 214), Engel (2014: 7), Smerick (2009: np), Weber (2008: 73).

## 53 Translational fidelity (2): what else might it mean?

> Zwar sieht ihre herkömmliche Verwendung diese Begriffe stets in
> In fact sees their conventional use these concepts always in
>
> einem unauflöslichen Zwiespalt. Denn was kann gerade die Treue für die
> an irresolvable conflict. For what can frankly the fidelity for the
>
> Wiedergabe des Sinnes eigentlich leisten?
> reproduction of the sense actually accomplish?

*Paraphrase*: To be sure the usual understanding of these notions invariably sees them as irresolvably at odds with each other. For what in the end can fidelity achieve for the reproduction of meaning?

*Commentary*: This is more polemical posturing, and not a particularly coherent example of it. Yes, sense-for-sense "freedom" and word-for-word "fidelity" are traditionally seen as mutually exclusive—though that radical binarization of the two has always been an artifact of bad theory. Translators and sensible translation scholars have always known that every translation is a mixture of the two; dicta like "as faithful as one can and as free as one must" are legion. Arguably the reason Benjamin despised the practical work of translating was that he too accepted that dictum, and hated not only the middling compromises it required but the inevitable failure to capture the brilliance of say Baudelaire or Proust that he felt always resulted. The astonishing gap between Benjamin's practical experience of translating and his understanding of translation theory is very much on display here.

A superficial reading of this passage would protest that in #52 he shifted the terms, so that "freedom to reproduce the sense" and "fidelity against the word" are *not* "irrevocably at odds with each other"; but presumably what he means by "the usual understanding of these notions" is not that reversal but the bare binary with which he begins #52: *Treue und Freiheit* "fidelity and freedom."

The real problem in this passage is the second sentence: "For what in the end can fidelity achieve for the reproduction of meaning?" What "fidelity against the word" can achieve for "the reproduction of meaning" is not perfect, not transcendental, indeed nothing like the brilliant metaphysical vision that he outlines in this essay—but it is good enough for the multibillion-dollar translation marketplace. Yes, Benjamin despises that marketplace, and indeed all marketplaces; but the rhetorical question he should be asking to diminish that whole set of assumptions is not "what can it achieve?" but "what *good* is it?" If commonsensical approaches to the translation marketplace see not only great achievements but good enough quality, the leading edge of his critique should actually be the quality, not the achievements. Okay, sure, you have your achievements; but because "good enough" is *not* good enough, the achievements are worthless. Because the quality that you prize is defined on the wrong grounds, you have no way of knowing just how bad it is, and therefore, secondarily, just how inconsequential your achievements are. The inconsequentiality of those achievements in Benjamin's eyes makes him want to deny their very existence; that implied denial misses the point that Benjamin himself wants to make.

*Other commentators*: Berman (2008/2018: 187–88).

## 54 Translational fidelity (3): the power of words' feeling-tone

> Treue in der Übersetzung des einzelnen Wortes kann fast nie den
> Fidelity in the translation of the single word can almost never the
>
> Sinn voll wiedergeben, den es im Original hat. Denn dieser erschöpft
> sense fully reproduce that it in the original has. For this exhausts
>
> sich nach seiner dicterischen Bedeutung fürs Original
> itself in accordance with its poetic significance for the original
>
> nicht in dem Gemeinten, sondern gewinnt diese gerade dadurch, wie das
> not in the *intendendum*, rather obtains this directly through how the
>
> Gemeinte an die Art des Meinens in dem bestimmten Worte
> *intendendum* to the way of the intending in the specific word
>
> gebunden ist. Man pflegt dies in der Formel auszudrücken, daß die Worte
> bound is. One tends this in the formula to express that the words
>
> einen Gefühlston mit sich führen.
> a feeling-tone with themselves carry.

*Paraphrase*: Translational fidelity is almost totally incapable of fully reproducing the meaning of each individual source-textual word. For that meaning is exhausted in accordance with its poetic significance for the source text, and that relationality is channeled not through what is intended but through the way the *intendendum* is bound up with the way it is intended in each individual word. We tend to formulate this by saying that words carry a feeling-tone.

*Commentary*: Even in the commonsensical terms that Benjamin attacks in this essay, that first claim is true. Translators and traditional translation scholars have always known that perfect fidelity is impossible, even for the most mundane utilitarian text. The next sentence, with its reference to "poetic significance," limits the range of applicability of his critique to literary translation, of course, as does the entire essay; but even without that limitation that second sentence could easily be accepted by nonliterary translators as an accurate account of what they do. If the "significance for the source text" is not poetic but technical, or commercial, or legal, or medical, and in each case saturated in the text's cultural implications for the source culture, and problematized by cultural shifts in the transfer to the target culture, there remains a lesson to be gleaned by the nonliterary translator from the observation that "that relationality is channeled not through what is meant but through the way what is meant is bound up with the way it is meant in each individual word."

If I were to adapt that lesson for the next edition of *Becoming a Translator* (Robinson 1997/2020), for example, I would have to give a great deal of thought to explaining *wie das Gemeinte an die Art des Meinens in dem bestimmten Worte gebunden ist* "the way the *intendendum* is bound up with the way it is intended in each individual word" for practical translators of nonliterary texts; but it could be done. *Das Gemeinte* "what is meant/intended" is the semantics of the word; *die Art des Meinens* "the way it is meant/intended" is not only how the culture has conditioned us to mean that particular thing by the word, but how that cultural conditioning has led us to the feeling that each language *wants* us to say things in a certain way, to mean certain things by saying them in that certain way.

But how does culture condition us into those "certain ways"? Benjamin doesn't explain, and he wouldn't be happy with the post-Kantian/post-Romantic constructivism of "cultural conditioning"; but his final sentence in this passage does give us a hint: "We tend to formulate this by saying that words carry a feeling-tone." Mikhail Bakhtin (1895–1975, three years younger than Benjamin) developed his theory of internal dialogism just a few years after Benjamin's essay on the translator's task, based precisely on the conditioning effects of those "feeling-tones" that Benjamin mentions. "The culture" is hundreds of thousands of dialogues in each language user's life, each saturating the speaker's and writer's sense of "meaning" or "intention" with myriad attitudinal feeling-tones that are conative in nature, putting pressure on us to act and think and feel in collectively guided ways.[44]

---

44 The collective guidance that I attribute here to Bakhtin's internal dialogism of the word is indeed part of his theory, but only as a directionality that is intertwined with its opposite, toward idiosyncratic deviations; the tensions between the two opposite tendencies are part of what he calls "heteroglossia."

Obviously Benjamin cannot possibly have known anything about Bakhtinian dialogism in 1923, as Bakhtin's *Problems of Dostoevsky's Poetics* did not appear in Russian until 1929(/1984), and "Discourse in the Novel" (1934–35/1981), his first full theorization of internal dialogism, wasn't even written for five more years after that, and it didn't begin to be translated into German until a half century later. Even if he had known about it, he probably wouldn't have appreciated it—it's too focused on the phenomenology of human communication for his metaphysical tastes; but that would be one way of helping less transcendentally oriented readers understand his point. And indeed without the conative effects of Bakhtinian internal dialogism, Benjamin's remark about feeling-tones seems like a throwaway. So we feel words: so what?[45]

One line of speculation might go like this. We are to translate literally, yes; but more holistically speaking we are to translate not the meanings of individual words but *how they are intended*, how the vitalistic intentions of the target language *want* us to translate them; and we are to *feel* our way into those intentions, guided by those feeling-tones. Tonalizations are prosodic features of texts, and prosodies perform bodily orientations, attitudinalizations—in this case not human attitudes, not the source author's wishes, but the attitudinal *Intentionen* "intentions" of the language(s).

Of course if this line of speculation is at all useful, what Benjamin would be fleshing out in it would be a somatic mirroring/mapping not from human to human but from language to human, through the mediation of the source text and its echo in the target language. His idea would be that what is channeled *somatically* to the translator is a transcendental impulse sent down through the languages by (#17–19) the vitalistic Forms in Plato's Realm, guided by (#59) the mystical divine agent that Philo Judaeus called the Logos. In this reading the *feeling* of working to bring what seem like the intentions of the source and target languages into rough alignment would be understood as a tonalizing *Andeutung* "intimation" or *Offenbarung* "revelation" of the transcendental/vitalistic supplementation of the intentions of ideal Forms and their Essences. Benjamin would thus be construed as believing that the translator is "given" the transcendental truth in phenomenological form; that the translator apprehends that truth phenomenologically through the *Gefühlston* "feeling-tone" in and of the SL/TL intentions. Our path to understanding what we need to know while translating would thus run through situated embodiment, lived experience.

---

45 This is the domain that I have been exploring since the mid-1980s, under the rubric of "the somatics of language"; see Robinson (1991, 1996, 2003, 2008, 2011, 2013a, and 2015). A more focused effort to theorize the cultural conditioning of those "certain ways" through somatic theory led to the development of "icotic theory" in early drafts (from about 2009) of what eventually became Robinson (2016a); see also Robinson (2013b, 2016b, 2016c, 2017b, 2017c, and 2019).

*Other commentators*: Berman (2008/2018: 140–41), Ferris (2008: 65), Hamacher (2001/2012: 508), Pfau (1988: 1083–84), Smerick (2009: np), Weber (2005: 76, 2008: 73, 93).

## 55 Translational fidelity (4): Hölderlin (2)

| | | | | | |
|---|---|---|---|---|---|
| Gar die Wörtlichkeit | hinsichtlich der | Syntax wirft | jede | | |
| Even the word-for-wordness | with respect to the syntax | throws that | | | |

Sinneswiedergabe vollends über den Haufen und droht geradenwegs
sense-reproduction totally over the heap and threatens straightaway

ins Unverständliche zu führen. Dem neunzehnten Jahrhundert
into the incomprehensible to lead. To the nineteenth century

standen Hölderlins Sophokles-Übersetzungen als monströse Beispiele
stood Hölderlin's Sophocles translations as monstrous examples

solcher Wörtlichkeit vor Augen.
of such word-for-wordness before eyes.

*Paraphrase*: In fact a literal rendering of the syntax totally flips the reproduction of meaning on its head and threatens to lead straight into the incomprehensible. To the nineteenth century Hölderlin's translations of Sophocles stood as monstrous examples of such literalism.

*Commentary*: The image of literalism flipping the reproduction of meaning upside-down and threatening to lead straight into the incomprehensible seems negative, perhaps, especially to those of us who have spent our entire lives seeking to be understood, and our professional lives seeking to translate comprehensibly; but I'm guessing for Benjamin there would have been an air of the *salto mortale* to it, the exhilaration of virtuoso daredevil acrobatics involving a serious risk to life and limb (flips it on its head!). A threat of incomprehensibility? So what? Go for it! Feel the adrenalin surge! Take the leap! (See also the footnote on Austin in #51, p. 125n42, for a similar moment.)

There is also an intriguing link between *das Unverständliche* "the incomprehensible" in this passage and *sich nie verständigen* "never correspond" in #47. Both *unverständlich* and *sich nie verständigen* have the negation of understanding in them—here, because literalism threatens to block understanding, and in #47 because without the ministrations of literal translation the individual elements in the source and target texts can't "communicate," can't hear and understand and explain each other. The difference between the two, obviously, is that the threat here is that the *reader* won't understand, and in #47 it is that the intentions in the two languages won't be brought into communicative tension with each other, and the holy growth of languages to the messianic end of pure language will not be advanced. The takeaway is that in order to contribute to that holy growth, the translator has to relinquish all desire to be understood by readers and focus on setting up transcendental echoes between the source and target tongues.

As for Friedrich Hölderlin, Benjamin was one of the first German scholars to rescue his radical translations from obscurity, and, as he says in #75–76, to celebrate them as *Urbilder ihrer Form* "prototypes of their Form." (See also his article on Hölderlin: Benjamin 1914–15/1991.) Antoine Berman (2008/2018: 104) also makes a useful point:

> Hölderlin can help us understand this essence of translation [as performing signification]. For Benjamin, Hölderlin the translator was a crucial reference point. But this is perhaps even more the case for us, if only because it appears that Benjamin didn't read Hölderlin's translation of Sophocles' *Antigone* very closely; rather he read his translations of Pindar, which do not exhibit the same characteristics.[46]
>
> What is key in Hölderlin's translation of Sophocles is that the translation does violence to the original text to force the emergence of its tragic truth, that is to say, of its original speaking power.

*Antigone* is a violent play about violence; Berman's point is that Hölderlin *performs* that tragic violence, embodies it, repeats and intensifies it, in and through the radicalism of his etymological experiments.

The nineteenth-century perception of the "monstrosity" of Hölderlin's translations, even among his fellow Romantics, was in large part provoked by the extreme difficulty of those translations, "flipping [as they did] the reproduction of meaning on its head and threatening to lead straight into the incomprehensible." That difficulty was compounded for his contemporaries, or perhaps "explained" in their minds, by his mental disorders. He was diagnosed with what is now understood to be schizophrenia in the late 1790s, and wrote his great translations and many of his great poems during the next few years, before being remanded to a mental institution affiliated with the University of Tübingen in September, 1806. Discharged the following year as incurable and given three years to live, he was taken in by Ernst Zimmer, a carpenter who, an avid reader, had read

---

46 See also Louth (1998) for a book-length discussion, especially perhaps his chapter on Hölderlin's Pindar translations (103–49), which does not mention Berman's dismissive claim here but can be read as brilliantly refuting it nonetheless. In any case "performing or not performing signification" is not an explicit textual fact but an interpretive construct, one that can equally persuasively be constructed for the Pindar as for the Sophocles. And if what Berman means is that the two Sophocles translations perform the *dramatic* performativity of *Oedipus* and *Antigone*, it is easy to show that the Pindar translations perform the *vocal* performativity of those odes, which were specifically written to be sung.

Hölderlin's epistolary novel *Hyperion* (written in the second half of the 1790s, around the time his schizophrenia was diagnosed, and published in two volumes in 1797 and 1799). Hölderlin ended up living out the rest of his life, 36 more years, in Zimmer's tower, since renamed the Hölderlin Tower (and his output of those years is called "the tower period").

*Other commentators*: Ferreira Duarte (1995: 273–74), Jacobs (1975: 761–62), Menke (2002: 90), Smerick (2009: np), Weber (2008: 74).

## 56 Translational fidelity (5): rethinking literalism

> Wie sehr endlich Treue in der Wiedergabe der Form die des Sinnes
> How much finally fidelity in the reproduction of the form that of the sense
>
> erschwert, versteht sich von selbst. Demgemäß ist die Forderung
> aggravates, understands itself from itself. Consequently is the requirement
>
> der Wörtlichkeit unableitbar aus dem Interesse der Erhaltung
> of the word-for-wordness underivable out of the interest of the preservation
>
> des Sinnes. Dieser dient weit mehr – freilich der Dichtung und
> of the sense. This serves far more – admittedly of the poem and
>
> Sprache weit weniger – die zuchtlose Freiheit schlechter Übersetzer.
> language far less – the dissolute freedom of bad translators.
>
> Notwendigerweise muß also jene Forderung, deren Recht auf der Hand,
> Necessarily must also that requirement whose right on the hand,
>
> deren Grund sehr verborgen liegt, aus triftigeren
> whose ground very concealed lies, out of more compelling
>
> Zusammenhängen verstanden werden.
> together-hangs understood become.

*Paraphrase*: It should be obvious just how much harder fidelity in reproducing the form makes fidelity in reproducing the sense. One cannot, therefore, deduce the demand for literalism from an interest in retaining the sense. And indeed retaining the sense serves the dissolute freedom of bad translators far better than it does poetry, or language. The demand for literal translation, therefore, whose justification is plain as day but whose ground is buried deep, must necessarily be understood through more compelling intertwinings.

*Commentary*: Because translating each source-textual word in turn, retaining the source-textual syntax—i.e., "reproducing the form"—obviously devastates the sentential "sense" preserved in sense-for-sense translation, it makes no sense to start with the aim to reproduce the sense and from that aim deduce a need for word-for-word translation. In fact, of course, the "obvious"—commonsensical, which is to say ideologically normative—conclusion to draw from the ruination of sense through literalism is that literalism is the enemy and must be avoided. Due in large part to Christian exotericism—the demand that Christian salvation and the texts that make salvation possible be open and easily accessible to everyone—"we" (let's say Westerners since the Renaissance and the sixteenth-century Reformation) tend to assume unthinkingly that the "spirit" or meaning of a text is the only important thing, and everything else must be sacrificed to a clear translation or other articulation of it. For most of us, this isn't an historical prejudice; it's simply the nature of translation, and, beyond that, the nature of human communication. The sense has to be given pride of place, and it has to be clear. Benjamin seeks to overturn the unthinking (in the West originally Christian) normativity of that historical prejudice, for reasons, as we'll see in the commentary to #78, that are grounded in Jewish hermeneutics.

There is, perhaps, a certain circularity to Benjamin's claim that "retaining the sense serves the undisciplined freedom of bad translators far better than it does poetry, or language": he has defined "bad" translators as those who seek to retain the sense—to translate "freely"—and here he warns that the aim to retain the sense will only exacerbate "the dissolute freedom of bad translators." What makes a translator "bad" will only make that translator worse; what makes a translator sin will only make him or her proud of that sin. Whether that circular causality can be laid at the feet of every innovative translation is of course empirically an open question; but Benjamin isn't interested in the empirical questions. His argument is *a priori*. Translators who seek freedom through sense-for-sentence translation are *fundamentally*, transcendentally bad. They deviate so egregiously from the Platonic Form of translation that they can hardly even be called translators.

We know why Benjamin believes that retaining the sense doesn't serve "language": because translation, and especially literal translation, activates the intentions in the source and target languages and so hastens the advent of pure language. But how does it not serve poetry? Does a free translation of free verse not retain the *poetry* of the source text? Does a verse translation that retains the meter and rhyme of the source text and to that end retains *something like* the sense of the source text not serve poetry?

Benjamin would say no—because "the *poetry* of the source text" as reimagined and reframed in the target language only has anything (very remotely) to do with the source text in a rarefied, "spiritualized," abstract way. Translated poetry is *target-textual* poetry, and Benjamin has no interest in serving that. For him, as for Vladimir Nabokov in his literal translation of Pushkin's *Eugene Onegin*, it's all about the poetry of the source text. The attempt to retain the verse form and the semantic content of *Onegin* ruins both—not just because no translator can ever hope to write poetry as brilliantly as Pushkin does, but because the translation exists to serve the original, not to mimic it. The translation is a crib, period—not a poem. The idea of translating *Onegin* with the aim of "competing" with Pushkin was anathema to Nabokov—and would have been to Benjamin as well. Not only is the translator unlikely to be as brilliant a poet as Pushkin; the translator's legs, to use John Dryden's trope, are shackled. Precisely because a verse translation is derived from an original, because it is secondary, belated, and because in order to "compete" or "imitate" it must follow the poet's forms and images and wordings in another language and another culture, it will always be stiff at best, and most likely groanworthy.

Nabokov's translation is often hailed (or despised) as radically literal, but it's not; it's basically just a pedestrian prose paraphrase with poem-like line-breaks. It gives us the sense—what Pushkin's verse novel is about, line by line.[47] It makes a good example of Benjamin's dictum that sense-for-sense translation ill serves poetry; but it would be a terrible example of the kind of translating that Benjamin prefers. Nabokov never even tries to follow Friedrich Hölderlin's example and track the etymologies that join Russian with English, with no thought at all for the sense. But then in Benjamin's terms, Nabokov's *Onegin* is not really a translation at all: it's a crib, a prose rundown of the sense. All it can do at best is whet the reader's appetite for Pushkin in Russian—to motivate the reader without Russian to go out and learn enough Russian to read the novel in the source language.

Benjamin's last sentence in this passage insists that *der Recht* "the justification" for *jene Forderung der Wörtlichkeit* "that demand for literal translation" is *auf der Hand* (lit. "on the hand") "plain as day" but *deren Grund sehr verborgen liegt* "whose ground is buried deep." Or, as the other translators have it: "[its] justification is obvious [but its] legitimate ground is quite obscure" (Zohn 78), "the reason for which is obvious, though the underlying motive may be deeply concealed" (Hynd and Valk 304), "[its] justice is obvious [but its] ground is deeply concealed" (Rendall 161), and "[it is] clearly just but very hard to justify" (Underwood 40).[48]

I have to say, if some readers find any of that "on the hand" or "plain as day" or "obvious," my hat is off to them. It's obvious, certainly, that things we believe deeply seem obvious to us, and whatever seems obvious to us also seems like it ought to be obvious to everyone else as well. And Benjamin did believe deeply that the task of the translator demanded literalism. What *der Grund* "the ground/

---

47 See Robinson (2021) for a discussion of the wish that Nabokov had translated *Onegin* not as a boring prose paraphrase but on the model of *Pale Fire*.
48 It's interesting that Hynd and Valk translate *der Recht* "the law, justice, the title/claim" as "reason," though *der Grund* can also be translated "reason," and *der Grund* as "the motive," though metaphorically *Grund*/ground is stable and a motive is in motion; and that Underwood made it about two kinds of justice, the *prima facie* kind ("clearly just") and the rhetorical kind ("hard to justify"). Each pair there—reason/motive, just/justify—is manifestly based on guesses. Zohn, Rendall, and I all played it safe by sticking closely to the core meanings of the two nouns, *der Recht* and *der Grund*—but that also means that our translations don't go very far as explanations (let alone as justifications).

reason/basis" for that demand is, though, and where and why and how it lies buried deep, is an open question.

I suppose if I were to venture a guess I'd say that Benjamin can feel just how hard it is to explain and justify his demand for literal translation, and the discrepancy between that feeling of difficulty and his own inner sense of the absolute rightness of that demand has been nagging at him, making him wonder how his address to the issue could possibly be pulled so insistently in two directions.

Guessing further—one layer down, let's say—I would say that *der Recht* of the demand seems obvious to him in 1921 because he's a mystical Jew whose best friend is an expert on Kabbalah (see #57), and they have been reading about and discussing these matters intensely for years; and yet the whole thing feels buried deep under the ponderous weight of normative Christian ideology (see the commentary to #78). *Der Grund* "the ground" of fringe esoteric Jewish hermeneutics lies buried deep beneath *der Grund* "the ground" of the dominant exoteric Christian hermeneutics.

And speaking of hermeneutics: again here we find Wilhelm Dilthey's hermeneutical term *Zusammenhang*, which I continue to render "intertwining." For *triftigere Zusammenhänge* Zohn has "more meaningful context" (78); Hynd and Valk have "more convincingly grounded" (304); Rendall has "more pertinent relationships" (161); and Underwood has "more convincing links" (40). See the commentary to #13 for the full Diltheyan work-up of this term; the important thing to remember here is that the hermeneutical phenomenology behind the *triftigere Zusammenhänge* "more compelling intertwinings" is the *experience* of relationalities: not just relationships or links, as Rendall and Underwood have it, but the experiential *perception and interpretation* of those things.

*Other commentators*: Bellos (2010: 214), Berman (2008/2018: 189), Johnston (1992: 43–44), Smerick (2009: np), Uhl (2012: 456–57), Vermeer (1996: 176).

## 57 Translational fidelity (6): reassembling the broken vessel

> Wie nämlich Scherben eines Gefäßes, um      sich        zusammenfügen
> As  namely  shards   of a  vessel,  in order themselves to assemble
>
> zu lassen, in den kleinsten Einzelheiten einander     zu folgen, doch   nicht
> to let,   in the smallest   details     one another to follow,  though not
>
> so zu gleichen haben, so muß, anstatt dem Sinn des   Originals sich
> so to resemble  have,  so must, instead of the sense of the original  itself
>
> ähnlich zu machen, die Übersetzung liebend vielmehr    und bis  ins
> alike   to make,   the translation  lovingly much more and until in the

> Einzelne hinein dessen Art des    Meinens in der eigenen Sprache  sich
> single    into    this's  way of the intention in the own    language itself
>
> anbilden, um      so beide wie Scherben als Bruchstück eines Gefäßes, als
> to mimic, in order so both  like shards   as fragments of a    vessel, as
>
> Bruchstück einer größeren Sprache  erkennbar     zu machen.
> fragments of a   greater   language recognizable to make.

*Paraphrase*: You know how when you're reassembling a broken pot by fitting the shards back together, the pieces don't have to be alike, but they do have to follow each other perfectly, down to the tiniest detail? The same is true in translating: rather than replicating the source text's meanings, the translation must work lovingly and in minute detail to mimic the *way* the source text means those things into the target language, so as make the source and target languages recognizable, as with the shards of a broken pot, as pieces of the same greater language.

*Commentary*: The reassembly of a shattered pot in this passage is the essay's first strong imagistic hint that the metaphysics behind the essay is not just the Neoplatonist Logos mysticism of Philo of Alexandria but the Jewish Kabbalah, about which Benjamin learned from his close friend Gershom Scholem.[49]

The basic esoteric aim of Kabbalah is to explain the relation between the Ein Sof (אֵין סוֹף) or "the Infinite" and the created finite universe. The creation myth in Kabbalah is that the Ein Sof constricted its light, creating a void and pouring the divine light of existence into it; this is called the Tzimtzum, or construction/concentration. The process began with the Ein Sof's Atsilut (emanation) of the ten Sephirot or "vessels," which the early (polytheistic) chapters of the Hebrew Bible call the Elohim. Later monotheistic Judaism fell into the habit of singularizing the Elohim, taking that plural as the name of the One God; but the Elohim,

---

49 As Tamara Tagliacozzo (2018: 160–61) notes, while "the principal source [for Benjamin's knowledge of Kabbalist theories of language] was his friend Gershom Scholem, … Scholem was reading Baader and Molitor, along with the available editions of the Kabbalist theories of language of Abraham Abulafia [1240–1291]." Scholem also got Benjamin reading Franz von Baader (1765–1841) and Franz Joseph Molitor (1779–1860), the main channels of the Christian Kabbalah from Johann Reuchlin (1455–1522) and Jakob Böhme (1575–1624) to the Romantics; Benjamin was also reading Friedrich Schlegel, Novalis, Tieck, Schleiermacher, and others. For other studies of Benjamin's Kabbalism, in addition to Tagliacozzo (2018: ch. 4), see McBride (1989), Jacobson (2003), and Shapiro (2011).

There are plenty of nay-sayers as well. João Ferreira Duarte (1995), for example, citing George Steiner's (1975/1998: 63–67) and Willis Barnstone's (1993: 242) tracking of Benjamin's Kabbalism, calls this "a gross misunderstanding and a biased misreading of Benjamin's theoretical manoeuvres and objectives" (275–76), arguing that "we could say of Benjamin what Althusser once said of Marx, that he is playing with empty formulae in order to name something that is indeed nameless and can only be grasped through a 'symptomatic' reading of the text (Althusser 1970: 29)" (276).

originally the gods of polytheistic Canaanite religion, are explained in Kabbalah as the plural emanations of the Ein Sof.

Some Kabbalists believed that evil was an attribute of the Ein Sof: because the Ein Sof is infinite, it must contain negativity as well as positivity and everything else. Other Kabbalists believed that evil emerged in the Sephirot, the vessel-emanations, through an unfortunate imbalance in Gevurah, the power of strength/judgment/severity. Still other Kabbalists theorized that evil originated as a demonic parallel to the holy, called the Sitra Achra (the "other side"). Gershom Scholem called this dualistic (good/evil) line of thought a "Jewish Gnostic" motif. Where this belief arguably appears imagistically in Benjamin's text is the Kelipot (also written Qliphoth), the "impure shells" or "husks" that cover and conceal the holy. The Kelipot originate in the Sitra Achra, the demonic other side; but they also feed off the holy, and protect the holy by placing limits on its power to reveal the truth. Evil as a necessary limitation—at least for a while, until the messianic end.

Where are the Kelipot or "shells" in Benjamin? In #39, where Benjamin compares the tenor and language of the source text to the duality of *Frucht und Schale*, loosely translated as "fruit and skin," but literally "fruit and shell": the kernel of pure language is wrapped in the impure Kelipot shells of historical existence. Because translation brings languages into contact, however, in effect rubbing them up against each other, the abrasions begin to wear away at the shells and eventually break them, so that pure language begins to emerge. This of course is a somewhat sketchy link: the Kabbalistic reading works, but is not demanded by Benjamin's imagery.

The shards of the broken vessel here in #57, on the other hand—as Jacobs (1975: 763n9) points out, a key image in Kabbalah[50]—point far more insistently

---

50 Carol Jacobs, noting that "Gershom Scholem, in writing about this text, relates the figure of the angel of history to the Tikkun of the Lurianic Kabbalah" (1975: 763n9), suggests that Scholem could have applied the Tikkun—the reassembly of the broken vessels—more germanely to this passage in the "Task." Scholem writes:

> Zugleich steht in Benjamins Sinn aber der kabbalistische Begriff des *Tikkun*, der messianischen Wiederherstellung und Ausbesserung, die das im "Bruch der Gefässe" zerschlagene und korrumpierte ursprüngliche Sein der Dinge und auch der Geschichte zusammenflickt und wiederherstellt. (1972: 132–33)

> Yet at the same time, Benjamin has in mind the kabbalistic concept of the Tikkun, the messianic restoration and mending that patches together and restores the original being of things and of history that was shattered and corrupted in the "Breaking of Vessels." (translated/quoted in Jacobs 763n9; translation modified)

For a fuller account of the Tikkun, Jacobs also directs us to Scholem (1973).

One more observation in that same Jacobs footnote:

> Harry Zohn's (mis)translation of this passage ["as fragments of a greater language, just as fragments are part of a vessel" (78)] along with Benjamin's carefully articulated messianic rhetoric seem to speak here of the successful realization of the Tikkun. Yet whereas Zohn suggests that a totality of fragments are brought together, Benjamin insists that the final outcome of translation is still "a broken part".

from Benjamin to the Kabbalah. The cosmic creative act of Tzimtzum began by emanating the Sephirot-vessels and ended by shattering them, causing them to fall into the lower realms. There they were animated—given "fully unmetaphorical" life (#13)—by what remained of divine light, making them available for revelation, but also exiling the Divine Persona, requiring humans to undertake the process of rectification called Tikkun Olam, involving the reassembly of the vessels by fitting the broken shards back together. Perhaps, though, this is another sketchy link, not demanded by Benjamin's imagery? No: "You know how," as I paraphrased Benjamin above, "when you're reassembling a broken pot by fitting the shards back together, the pieces don't have to be alike, but they do have to follow each other perfectly, down to the tiniest detail?" There the submerged allusion to Kabbalah—not just translation but literal translation as part of Tikkun Olam—makes more sense than the surface level of the imagery, where the shards "don't have to be alike," they only need to "follow each other perfectly." ("Be alike" obviously refers to the equivalence theory of translation, but doesn't make sense in the reassembly of a shattered pot: who would ever assume that those shards might all be identical?) The catastrophe that brought about the separation of natural languages—what Kabbalists call the three stages of Tzimtzum (construction/concentration), Tohu (chaos), and Shevirah (the shattering of the vessels)—begins to be rectified when the exile of the Divine Persona in the lower levels (the physicality of earth) leaks the light of revelation and makes it possible for Creation to become self-aware, leading eventually to the breaking of the impure Kelipot-shells and the reassembly of the Sephirot-vessels, by fitting those shards back together. By "work[ing] lovingly and in minute detail to mimic the *way* the source text means those things into the target language," the literal translation can "make the source and target languages recognizable, as with the shards of a broken pot, as pieces of the same greater language."

One final point: the Kabbalists appropriated both the rabbinical term Shekhinah (the Divine Presence) and the earlier Jewish Neoplatonist mystical tradition elevating Sophia or Wisdom as a feminine manifestation of God in order to imagine a Divine Queen as the indwelling/immanent feminine presence of God. This Divine Queen was the tenth emanation of the Ein Sof, the tenth of the Sephirot-vessels, called the Malkuth or Kingdom. It is of course completely speculative that this is what Benjamin meant by *Bereich* in passages like #10 and #37:

---

That seems like a stretch to me. Benjamin's word is *Bruchstück*, which does morphologically mean "break-piece" or "breach-piece" but actually is a shard, a fragment—something that *was* broken, not necessarily something that *still is* broken. Once the broken vessel has been reassembled and glued back together, one can trace the outline of each "break-piece" or shard and recognize that it has that outline because it was once broken; but it isn't *still* broken. (Cf. also the Jacobs quotation in the commentary to #45, p. 111, to the effect that "the vase of translation built unlike fragment on unlike fragment only to achieve a final fragmentation": she gets that "final fragmentation" too from her tendentious reading of *Bruchstück*.)

> den Verweis auf einen Bereich enthalten, in dem ihr entsprochen wäre: auf ein Gedenken Gottes (#10)

a reference to a kingdom in which it would be fulfilled, namely God's memory

> In ihr wächst das Original in einen gleichsam höheren und reineren Luftkreis der Sprache hinauf, in welchem es freilich nicht auf die Dauer zu leben vermag, wie es ihn auch bei weitem nicht in allen Teilen seiner Gestalt erreicht, auf den es aber dennoch in einer wunderbar eindringlichen Weise wenigstens hindeutet als auf den vorbestimmten, versagten Versöhnungs- und Erfüllungsbereich der Sprachen. (#37)

In the translation the source text grows as it were into a higher and purer realm of language—and even though it can't live there forever, because it never attains that realm in every aspect, it still points in a wonderfully haunting way toward the predestined yet inaccessible kingdom of linguistic reconciliation and fulfillment.

But the mystical/religious imagery there is at least strongly redolent of Kabbalistic thinking, where the Divine Queen is exiled among humans, and generally among the Kelipot shells of impurity, and must await redemption above—back into her kingdom above—by the humans below. The Hasidic Reb Nachman of Breslov (1772–1810) retold this story allegorically in "The Lost Princess" (Nachman 2006–7), in which the Divine Queen is accidentally banished into the place of evil by her father the King, and he sends emissaries to find her and bring her back.[51]

*Other commentators*: Bellos (2010: 214), Baltrusch (2010: 122), Benjamin (1989/2014: 97–102), Berman (2008/2018: 138–39, 189–90), Chapman (2019: 78–81), de Man (2000: 31–33), Derrida (1985: 189–90), Ferreira Duarte (1995: 279), Flèche (1999: 100–2), Gelley (2015: 143), Gold (2007: 621), Johnston (1992: 44), Liska (2014: 240–41), Menke (2002: 94), O'Keeffe (2015: 377), Pan (2017: 41–42), Pfau (1988: 1084–85), Regier (2006: 625–26n10), Rothwell (2009: 260–61), Sandbank (2015: 217), Uhl (2012: 457), Vermeer (1996: 180).

---

51  I confess that I had no idea of this link to Kabbalistic fairy tales when I wrote *Translation and Taboo* (Robinson 1996), and there fortuitously read Benjamin's "Task" as a cryptic fairy tale in which the grammatical gender of the various players in his essay indicates their symbolic gender as actors in a story (207–8): *der Übersetzer* "the translator" (gendered male in German) mobilizes *die Übersetzung* "translation" (gendered female) to stir up *die Intentionen* "the intentions" (gendered female) in the source and target *Sprachen* "languages" (gendered female) to do battle against the evil witch (*die Mitteilung* "transmission, communication," gendered female) and wizard (*der Sinn* "sense," gendered male) and ultimately to rescue from bondage *die reine Sprache* (gendered female), the maiden in distress. I didn't know to call her the Divine Queen, or Malkuth, the Kingdom as the tenth and final Sephirot emanation of God, the last vessel to be broken and scattered as fragments in the lower realms. See also #59 for another possible allusion to Sophia as the female Divine Presence, and #69 for the passage that suggested the fairy-tale rescue to me in the first place.

## 58 Translational fidelity (7): the source text relieves the translator of the need to communicate

> Eben darum muß sie von der Absicht, etwas mitzuteilen,
> Even therefore must it from the impulse something with to share,
>
> vom Sinn in sehr hohem Maße absehen und das Original ist ihr in
> from the sense in very high measure refrain and the original is to it in
>
> diesem nur insofern wesentlich, als es der Mühe und Ordnung des
> this only insofar essential, as it of the trouble and ordering of the
>
> Mitzuteilenden den Übersetzer und sein Werk schon enthoben hat.
> with-to-be-shared the translator and his work already relieved has.

*Paraphrase*: In the same way must the translation also, and for the same reason, to a very high degree refrain from the impulse to communicate something of the meaning of the source text; the source text should only be essential to it insofar as that text has already relieved the translator-while-translating of the effort of construing and framing a content to be communicated.

*Commentary*: The first question that leaps out of that paraphrase has to do with the scalar pronouncement *in sehr hohem Maße* "to a very high degree." Benjamin's reader has come this far in the essay believing that for its author the attempt to communicate *at all* is a sign of bad translation; here, however, it seems that maybe it's okay to communicate *a little bit*. But not so fast: the second part of that passage, from the semicolon in my paraphrase to the end, suggests that the source text, as a vitalistic agent in its own right, has relieved the translator of the *entire* effort traditionally assigned to translators, "construing and framing the to-be-communicated." Which is it? Could it be that the "good" translator, resting assured in the certainty that the source text has removed that burden from the job, translates in the mystically right way, aiming only to (#36) ripen the seed of pure language by stirring up the intentions in the two languages, but somehow inadvertently, perhaps unconsciously, lets a tiny smidgen of source-textual sense seep over into the target language?

The second question is: does the restriction of the source text's *Wesentlichkeit* "essentiality" to that liberation from sense mean that the source text should not be important to the translator at all? That the source text should not matter? That the translator should not care about what s/he is translating? Benjamin does say specifically that *das Original ist ihr in diesem **nur** insofern wesentlich, als es* "the original is in this essential to the translation *only* insofar as"—but is *wesentlich* "essential" here broadly synonymous with "important, significant, valuable"? Or does it mean simply that the source text is essential exclusively to the translator's *work*, not to his or her general evaluation of that text?

Underwood takes an intelligent guess at this: "in this respect the original is essential to it only in so far as, *through its existing*, the translator and the work of translation have been spared the effort and ordering of what is to be communicated" (41; emphasis added). The adverbial phrase I've italicized is not in Benjamin, but it does help clarify what seems like Benjamin's careless phrasing—though perhaps problematically. The import of Underwood's rendition would appear to be that the translator is going to communicate something, and s/he has no idea what, but by already having ordered or framed a content to be communicated the source text relieves the translator of the effort.

Part of this confusion may be Benjamin's: instead of writing *die Mühe und Ordnung* **eines** *Mitzuteilenden* "the effort and framing of *a* to-be-communicated," he wrote *die Mühe und Ordnung* **des** *Mitzuteilenden* "the effort and framing of *the* to-be-communicated," implying that *there is a specific thing* that *is* to be communicated. Preventing that misreading would seem to require the indefinite article, or perhaps an indefinite pronoun like "some": the source text relieves you of the effort of framing *a/some/any* to-be-communicated. But Underwood also adds to the confusion, by suggesting that the source text doesn't actively *intervene* in the translation process in order to block the communicating of its sense but has the passive effect of blocking communication just by existing. I look at the book by my keyboard and *know*, without opening it, that I don't have to reproduce its semantic payload. Or else—and for Benjamin this would be even worse—I look at the book and know that I don't have to *decide what* to communicate or *how to frame* that communication, because the source text must already have done it for me.

*Other commentators*: Berman (2008/2018: 190–91), Ferreira Duarte (1995: 273), Pfau (1989: 1068), Smerick (2009: np), Uhl (2012: 457), Vermeer (1996: 180).

## 59 The Logos of translation

| Auch im | Bereiche der | Übersetzung gilt: | ἐν ἀρχῇ | | ἦν ὁ | λόγος, |
|---|---|---|---|---|---|---|
| | | | en arkhē | | ēn ho | lógos, |
| Also | in the realm | of the translation | yields: in beginning | | was the | Logos, |
| im | Anfang | war das Wort. | | | | |
| in the beginnning | | was the word. | | | | |

*Paraphrase*: The pronouncement ἐν ἀρχῇ ἦν ὁ λόγος—"in the beginning was the word/*logos*"—is in force in the realm of translation too.

*Commentary*: It may seem odd that a devotee of ancient Jewish mystical traditions like Benjamin should cite the opening line of the Christian Gospel according to

John[52] (final form 90–110 CE)—but presumably John (whoever he was) was a Jew before he was a Christian, and almost certainly he learned his Logos mysticism from the Hellenistic/Neoplatonist Jewish mystical traditions developed and promoted by Philo of Alexandria, also known as Philo Judaeus (Philo the Jew, c. 20 BCE–c. 50 CE). Philo theorized the Logos as a bridge between the perfection of Plato's transcendental Forms and the imperfections of earthly matter, including human beings: for him the Logos was the highest form of a whole hierarchy of intermediary divine beings. In fact the Platonic Forms resided *within* the Logos, who was also, however, God's agent on earth. In *De Profugis* Philo wrote that "the most ancient Logos of the living God is clothed by the world as with a garment. ... For the Logos of the living God is the bond of everything, holding all things together and binding all the parts, and prevents them from being dissolved and separated" (quoted in Friedlander 1912: 114–15). The Logos mysticism that begins John's Gospel is manifestly steeped in the Jewish Neoplatonism of Philo; as Friedlander writes, "according to Philo the Universe arrived at creation through the Logos, who is also the bond holding all things together. This description of the Logos reappears in the New Testament" (115). In the first line of John's Gospel, specifically, "the Christ not only creates the universe, but he also holds it together" (115): "In the beginning was the Word, and the Word was with God, and the Word was God. The same was in the beginning with God. All things were made by him; and without him was not any thing made that was made" (John 1: 1–3, *KJV*).

This all has several interesting implications for a reading of Benjamin's essay.

First, the way in which the primordiality of "the word" is "in force in the realm of translation too" has almost nothing to do with the fact that translators translate words. Individual human words in this Neoplatonist mystical tradition are ephemeral copies of the transcendental Form of "word," which in Neoplatonist/Hellenistic Logos mysticism is specifically the Logos.

Second, the Logos for Philo is not an idealized Word/Form as a stable perfected model or picture of the debased human activities of (say) "translation" or "poetry," as Benjamin has seemed to mean by "Translation is a Form" all

---

52 Cf. Vermeer (1996: 17):

Als viertes findet sich im Rahmen dieser Geistesgeschichte auch das christliche Element. Gerade darin z. B., daß Benjamin in seiner Hauptarbeit zum Übersetzen den ersten Satz des sog. Johannesevangeliums zitiert ..., scheint mir u. a. *eine* Problematik seines translatologischen Denkens aufzulassen und läßt sich aus ihm entwickeln und in ihm darstellen.

Fourth, there is to be found in the framework of this intellectual history a Christian element as well—for example, the very fact that in his main work on translation Benjamin quotes the first sentence of the so-called Gospel According to John ... seems to me among other things *one* problematic of his translatological thinking that can be derived from it and represented in it.

He returns to this theme, including Sophia, on pp. 176–77.

along—until this very passage—but a divine demiurge, God's transcendental agent on earth, the Messiah and High Priest, who has divine powers to create and to hold creation together. All the cryptic signs of Benjamin's mystical vitalism that we have been noticing throughout this commentary would seem to point directly to this Logos, whose father is God and mother is Wisdom (σοφία/Sophia).[53] To the extent that the growth of languages toward the ἔσχατον/*éskhaton* "end" of pure language is *holy* and *messianic*, it is guided and overseen by the Logos.

And third, "in the beginning was the Logos" is in force in the realm of translation in the very specific sense that the translator is *guided* (#46) only at second or third hand by the source author and the source text—at first hand by Philo's demiurgical Logos. The translator is *mobilized* by the Logos as a producer of fuel for the mystical engine that drives the holy messianic growth. In translating the translator is doing the Lord's work.

One last note: Chantal Wright (2018: 201) observes that "Benjamin's Messianic framework makes [Antoine] Berman uncomfortable," and that in response to that discomfort Berman argues passionately for a strategically secular reading of Benjamin's essay. See the commentary to #1 for his Romanticizing reading in general, and the commentaries to #48, #65, #68, and #78 for discussions of his claim that "pure language" can mean nothing more mysterious than *dialect*. Here note only that when Berman quotes this passage from John's "In the beginning" opening (191)—without citing Benjamin's contextualization "The pronouncement … is in force in the realm of translation too"—his only comment is that "this citation from the Bible has such autonomy that it is barely a citation. It certainly cannot be treated in the same way as the Mallarmé [#50] and Pannwitz [#72] citations" (192). That "same way" that he feels obliged to avoid would evidently mean something like "at length" or "in detail": he deals with the Mallarmé (182–83) and Pannwitz (183–84) quotations for one full page each, and with the quotation from John's Gospel for exactly those two lines above. It is

---

53 Sophia was a mystical female figure developed in the Hellenistic period by the Neoplatonists and Gnostics, shaped by Plato's use of φιλοσοφία "philo-sophía," the love of wisdom, to refer to the philosophizing that he did. It is easy to "forget" the extent to which Plato's so-called rationalism was soaked in the mysticism of the Eleusinian and other ancient mysteries; and the Neoplatonists in the following centuries worked very hard to reverse any rationalist tendencies promoted by Aristotle and his followers. Whenever Benjamin writes of the "task of the philosopher" (#15), the philosophy of language (#31), the philosopher achieving perfection (#48), the philosophical *ingenium* (genius or engine) (#49), or philosophical coherence (#50), therefore, we should imagine "philosophy" not as reductivist rational deduction but as a love of the mystical wisdom/Sophia. See also the commentary to #57 for the incorporation of Sophia into the Kabbala as the Shekhinah or female Divine Presence who, as the last Sephirot-vessel, is shattered and scattered among the lower levels, where the shards must be gathered and fitted together so as to reassemble the vessel.

difficult to imagine any other Bermanian gloss on the word "autonomy" in that remark than "irrelevancy, not worth discussing."

*Other commentators*: Balfour (2018: 748), Benjamin (1989/2014: 103), Ruin (1999: 147–48, 158n23), Thobo-Carlsen (1998: 7), Uhl (2012: 457), Weber (2005: 76, 2008: 92).

## 60 Translational fidelity (8): stepping away from meaning in order to tonalize its intention

| | | | | | | |
|---|---|---|---|---|---|---|
| Dagegen | kann, ja | muß dem | Sinn | gegenüber ihre Sprache | sich |
| By contrast can, | indeed must to the sense opposed | | | its | language itself | |

gehen lassen, um    nicht dessen intentio als Wiedergabe,  sondern als
to go let,    in order not    this's *intentio* as reproduction, rather    as

Harmonie, als Ergänzung    zur    Sprache, in der    diese sich
harmony,  as supplementation to the language in which this    itself

mitteilt,    ihre eigene Art    der    intentio ertönen    zu lassen.
communicates, its    own    mode of the *intentio* to resound to let.

*Paraphrase*: By contrast, it's clear that the language of translation must step away from meaning, turn its back on it, so as to tonalize the *intentio* of that meaning not as playback but as harmony, as a supplement to the language in which it transmits itself, as its own kind of *intentio*.

*Commentary*: One interesting question in this passage is how one tonalizes the *intentio* of a meaning if one has *dem Sinn ... sich gehen lassen*, literally "from [with respect to] the meaning let oneself go," or, as I paraphrase it, "stepped away from meaning." At work behind that scene, though, is the tension between *das Gemeinte* "what is meant/intended" (the *intendendum*) and *die Art des Meinens* "the manner of meaning/intending" (the *modus significandi*): #31–33, #54. For Benjamin the translation has to make a choice between rendering the meaning of the source text and the ways in which the source language intends that meaning: to step away from the one in order to engage the other.

It's interesting, in fact, that he never uses the Latin *modus significandi* in the essay (he does use *Darstellungsmodus* "performance mode" in #19) but switches to the Latin *intentio* here. Since Latin *intentio* looks so much like English "intention," it seems relatively safe for all four translators (and me) to leave it in Latin and assume that we know what it means; but perhaps things are more complicated than that. In #30–31 he Germanizes the Latin noun (in the plural) as *die Intentionen*;

should we speculate here that the Latin word *intentio* means something other than the agentive/vitalistic forces that he calls *die Intentionen*?

I wouldn't want to push this line of speculation too far, but it does seem potentially significant that Latin *intentio* does not mean just the intended goal or purpose of a course of action. It also means a *tension*, a straining—as does an obsolete use of "intention" in English. In Latin it can also mean an increase, an augmentation; and it can mean the exertion or the effort that goes into increasing or augmenting. In a legal context it can mean a charge or an accusation. Setting aside the legal context, we might imagine three different translations of *intentio* and their respective impacts on the sense of the passage:

1 By contrast, it's clear that the language of translation must step away from meaning, turn its back on it, so as to tonalize the *strain/tension* of that meaning not as playback but as harmony, as a supplement to the language in which it transmits itself, as its own kind of *strain/tension*.
2 By contrast, it's clear that the language of translation must step away from meaning, turn its back on it, so as to tonalize the *exertion/effort* of that meaning not as playback but as harmony, as a supplement to the language in which it transmits itself, as its own kind of *exertion/effort*.
3 By contrast, it's clear that the language of translation must step away from meaning, turn its back on it, so as to tonalize the *increase/augmentation* of that meaning not as playback but as harmony, as a supplement to the language in which it transmits itself, as its own kind of *increase/augmentation*.

In (1), the *intentio* of meaning is not just a vitalistic agent in a language: it is a vitalistic strain, an agentive tension. This works well with Benjamin's vision, in fact, because the mystical task of translation in that vision is to agitate those intentions into conflict, into tension with the intentions of other languages. For Benjamin, in fact, the ideal "state" of the intentions is not stasis but tension or strain. It is precisely through their straining that they advance the holy growth of language toward pure language.

The same seems to hold for (2): the strain is not the kind of tensile strain that one finds in a rope from which a heavy weight dangles, say; it is a *straining*. It is an effort, an exertion. The *intentio* of meaning is working hard. And at what is it working? At (3) the increase or augmentation of language.

To be sure, *intentio* as (1) "strain/tension," (2) "exertion/effort," and/or (3) "increase/augmentation" would seem to clash with "harmony": how might a translator tonalize strain, tension, and so on as harmony? But perhaps the harmony he means is not euphony, the sound of agreement or accord, but a tensile resonance, the in-synch vibrations of two plucked strings as they stretch toward each other and restlessly intertwine.

*Other commentators*: Bellos (2010: 214), Berman (2008/2018: 192).

## 61 Translational fidelity (9): literalism reflects the great yearning for the supplementation of languages

| | | | | | | | |
|---|---|---|---|---|---|---|---|
| Es ist daher, | vor | allem im | | Zeitalter ihrer | Entstehung, | das höchste |
| It is, therefore, before all | | in the era | | of its emergence, | | the highest |

Lob   einer Übersetzung nicht, sich wie ein Original ihrer Sprache  zu
praise of a  translation     not,  itself as  an original of its language to

lesen. Vielmehr ist eben das die Bedeutung der   Treue, welche durch
read. Rather   is even that the significance of the fidelity, which   through

Wörtlichkeit         verbürgt   wird,     daß die große Sehnsucht nach
word-for-wordness guaranteed becomes, that the great yearning    for

Sprachergänzung           aus dem  Werke spreche.
language-supplementation out of the work   speak.

*Paraphrase*: It is, therefore, especially in the era of its genesis, the highest praise of a translation—NOT!—for it to be read as if it had originally been written in the target language. It is rather the fact that word-for-word fidelity has the power to make the yearning for the supplementation of languages call out from inside the work.

*Commentary*: Sorry, that NOT! was an old joke that I couldn't resist repeating. Back in the early 1990s I was taking my first close look at Benjamin's "Task" in both German and Zohn's English translation, and also avidly watching *Saturday Night Live* every week—and one of the most popular sketch series on *SNL* was "Wayne's World" with Mike Myers and Dana Carvey. Those sketches left an indelible imprint on fans' speech back then: "Shwing!", "Party on!", "A sphincter says what?", "Exsqueeze me? Baking powder?", "We're not worthy!", "No way! Way!"—and "NOT!" The NOT! joke was that Wayne (Myers) would say something "grown-up" in an ostentatiously serious tone, and then negate the whole thing by adding NOT! to the end. I had the idea of writing an article about "Foreignism and the Phantom Limb" (Robinson 1997: 113–31), organized around a literal or foreignizing translation of Benjamin's phrase in this passage, "Es ist daher, vor allem im Zeitalter ihrer Entstehung, das höchste Lob einer Übersetzung *nicht*, sich wie ein Original ihrer Sprache zu lesen," as "It is therefore, before all in the time period of its origin, the highest praise of a translation—NOT!—that it reads like an original of its language" (117).[54]

54 Burghard Baltrusch (2010: 121) correctly identifies my reading of that line in Benjamin as "carr[ying] out a negotiation between foreignization and domestication, by comparing the practice of translation with the physiological phenomenon of proprioception, and its continued

"Rather than fetishizing strangeness or foreignness as an awkward or difficult obstacle to easy English appropriation," I noted, "I've assimilated Benjamin's elitist postromantic German text to an extremely anti-elitist masscult American text, a text that typically gives us the 'un-English' NOT! after a chipper parody of elitist academic discourse" (117). Given the fact that this translation "is a perfect example of the kind of fidelity to foreign syntax that the foreignists have tended to favor," I asked: "Does a foreignizing translation have to be serious, respectful, and worshipful to count?" (117). Probably so, I surmised: literal and foreignizing translations originally emerged out of worshipful attitudes toward sacred texts—out of what V.N. Voloshinov (1930/1973) suggestively called the mystifying impact of чужое слово/*chuzhoe slovo* "the alien word." But is that esoteric disposition still in force—*gilt es?* (see the commentary to #2)—in contemporary defenses of literalism and foreignism?

It certainly seems to be in Benjamin's "Task." But then Benjamin forecloses on the shaping effects of target readers (#1–6), and that poses a significant impediment to essentializing claims about the stable "nature" of literalism or foreignism. Asking whether my literal translation of Benjamin was foreignizing or domesticating, I found myself unable to answer without taking readers into consideration. "It does probably still feel alien," I wrote, "syntactically malformed, therefore (potentially) foreignizing, to many native speakers of English—especially those who don't watch *Saturday Night Live*, who don't like or don't approve of that kind of humor, who would find Wayne and Garth's breezy populist anti-academicism repellent" (117–18). But to fans of the sketch and the movies it spawned, especially fans who had adopted the NOT! structure allusively in their everyday speech, my literal translation would probably feel domesticating. It did, after all, assimilate a German text published in 1923 to the popular argot inspired by an American comedy show around seven decades later. In the early nineties, the era of the translation's genesis, it could very well be read as if it had originally been written in the target language—but only by fans of the sketch, or by *SNL* viewers who disliked "Wayne's World" but knew it well enough to be able to despise the translation as a domestication. To other readers—those who would have needed an explanation like this to get the joke, and who perhaps need it even more now, three decades after "Wayne's World" aired—it would be a foreignization.

"Once again," I noted, "a reader-response approach to foreignism throws a good many wrenches into the essentialist works" (118).

---

existence in cases of amputation," and adds intriguingly that "The intensification of the negation ['NOT!'] takes on a marked political character which specifically allows for the fact that 'established words also have their after-ripening' [#25] in discourses, a practice that Benjamin had demanded, but only considered possible from a certain distance in time."

*Other commentators*: Berman (2008/2018: 192–94), Chapman (2019: 78), Engel (2014: 7), Ferreira Duarte (1995: 274), Rendall (1997b: 182), Weber (2005: 75), Wurgaft (2002: 379).

## 62 Translational fidelity (10): literalism is the arcade

> Die wahre Übersetzung ist durchscheinend, sie verdeckt nicht das
> The true translation is translucent, it enshrouds not the
>
> Original, steht ihm nicht im Licht, sondern läßt die reine Sprache, wie
> original, stands to it not in the light, rather lets the pure language, as
>
> verstärkt durch ihr eigenes Medium, nur um so voller
> strengthened though its own medium, only in order so more fully
>
> aufs Original fallen. Das vermag vor allem Wörtlichkeit in
> upon the original to fall. That enables before all word-for-wordness in
>
> der Übertragung der Syntax und gerade sie erweist das Wort, nicht den
> the transposition of the syntax and directly it confirms the word, not the
>
> Satz als das Urelement des Übersetzers. Denn der Satz ist die
> sentence, as the ur-element of the translator. For the sentence is the
>
> Mauer vor der Sprache des Originals, Wörtlichkeit die Arkade.
> wall before the language of the original, word-for-wordness the arcade.

*Paraphrase*: True translation is translucent: it does not enshroud the source text, does not stand in its light, but rather allows pure language, as if intensified by its own medium, to illuminate it all the more brightly. What enables this is above all a word-for-word transposition of the syntax, which confirms that the word, not the sentence, is the translator's primordial element. For the sentence is the wall before the source language, the word the arcade.

*Commentary*: In that famously aphoristic last line, "the sentence" means sense-for-sense translation, and its obvious counterpart, "the word," signifies word-for-word translation. Benjamin has *der Satz* "the sentence" and *die Wörtlichkeit* "wordliness," an abstract noun that doesn't exist in English but in German maintains the sentence/word opposition more or less clearly.

Antoine Berman (2008/2018: 202) has an interesting riff on the opposition here between "the sentence" and "the word." For isn't word-for-word translation also meaning-based? Sense-for-sense translations render the meanings of whole sentences; word-for-word translations render the meanings of individual words. Isn't the difference between them, as indeed several centuries of *ad hoc* thinking about translation has tended to assume, simply a matter of the length of the *segment* of meaning isolated for translation? So how does that pragmatic difference get blown up into a mythical battle between the forces of good and the forces of evil?

Berman's suggestion is that the key word in that distinction is "syntax": we often think of the sentence as structured by syntax, and of literalism as *disrupting* that sentential syntax; but that is because we're thinking of target-language syntax. What radical literalism does is *preserve* the syntax—of the source text. That source-textual syntax is precisely what sense-for-sense translation despises and discards as dross. I have elsewhere (Robinson 1996: 59–66, 118–20) called this model the "metempsychotic" theory of translation: the translator discards the mere physicality (the "letter," which is to say here the syntactic structure) of the source text so that the spirit can be reincarnated intact. "The letter [body] killeth," as St. Paul says, "but the spirit giveth life" (2 Corinthians 3:6, *KJV*). The literalism that Benjamin champions as the arcade, by contrast, not only gives us a clear view of the source-textual syntax, but *showcases* that syntax with the new verbal performance that is the target text. As Berman puts that, "the syntactic letter of the original text … strives to separate itself from meaning, acquiring a peculiar autonomy" (202)—or, since I feel less comfortable with the assumption that "the syntactic letter" is an agent capable of "striving" to do anything, the translator showcases the source-textual syntax bare-bones by stripping away the attempt to communicate coherently in the target language. This is what Benjamin describes in #37 as "in the translation the source text grows as it were into a higher and purer realm of language—and even though it can't live there forever, because it never attains that realm in every aspect, it still points in a wonderfully haunting way toward the predestined yet inaccessible kingdom of linguistic reconciliation and fulfillment."

See also Wright (2018: 181–82) for a discussion of Berman's insistence that *durchscheinend*, which can be translated either "transparent" or "translucent," should here be rendered "translucent" (195). I agree that "transparent," favored not only by Zohn, Rendall, and Underwood, but by Gandillac in French as well, "has the unfortunate consequence of resonating with those metaphors that would view translation as a window or a pane of glass" (181), and thus also as providing an unimpeded view of the source text's semantic contents. "Translucent," by contrast, or Hynd and Valk's French-inspired "translucid," soaks the imagery in mystical light. Benjamin's diction here is ecstatic. We are clearly approaching the full religious peroration now. The light that shines in this passage is the mystical light that shines in the darkness, the light that only the initiate with eyes and mouth closed can see and describe.

The only possible problem with that analysis is that if seeing clearly through to something on the other side resonates with the old "dead theory of translation," Benjamin's insistence that literalism is the arcade might arguably be tarnished with the same brush. At the beginning of this passage, according to Berman, seeing clearly is bad, but at the end of it, as he apparently doesn't notice, seeing clearly is good. In the beginning, if Berman is right, it's better to diffuse the light; but there is nothing in the clear straight vista through an arcade that diffuses the light. A mixed metaphor? Possibly—though in German *durchscheinend* can be either "translucent" or "transparent." It is Berman's interpretation that inclines Benjamin in the former direction, and thus also Berman's interpretation that creates the possible mixed metaphor. If we restore transparency to the true translation, the mixed metaphor disappears.

Then again, see O'Keeffe (2015: 375–76) for an account of Benjamin on *durchscheinend* translation based primarily on Zohn's translation, and indeed assimilating Berman's "translucidity" to Zohn's "transparency":

> Here would be translation so transparent, or following a suggestion of Antoine Berman, so "translucid" (2008, 168), that if it envelops the text at all, it is in the form of a gossamer film, as light and limpid as is possible to imagine. Call it the "Saran Wrap" theory of translation. But how would we see that translation? Would we simply look through it? How, then, shall we know the translation from the original?

David Pan (2017: 40) relies on Zohn to the same effect. If Benjamin's "*shining through*" makes translation a medium for *seeing* through, we end up with the disparaging image of Saran Wrap (aka cling wrap).

If on the other hand it makes translation a conduit of unseen mystical light, the glow of the holy in the darkness, "seen" with eyes closed, the image no longer conflicts with the arcade. And indeed the first sentence of this passage nowhere suggests that we *see* through the translation, only that *light* passes through it—and indeed that translation is the *medium* of the light source (pure language) and intensifies the light it emits.[55]

*Other commentators*: Bellos (2010: 215), Bradbury (2006: 142), Britt (1996: 55), Derrida (1985: 187–88), Engel (2014: 7), Ferris (2008: 66), Pan (2017: 36), Rendall (1997b: 182), Smerick (2009: np), Vermeer (1996: 204), Weber (2005: 75, 2008: 74, 329n10), Zathureczky (2004: 201).

---

55 It is interesting to speculate here on the imagistic links between the translation as the medium of pure language's light here in #62 and *die (Un)mittelbarkeit* "the (im)mediability" of the source and/or target text in #36, #46, and #77. If in the commentary to #46 the translation is immediable in the sense of being incapable of conveying a message to readers, and in #36 religion has the mediability that translations lack, the convergence in #77's sacred text of #36's religion with #62's mystical light arguably makes the "true translation" transcendentally mediable as well.

## 63 Translational fidelity (11): denying legitimacy to sense-for-sense "freedom"

> Wenn Treue und Freiheit der Übersetzung seit jeher als
> If fidelity and freedom of the translation since always as
>
> widerstrebende Tendenzen betrachtet wurden, so scheint auch diese tiefere
> opposing tendencies regarded became, so seems also this deeper
>
> Deutung der einen beide nicht zu versöhnen, sondern im
> interpretation of the one both not to reconcile, rather on the
>
> Gegenteil alles Recht der andern abzusprechen. Denn worauf bezieht
> contrary all right of the other to deny. For whereto refers
>
> Freiheit sich, wenn nicht auf die Wiedergabe des Sinnes, die
> freedom itself, if not to the reproduction of the sense, which
>
> aufhören soll, gesetzgebend zu heißen?
> cease should, law-giving to call?

*Paraphrase*: It has long been assumed that fidelity and freedom pull in opposite directions, and this deeper interpretation does nothing to reconcile them; rather, it denies the other one all legitimacy. For what could freedom refer to if not the reproduction of meaning, which should stop being thought of as laying down the law?

*Commentary*: There is very little that needs to be said about this; Benjamin's polemic against sense-for-sense translation is clear and unadorned. The idea in "what could freedom refer to if not the reproduction of meaning," understood through the commentary to #62, is that "freedom" (sense-for-sense translation) is specifically freedom from the constraints of source-textual syntax, which for Benjamin is the gateway to pure language. Why would one want to be freed from that? The shift from "pull in opposite directions" to "denies the other one all legitimacy" may seem counterintuitive at first; but presumably Benjamin takes "pull in opposite directions" to imply a pluralistic tolerance for both, and his steadfast message is "no mercy." Pulling in the wrong direction is just wrong full stop.

## 64 Translational fidelity (12): the hidden yet mighty remnant

> Allein wenn der Sinn eines Sprachgebildes identisch gesetzt werden
> Alone if the sense of a language-construct identical set become
>
> darf mit dem seiner Mitteilung, so bleibt ihm ganz nah und doch
> may with that of its with-sharing, so remains to it wholly near and yet

| | | | | | | |
|---|---|---|---|---|---|---|
| unendlich fern, | unter ihm verborgen oder deutlicher, durch | | | | | ihn |
| infinitely distant, under it | | concealed or | | plainer, | through it | |
| gebrochen oder machtvoller über alle Mitteilung | | | | hinaus | ein Letztes, | |
| broken or | | mightier | over all | with-sharing | beyond a | last, |
| Entscheidendes. | | | | | | |
| decisive. | | | | | | |

*Paraphrase*: Even were the sense of a verbal construct to be presumed identical with the thing that it communicates, something ultimate and decisive remains, something that is intimately close to it and yet at the same time infinitely distant; something that is hidden beneath it and yet crystal-clear; something that is crushed and broken by it and yet far mightier—something beyond all communication.

*Commentary*: This passage begins in German with *allein wenn* "alone/only if"—and so all four full translators dutifully begin with "only if":

- "Only if the sense of a linguistic creation may be equated with the information it conveys does some ultimate, decisive element remain beyond all communication" (Zohn 79)
- "Only if the sense of a linguistic creation can be taken as identical with the sense it communicates, it retains over and above all communication" (Hynd and Valk 305)
- "Only if it can be posited that the meaning of a linguistic construction is identical with the meaning of its communication, does something ultimate and decisive remain beyond any message" (Rendall 162)
- "Only if the sense of a linguistic construct may be equated with what it communicates is it left with something that" (Underwood 41).

The problem with that reading, though, is that it makes the despised reproduction of meaning the precondition for the existence of the seed of pure language, the kernel, the tenor, the nugget of Rhine gold that the true translator must retrieve from river-hiding in the source text and translate—and that kind of precondition is simply not Benjamin. That mystical nugget of "beyond-communicationness" or immediability (#36, #46, #77) is what is close to the reproduction of meaning and yet infinitely distant; it is what is hidden beneath sense yet crystal-clear; it is what is crushed under the wheel of mundane workaday equivalence but possessed of a far greater transcendental power, indeed the mystical light of #62. The only translator to break out of that *allein* trap is Chantal Wright (2018: 203), who has "*Even if* the meaning of a linguistic unit were to be considered identical"—and it is her lead that I follow in the paraphrase.

*Other commentators*: Bellos (2010: 215), Berman (2008/2018: 202–4).

## 65 Pure language (1): symbolizing and symbolized (1): the latter is found in the becoming of language

Es bleibt    in aller Sprache   und ihren Gebilden    außer dem
It  remains in all    language and its     constructs outer  to the

Mitteilbaren   ein Nicht-Mitteilbares, ein, je       nach       dem
with-sharable a    non-with-sharable, one, always according to the

Zusammenhang, in dem   es angetroffen wird,        Symbolisierendes oder
together-hang,   in which it  met with       becomes, symbolizing     or

Symbolisiertes. Symbolisierendes nur,  in den endlichen Gebilden   der
symbolized.     Symbolizing       only, in the bounded  constructs of the

Sprache; Symbolisiertes aber      im     Werden   der    Sprachen selbst.
language; symbolized       however in the becoming of the language itself.

*Paraphrase*: There remains in all language and its constructs not only what is communicable but what is not; depending on the intertwining in which it is found, the latter may be either symbolizing or symbolized. It is only symbolizing in the bound constructs of language, but symbolized in the becoming of language itself.

*Commentary*: Antoine Berman (2008/2018: 204) has a rather wild and woolly commentary on this passage: "Symbol also implies a lacunary, fragmentary performance. The symbol is where the fragment reigns. Pure language is symbolized, which means that it arrives at a broken performance of its being in the becoming of languages." A lacuna, of course, is a gap, a hiatus, a break; a fragment is a broken-off piece of some larger whole, a shard; a performance is the staging of an action. How those three go together, I'm not sure, but let's try to work it out.

One way of thinking about it might be that a lacuna is what is missing from a notional or projected whole, leaving only a fragment behind. The symbol, therefore, isn't itself a lacuna or a fragment; it just performs pure language gapingly, as an absence performing an invisible presence, and "is"—those are scare quotes, interrogating the is-ness of its being there—"where the fragment reigns." The fragment reigns somewhere, and that place is pure language—but it isn't a place, any more than it's a being. What it means for "the fragment" to "reign" anywhere is a mystery to me as well; perhaps the fragment is the king, with the wide folds of his royal mantle, which symbolizes his power in the kingdom and language in the "Task" (#39)? Presumably "the fragment" is not a single specific fragment but "the" concept of "the" fragment—or perhaps "the" (fragmentary?) symbol of fragmentariness. And since what the fragment symbolizes is the symbolicity of pure language, what reigns is the symbol of a symbol. To put that differently, "symbol" and "performance" are both ways of *not* translating *die Darstellung* as "representation," which is to say that pure language doesn't exactly "arrive at a broken performance of its being in the becoming of languages"—it doesn't arrive anywhere, and it's also a mystery to me why Berman would suggest that it does—but simply points (*deutet*) beyond itself to something unseen, *stellt etwas dar*, places something there, in the dual sense of placing something visible before our eyes to point to something invisible and also using that visible thing to place the invisible thing there (before our inner eyes). Morphologically in German an interpretation is a pointing and a representation is a placing-there. To the extent that there is a break anywhere, it is between the symbol and the notional or projected beyondness for which the symbol stands. The symbol and the performance are attempts to mend that break, but their very existence depends on the break—is made possible and necessary by the break. The break reigns, then. Symbolicity and performativity are of course human artistic attempts to convince us that the break doesn't reign—art does—but the very need for the attempt suggests that the break reigns after all.

I submit, however, that there's an easier way of glossing this puzzling binary between "the symbolized" and "the symbolizing": the role of symbolism in the Kabbalah. The Ein Sof, the infinite ground of all being, is not symbolized. It is neither symbolizing nor symbolized. No symbol is adequate to the Infinite. But when the Ein Sof emits its ten emanations in the Atsilut, they are symbolized: as the Sephirot (divine attributes), as the Partzufim (divine faces), as the Olamot (spiritual worlds), as the Ohn (spiritual light and flow), as the holy names of God, and so on. The last of the ten emanations, as we saw in the commentary to #57, is the only female one, the Divine Queen; Nachman's allegorical story about her in human form is a secondary symbol, a symbolic story about a symbol. Lower levels of the divine manifestation are symbolized as "enclothed layers of reality." There is a Divine Tree of Life, which puts its roots down into the Edenic ground; there is an Archetypal Man named Adam Kadmon or Adam Elyon; there is, taken over from early Merkabah or chariot mysticism, the Angelic Chariot of the first chapter of Ezekiel; in the Heikhalot or palaces traditions there are stories of ascents to the Throne of God in the heavenly palace. "Male and female" as the two aspects of the divine creation are holy symbols. The Kelipot shells are part of an inside/outside symbolism, with the deathly externality of the shells counterpoised with an inward holy vitality. Like almost any religion, Kabbalah uses anthropomorphic symbolism to open a place of understanding in the human imagination for the divine, and Kabbalists have long debated the value and the validity of such symbolism: whether it unveils the truth or simply figures the ineffable.

So let us try to navigate through these symbolic waters. Think, to begin with, of the aura about which Benjamin (1935/2007) wrote in "The Work of Art in the Age of Mechanical Reproduction." That aura was a religious symbol, obviously, one used in many religious traditions; but most probably for Benjamin the tradition of choice was Kabbalah, where in Zohar 1.15a we read that "Zohar-radiance,

Concealed of the Concealed, struck its aura. The aura touched and did not touch this point."[56] Benjamin's point in that essay is that an aura gives an original work of art an authenticity that the mechanically reproduced work of art lacks. As a result, the reproduction is never fully "present": only the original is.

Note next the telling parallel between the aura "touching and not touching this point" and Benjamin's analogy in #70, where,

> In the same way as a tangent touches a circle fleetingly and at a single point, and as that tangent keeps pursuing its straight line to infinity in accordance with the law that prescribes that touch—but not the point at which it touches—so too does the [true] translation touch the source text fleetingly and only at that infinitesimal point of sense before, in accordance with the law of fidelity, pursuing its own path in the freedom of language-in-motion.

The traditional translation, in its efforts to *reproduce* the sense of the source text in its entirety, is like the reproduced artwork: by reproducing the original it smothers its aura. In #73 we read:

> The more mired in communication the source language is, the less value and dignity it will be found to have, and the less translation has to gain from it, until its sense becomes so grossly overweight that, far from providing the leverage that a translation needs to become Form-perfect, it thwarts all salutary efforts. The higher the source text's artistic quality has become, by contrast, the more translatable it will remain—even in the most fleeting touch of its sense.

Could it be that by *das Symbolisiertes* "the symbolized" Benjamin means something like the aura of religious symbolism, which "touches and doesn't touch" the human sublunary meanings of words like "pure" and "language," and by *das Symbolisierendes* "the symbolizing" he means the (mass) reproduction of meaning? If pure language is his primary religious symbol in the "Task," the holiest "symbolized" manifestation of the divine—not dialect, as the secularizing Berman would have it, but the Edenic language of the Philonian Logos (#59)—the epitome of "the symbolizing," which for Benjamin was just poor old sense-for-sense translation, might be updated in our time to Google Translate, whose neural symbol-generating algorithms reproduce the communicative function of marketplace translation "mechanically," or banausically (#49). A computer algorithm is not really mechanical, of course; but that quasi-mechanical reproduction of interlingual communication would arguably be the supreme

---

56 https://www.wjcshul.org/wp-content/uploads/In-the-Beginning-Zohar-115a.pdf.

instantiation in the "Task" of what Benjamin attacks in "The Work of Art." (For a fuller working-out of this suggestion, see Robinson, forthcoming-b.)

*Other commentators*: de Man (2000: 31–34), Derrida (1985: 190–91), Ferris (2008: 65), Pfau (1988: 1083–84), Weber (2008: 91–92).

## 66 Pure language (2): symbolizing and symbolized (2): the symbolized as an active force

> Und was im Werden der Sprachen sich darzustellen, ja
> And what in the becoming of the language itself to perform, indeed
>
> herzustellen sucht, das ist jener Kern der reinen Sprache selbst. Wenn
> to propagate seeks, that is that kernel of the pure language itself. If
>
> aber dieser, ob verborgen oder fragmentarisch, dennoch gegenwärtig
> however this, if hidden or fragmentary, yet present
>
> im Leben als das Symbolisierte selbst ist, so wohnt er nur symbolisierend
> in the life as the symbolized itself is, so lives it only symbolizing
>
> in den Gebilden.
> in the constructs.

*Paraphrase*: That generative impulse in the becoming of languages that seeks to body itself forth is the very kernel of pure language. But while that kernel only lives in verbal constructs as a symbolizing factor, and though it is hidden and fragmented, it is vitally present as the symbolized.

*Commentary*: The various translators' decisions are quite varied this time:

*das Werden der Sprachen*
Zohn: "the evolving of languages" (79)
Hynd and Valk: "the evolution of the languages" (305)
Rendall: "the development of languages" (162)
Underwood: "the way languages develop" (42)
Wright: "the becoming of languages" (203)
Robinson: "the becoming of languages"

I like "becoming" not only because *das Werden* is literally "the becoming," but because it is reminiscent of *le devenir* of Deleuze and Guattari (1980/1988); and my impression is that, while Antoine Berman didn't specifically mention them, he was thinking along the same lines: "What he [Benjamin] has in mind is the becoming-pure-language of languages, not the empirically verifiable diachrony of the various natural languages" (2008/2018: 204). In #67, in fact, we will see Benjamin saying in essence that translation effects a symbolizing-becoming-symbolized in the kernel of pure language. The implication in Deleuze and Guattari is always that there are no stable categories or objects, only becomings, only de- and reterritorializations—and the emptying out of language into the transcendental "purity" of pure language does seem to be a deterritorialization, a liberating of pure language from the stabilized and stabilizing territory of meaning and expression. Just how and as what it is reterritorialized is never quite clear; like most mystical thought, Benjamin's narrative tends toward negation: whatever is there now won't be there at the end.

*sich darzustellen, ja herzustellen*
Zohn: "to represent, to produce itself"
Hynd and Valk: "to come forward, indeed to come to birth"
Rendall: "to be represented and even produced"
Underwood: "to set itself forth (more: to body itself forth)"
Wright: "performance, production"
Robinson: "That generative impulse … that seeks to body itself forth"

Again Underwood chooses "bodying forth" for *herstellen*, while I choose it for *darstellen*; either way, it's a compellingly kinesthetic kind of embodiment. I like Berman's preference for *présentation* as performance—that too is basically a kinesthetic kind of embodiment—but the word is not nearly as suggestive of movement as "body forth," or even Hynd and Valk's "come forward." Their "come to birth" for *herstellen* is another kinesthetic kind of embodiment—this time for a fetus in the birth canal, perhaps inspired by *Wehen* "birth pangs" in #28—much more eloquent a trope than, say, "produce." Apropos movement, Berman continues: "Or rather, within this *being-in-movement of languages*, Benjamin discerns an intention, an *intentio*. In the historical-being of languages, he asserts the symbolization of pure language" (204). For that Latin *intentio* and its possible semantic divergences from English "intention," see the commentary to #60. My paraphrase "that generative impulse" is an unpacking of the German interrogative pronoun *was* ("what"): "generative" from *sich herzustellen* "to propagate itself," "impulse" because seeking to perform and propagate itself means that it is a vitalistic agent. For "to propagate itself," see the commentary to #19.

*gegenwärtig im Leben*
Zohn: "active force in life"
Hynd and Valk: "present in actual life"
Rendall: "present in life"
Underwood: "present in life"
Wright: NA
Robinson: "vitally present"

*Gegenwärtig* is "present (as opposed to past or future)," and *die Gegenwart* is "the present (moment)," so it's not surprising that all but Zohn use "present"; but "present" is a much weaker image in English than *die Gegenwart* is in German, where the morphology says "against-ward." The present moment has a directionality (*-ward*), and the direction is *against*. Crash. It is a becoming on a collision course. My decision to paraphrase *gegenwärtig im Leben* "present in life" as "vitally present" (hinting at vitalism, of course) is an attempt to put that present moment in motion; I also like Zohn's "active force in life."

*die Gebilde*
Zohn: "linguistic creations"
Hynd and Valk: "works of art"
Rendall: "linguistic constructions"
Underwood: "linguistic constructs
Wright: "linguistic units"
Robinson: "verbal constructs"

The German noun *die Gebilde*, after all, does not specify *linguistic* constructions/formations/structures: hence presumably Hynd and Valk's decision to broaden the category to "works of art." Benjamin is, however, writing about *das Werden der **Sprachen*** "the becoming of *languages*," so it's unlikely that *die Gebilde* are visual patterns in a painting or kinesthetic patterns in a dance.

*Other commentators*: Berman (2008/2018: 202–4), Jacobs (1975: 757), Liska (2014: 232), Smerick (2009: np), Vermeer (1996: 70, 190), Weber (2005: 74–75, 2008: 91–92).

## 67 Pure language (3): symbolizing and symbolized (3): translation turns symbolizing into the symbolized

> Ist jene letzte Wesenheit, die da die reine Sprache selbst ist, in den
> Is that last essentiality, that there the pure language itself is, in the
>
> Sprachen nur an Sprachliches und dessen Wandlungen gebunden, so
> languages only to verbal and this's transformations bound, so
>
> ist sie in den Gebilden behaftet mit dem schweren und fremden Sinn.
> is it in the constructs trammeled with the onerous and alien sense.
>
> Von diesem sie zu entbinden, das Symbolisierende zum Symbolisierten
> From this it to release, the symbolizing to the symbolized
>
> selbst zu machen, die reine Sprache gestaltet der Sprachbewegung
> itself to make, the pure language formed of the language movement
>
> zurückzugewinnen, ist das gewaltige und einzige Vermögen der Übersetzung.
> to win back, is the colossal and singular power of the translation.

*Paraphrase*: In the languages, then, this ultimate Essence, this pure language, is bound up solely with the verbal and its transformations, and in the verbal constructs that binding trammels it with an onerous and alien sense-communicability. To undo those trammels, to make the symbolizing over into the symbolized itself, to win back pure language in symbolized form for language-in-movement: that is the colossal and singular power of translation.

*Commentary*: This passage does not expressly address the task of the translator, or even the task of translation, but rather the *power* of translation; but implicit in that claim, as in almost every other remark Benjamin makes in the "Task" about *das Werden* "the becoming" or *die Sprachbewegung* "language movement" of pure language, is the ethical demand that the translation, and by extension the translator, break *die Behaftung* "the trammels" of sense-communicability and commit to the project of *das Symbolisierende zum Symbolisierten selbst zu machen* "making the symbolizing over into the symbolized itself." As I suggested in the commentary to #66, this could be read in the spirit of Deleuzean *devenir* as advancing or helping advance the symbolizing-becoming-symbolized of pure language—or perhaps rather the symbolizing-becoming-symbolized of language-becoming-pure-language.

For *Sprachbewegung* here Zohn has "linguistic flux" (80), Hynd and Valk has "linguistic growth and movement" (305), Rendall has "linguistic development" (162), Underwood has "linguistic usage" (42), and Wright has "the movement of languages" (205). Zohn's "flux" seems to imply *chaotic* change rather than a steady teleological/eschatological movement toward a transcendental end; Rendall's "linguistic development" implicitly invokes the philological model that Benjamin dismisses as excessively earth- and culture-bound, and therefore "heavy"; and Underwood's "linguistic usage" lacks any indication of change or movement at all. Hynd and Valk's "*growth* and movement" adds to Benjamin's "movement," but very much in the spirit of Benjamin's metaphorics in general: it links the *Bewegung* here to the recurring figure Benjamin employs of *das Wachstum* "the growth" (#27, #35–36) of a plant from the *Keim* "germ or embryo" (#19, #50) to the *Samen* "seed" (#36) to the *Kern* "kernel or grain" (#38, #66) to the *Frucht und Schale* "fruit and skin" (#39).

Note also the heavy–light imagery that Benjamin has begun to develop here toward the end of the "Task." In German *schwer* can mean both heavy and difficult, and *leicht* can mean both light(-weight) and easy; here in #67 what is heavy and therefore difficult is the communication of sense. As Antoine Berman (2008/2018: 205) puts it, "meaning has *weight* in literary texts, infinite weight," and "translation *frees* the text (and therefore its language) from the *weight* of meaning" (emphasis Berman's). That would seem to imply that in liberating language from the weight of meaning, it *lightens* the load—that even in a communicative translation the language is lighter than in the source text, because it has been freed from the grounding of textuality in the communal sense-making of the source culture. And translating "the letter" or "the word" lightens the load even more, because what survives in the translation is then only the bare syntactic skeleton of the source text: all the source-cultural trammels of sense-communication have been cast off and, freed from that weight, the target language can begin (or continue) to rise toward the transcendental glory of pure language. The earthly weight of culture and sense-making versus the heavenly lightness of pure language.

The only slight hitch in this imagery comes in #72, when Benjamin quotes Pannwitz on transforming the target language through foreignizing translation, and Pannwitz concludes that this is possible *aber nicht wenn man sie allzu leicht sondern gerade wenn man sie schwer genug nimmt* "not if one takes a language all too lightly but only if one takes it with enough weight." That apparent reversal can be discounted, however, not only through the problematics of quoting, but by dint of the fact that *taking* a language "lightly" or "with enough weight" is not the same thing as language *being* heavy or light.

*Other commentators*: Baltrusch (2010: 119), Berman (2008/2018: 205), Britt (1996: 54), Ferreira Duarte (1995: 280), Ferris (2008: 65), Jacobs (1975: 757, 761), Pan (2017: 39), Smerick (2009: np), Vermeer (1996: 70, 190), Weber (2005: 74–75, 2008: 91–92).

## 68 Pure language (4): the extinction of all languages in the no-longer-expressive Creative Word

> In dieser reinen Sprache, die    nichts   mehr meint und nichts   mehr
> In this    pure   language, which nothing more means and nothing more
>
> ausdrückt, sondern als ausdrucksloses und schöpferisches Wort das in allen
> expresses, rather   as   inexpressive       and creative        word that in all
>
> Sprachen Gemeinte ist, trifft    endlich      alle Mitteilung,    aller Sinn   und
> languages meant     is,  meets eventually all    with-sharing, all     sense and
>
> alle Intention auf   eine Schicht, in der    sie  zu erlöschen  bestimmt sind.
> all   intention with a       shift,     in which they to extinguish destined   are.

*Paraphrase*: This is that pure language that no longer means anything and no longer expresses anything—that no-longer-expressive Creative Word that is precisely what is meant in all languages. In that Word all communication, all sense, and all intention will eventually undergo a shift in which they are destined to be snuffed out.

*Commentary*: Antoine Berman's (2008/2018: 206–7) commentary here is useful. His reading is that what remains when "all communication, all sense, and all intention ... undergo a shift in which they are destined to be snuffed out" is "the letter." "Translation," Berman says, "worries about *the pure letter of the text*. Or at least this is its most intimate *power* which is still hidden from it" (206). This does seem to be an accurate reading of Benjamin. There are, however, two problematic moments in his reading of the passage.

One is that, having asserted that "Benjamin's greatness, historically speaking, lies in having announced this pure power," Berman goes on to admit that "I am less concerned with the Messianic framework of his reflection" (206). He recognizes that messianic framework, but doesn't like it, so he doesn't concern himself with it. A few pages later, in claiming that "pure language is dialect" (209), he similarly admits that "in saying this, I am going beyond Benjamin" (209). His commentary is speckled with such moments. In his commentary on the current passage (#68), for example, he claims that the image of the tangent (#70, #73–75) as a figure for the translation, fleetingly touching the circle (figuring source-textual sense), "springs from here"—from the liberation of the letter as the pure essence and power of language. That is pretty vague. What is the connection between the letter-as-pure-essence and the tangent touching the circle? How does the latter "spring from" the former? This, I submit, is one cost of being "less concerned with the Messianic framework." Certainly as I track the Kabbalistic source in the commentary to #65, that source raises the image from the nebulous abstraction in which Berman leaves it into greater clarity.

The other problem is also loosely related to #70:

> It is crucial that Benjamin's position not be interpreted as a choice between the two potentialities of translation—meaning *or* the letter. Because Benjamin does not think this way—rather *he considers the relationship between the meaning and the letter of translation speculatively*. This relationship is of the kind where meaning does not disappear but for the first time is re-ordered in relation to the letter, the letter being an ineluctable element. (206; emphasis Berman's)

I agree with that assessment in a general way: precisely in the image of the translation touching the source-textual sense *flüchtig* "fleetingly" in #70 and #73–75 Benjamin does introduce an interesting (if unfortunately undeveloped) speculation on that relationship. My only hesitation stems from the fact that in #63 Benjamin also states flatly that there is *nothing* valid or valuable in the traditional focus on sense, which must therefore be denied all legitimacy. The rigid polemical binary in #63 gives the lie to Berman's insistence that "Benjamin's position not be interpreted as a choice between the two potentialities of translation—meaning *or* the letter." He's right, of course, if we read only the "tangential" metaphors of #70 and after; but wrong if we read #63 and the many other passages where his thinking is explicitly and even aggressively either-or.

Hans Vermeer (1996) intriguingly reads the *Schicht* "shift" Benjamin mentions here as a Hegelian *Aufhebung* "sublation" of sense (182–83): he equates *das Erlöschen*, a "dousing" or "quenching" or "extinguishing" that I have paraphrased as a "snuffing out," with *das Erlösen*, the redemption or salvation in which Jews are delivered from captivity and Christians are delivered from sin, and ties both to *die Auflösung* "re-/dissolution" (196; see the commentary to #51 for Berman's reflections on this concept). Communication, sense, and intention die in order to be reborn; are extinguished in order to be delivered; are dissolved in order to be resolved. (See also Vermeer 1996: 158–59 for a discussion of Benjamin's *Aufhebung* "sublation" of form.[57])

Rodolphe Gasché (1986: 75), in posing the question of *die Mitteilbarkeit* "communicability"[58] in Benjamin as the overriding philosophical problem of his early work in the theory of language, tracks *das ausdrucksloses und schöpferisches Wort das in allen Sprachen Gemeinte ist* "that no-longer-expressive Creative Word that is precisely what is meant in all languages" back to the 1916 essay "On Language as Such and the Language of Man":

> Communicability, understood as language's communication of itself as communicating, is, in things, "the residue of the creative word of God" (*Reflections*, p. 331), and thus oriented by the horizon of this divine source. Rather than a category of possibility, communicability is constituted by things' yearning to relate to the origin of their creation in the Word. In language, in a verbal sense of their expression, things communicate that they are of divine origin. It shows them in a process of wanting to communicate, to be heard, and redeemed.

This theological perspective makes far better sense of Benjamin's "Task" than Berman's pan-Romanticism. For a fuller discussion of "Benjamin's -abilities," see Weber (2008); he deals with this passage on pp. 77, 91, and 332n16.

---

57 See also Vermeer (1996: 192–93) for another enumeration of the three types of sense-sublation:

> Sinn wird aufgehoben, so daß nur die Form relevant wird; dies ist (zumindest für manche Leute) der Inbegriff des Poetischen. Sinn wird aufgehoben, so daß der gemeinte Gegenstand unmittelbar relevant wird; Rede wird durch Tat ersetzt. Zwischen beide Möglichkeiten schiebt sich die Sprache der Logik und Mathematik, die nur noch Tautologien vermittelt; es ist die Möglichkeit der "reinen" Wissenschaftssprache.

> Sense is sublated so that only form remains relevant; this, at least for some people, is the epitome of the poetic. Sense is sublated so that the intended object remains immediately relevant; speech is replaced by action. Between those two possibilities we find the language of logic and mathematics, which only conveys tautologies; this is the possibility of "pure" scientific language.

The question, Vermeer adds, is which of these Benjamin means; my guess would be the first, where only form remains relevant.

58 Note the close connection in Benjamin between *die Mitteilbarkeit* "communicability" (Gasché's theme, based on #65) and *die Mittelbarkeit* "mediality" (Werner Hamacher's theme—see the commentary to #46). German *mit* is "with," *Mittel* (cognate of "middle") is "means, medium, median," *Teil* is "part," and *mitteilen* is "to share, to disclose, to inform."

*Other commentators*: Ferris (2008: 65), Flèche (1999: 106), Hodge (2005: 28), Jacobs (1975: 761), Hamacher (2001/2012: 529–30), Kohlross (2009: 98), O'Keeffe (2015: 377), Pfau (1988: 1084), Roberts (1982: 120), Smerick (2009: np), Zathureczky (2004: 207).

## 69 Pure language (5): the translator's task (5): releasing pure language from bondage

> Und eben aus ihr bestätigt sich die Freiheit der Übersetzung zu einem
> And even out of it validates itself the freedom of the translation to a
>
> neuen und höhern Rechte. Nicht aus dem Sinn der Mitteilung, von
> new and higher right. Not out of the sense of the with-sharing, from
>
> welchem zu emanzipieren gerade die Aufgabe der Treue ist, hat sie
> which to emancipate straight the task of the fidelity is, has it
>
> ihren Bestand. Freiheit vielmehr bewährt sich um der reinen Sprache
> its vitality. Freedom rather proves itself for the pure language's
>
> willen an der eigenen. Jene reine Sprache, die in fremde gebannt ist,
> sake on the own. That pure language, which in foreign spellbound is,
>
> in der eigenen zu erlösen, die im Werk gefangene in der Umdichtung zu
> in the own to release, the in the work imprisoned in the re-poeming to
>
> befreien, ist die Aufgabe des Übersetzers. Um ihretwillen bricht er
> free, is the task of the translator. For its sake breaks he
>
> morsche Schranken der eigenen Sprache: Luther, Voß, Hölderlin,
> mortar barricades of the own language: Luther, Voß, Hölderlin,
>
> George haben die Grenzen des Deutschen erweitert.
> George haben die Grenzen des Deutschen erweitert.

*Paraphrase*: And it is precisely through that shift that translational freedom is validated and raised to a new and higher prerogative. That freedom's vitality issues forth, of course, not out of the communicable meaning of the source text, but out of fidelity's true task, which is to emancipate freedom from that meaning. Freedom actually demonstrates its fidelity to pure language in the target language: it is the translator's task to transcreate the source text in which pure language is imprisoned, in order to release in the target language that pure language that is spellbound in the source language. For pure language's sake the translator smashes through the target language's rotten barricades: Luther, Voß, Hölderlin, and George all pushed back the boundaries of the German language.

*Commentary*: Benjamin was clearly working out what he wanted to say by writing it down, and not going back to edit his earlier formulations so as to accord with his later. In #53 and #63 he wrote that fidelity and freedom have traditionally been understood as opposed to each other, but (#53) fidelity has nothing to offer the reproduction of meaning and (#63) freedom is entirely about the reproduction of meaning, so he wants to deny freedom all legitimacy; now in #69 freedom is to be made to serve the letter, and in #70 the literal translation will touch "only at that infinitesimal point of sense before, in accordance with the law of fidelity, pursuing its own path in the freedom of language-in-motion." The movement in those final passages, in fact, is toward the fusion of literalism and freedom: from the near-total freedom of "the letter" only touching source-textual sense fleetingly (#70, #73), through the even more perfect freedom of Hölderlin's prototypical translations touching the sense like the wind touching an Aeolian harp (#75), to the total fusion of the letter with freedom in the interlinear version of Holy Writ (#78). Also, of course, in #52 "fidelity" is reframed as "fidelity *against* the word," which is to say that there is a brand of fidelity that is not opposed to freedom but another face of freedom. The underlying problem, I suggest, is that Benjamin's eschatological imagination was pulled strongly toward binaries—fidelity and freedom are absolute opposites with no middle ground in between, and fidelity is good and freedom is bad; but the more he let the mythic resonances of that binary reverberate in his imagination, the more he began to recognize the need for varying degrees of crossovers and middle grounds, if only in the fleeting touch of literal translation on sense and the resulting "freedom of language-in-motion." That kind of freedom is not bad, not the *wrong* kind of freedom—it would be the *freeing* of pure language from bondage—and "fidelity *against* the word" would not be good, not be the kind of fidelity *to* the letter (word, SL syntax) that he favored.

The image of the translator's task as transcreating the source text in which pure language is imprisoned so as to liberate or unleash in the target language that pure language that is spellbound in the source language was the inspiration for the little fairy tale that I teased out of the "Task" in *Translation and Taboo* (Robinson 1996: 207–8), and reported at the end of the commentary to #57 (p. 140n51). Since *die reine Sprache* "pure language" is grammatically feminine in German, it seemed to me that Benjamin was himself imagining *der Übersetzer* "the translator" (who is of course grammatically masculine) as a fairy-tale hero that rescues the maiden from her imprisonment and the spell cast on her by the evil sorcerer (*der Sinn* "the sense," also grammatically masculine). (According to Dennis Porter [1989: 1068], Benjamin's discourse here "echoes the messianic and spiritual cult of the poetic associated with symbolism since Mallarmé, and that was given an even more sacerdotal character by the school of [Stefan] George in Germany.")

The German word that I have paraphrased as "transcreation" and literalized in the interlinear as a "re-poeming" is *die Umdichtung*, which projects the image of taking a poem and spinning it around poetically, making it dizzy and disoriented. It is generally used to refer to radically transformative translating that creates a whole new poem with some (usually fairly minor) link to the source text; my paraphrase "transcreation" generally means something similar.[59] That traditional sense of *Umdichtung*/transcreation obviously would ill suit Benjamin's metaphysical purpose here, which is to valorize a different kind of transformation or transposition—one that radically excises the communicative function of the source text in a new focus on the letter, a new literal highlighting and showcasing of the source text's syntax. That would be just as transformative as the "old" *Umdichtung*/transcreation, perhaps, but the directionality is very different: away from the enhanced mediability of the traditional *Umdichtung*/transcreation.[60]

The list of translators who have "smashed through the ... rotten barricades" of German and "pushed back" its boundaries—Martin Luther, Johann Heinrich Voß, Friedrich Hölderlin, and Stefan George—is surprising only in that Luther's Bible translation is typically venerated not only for establishing a German literary language (pushing those boundaries back) but for insisting on translating into a German that is actually spoken by native speakers: "You've got to go out and ask the mother in her house, the children in the street, the ordinary man at the market. Watch their mouths move when they talk, and translate that way. Then they'll understand you and realize that you're speaking German to them" (Robinson 1997/2014: 87). But see note 3 on p. 11 for the other side of Luther's Bible as tracked by Louth (1998: 9): Luther did affirm his willingness to translate certain passages literally, and he too revived obsolete German words for his purposes. Louth also tracks the transformative impact of Voß's brilliantly literal translations of Homer on the German Romantics (26–29); and of course his entire book is a close reading of the ways in which Hölderlin "smashed through the ... rotten barricades" of German and "pushed back" its boundaries, not only in his translations of Pindar and Sophocles but in the original poetry that was so powerfully shaped by his translation work.

*Other commentators*: Baltrusch (2010: 119–20), Bellos (2010: 215), Benjamin (1989/2014: 101–2), Bradbury (2006: 142), Britt (1996: 54), Engel (2014: 3–4),

---

59 "Transcreation" was coined by P. Lal (1964) for his transformations of Sanskrit plays for English and American readers, and later picked up by the Brazilian poet and translator Haroldo de Campos (1992); see Holmström (2006) for the Indian context and Vieira (1999) for de Campos. It has since been adopted by "a new wave of companies seeking to distance themselves from traditional translation firms" (Bernal Merino 2006: 32–33) through creative/transformative approaches to various commercial products, especially perhaps video games (see also Mangiron and O'Hagan 2006). My transcreation of Volter Kilpi's *Gulliverin matka Fantomimian mantereelle* as *Gulliver's Voyage to Phantomimia* (Robinson 2020) is also quite transformative.
60 None of the four full translations engages the traditional sense of *die Umdichtung*: Zohn (80) has "re-create," Rendall (163) and Underwood (42) have "rewriting," and Hynd and Valk (305) have just plain "translation." Wright didn't translate this passage, because Berman didn't select it for translation and commentary.

Felman (1999: 201–2), Johnston (1992: 44), Lacoue-Labarthe (2002: 11), Liska (2014: 232–33), Rendall (1997b: 172), Smerick (2009: np), Steiner (1975/1998: 67), Vermeer (1996: 173, 190), Weber (2005: 76, 2008: 93–94).

## 70 Translational fidelity (13): the translational tangent touching the circle glancingly (1)

> Was hiernach für das Verhältnis von Übersetzung und Original an
> What by this for the relationship of translation and original of
>
> Bedeutung dem Sinn verbleibt, läßt sich in einem Vergleich fassen.
> significance to the sense remains, lets itself in a simile to grasp.
>
> Wie die Tangente den Kreis flüchtig und nur in einem Punkte berührt und
> As the tangent the circle fleetingly and only in one point touches and
>
> wie ihr wohl diese Berührung, nicht aber der Punkt, das Gesetz
> as its well this touching, not however the point, the law
>
> vorschreibt, nach dem sie weiter ins Unendliche ihre gerade Bahn
> prescribes, after which it farther into the infinite its straight path
>
> zieht, so berührt die Übersetzung flüchtig und nur in dem
> pursues, so touches the translation fleetingly and only in the
>
> unendlich kleinen Punkte des Sinnes das Original, um nach
> infinitesimally small point of the sense the original, in order according
>
> dem Gesetze der Treue in der Freiheit der Sprachbewegung ihre
> to the law of the fidelity in the freedom of the language-movement its
>
> eigenste Bahn zu verfolgen.
> ownmost path to follow.

*Paraphrase*: What significance that leaves for sense in the relationship between the translation and the source text may be grasped through an analogy. In the same way as a tangent touches a circle fleetingly and at a single point, and as that tangent keeps pursuing its straight line to infinity in accordance with the law that prescribes that tangential touch—but not the point at which tangentiality occurs—so too does the translation touch the source text fleetingly and only at that infinitesimal point of sense before, in accordance with the law of fidelity, pursuing its own path in the freedom of language-in-motion.

*Commentary*: The image of the tangent touching a circle fleetingly at a single point as a figure for Benjamin's preferred mystical literalism, which we began to explore briefly in the commentary to #68, is quite evocative, as it seems to flesh forth an image of translation traveling like a spaceship into outer space, and only dipping slightly into the gravitational force field of a planet like earth. Out there somewhere is "heaven," or Plato's Realm of Forms, and translation is headed that way, with pure language in tow (or perhaps pure language is the spaceship with translation in tow, as its external fuel source).

Carol Jacobs (1975: 758–59) places this analogy in the larger context of Benjamin's essay, suggesting that

> The relation between translation and original then, although "seemingly tangible," is always on the verge of eluding understanding (IV. 1: I 1). And eluding of understanding (*Erkenntnis*) is precisely what translation performs (*darstellt*). Benjamin insists on the verb "*darstellen*," as opposed to "*herstellen*" or "*offenbaren*" (IV. 1:12), for translation neither presents nor reveals a contents. It touches the meaning of the original only by way of marking its independence, its freedom—literally—to go off on a tangent: the point it chooses remains irrelevant.

*Other commentators*: Balfour (2018: 751), Chapman (2019: 78), Derrida (1985: 189), Fenves (2011: 150), Ferreira Duarte (1995: 273), Gasché (1986: 86), Gelley (2015: 143), O'Keeffe (2015: 379), Pan (2017: 38), Smerick (2009: np), Weber (2005: 76, 2008: 93–94).

## 71 Pannwitz (1): the set-up

> Die wahre Bedeutung dieser Freiheit hat, ohne sie doch zu nennen
> The true significance of this freedom has, without it yet to name
>
> noch zu begründen, Rudolf Pannwitz in Ausführungen gekennzeichnet, die
> nor to justify, Rudolf Pannwitz in remarks characterized, that
>
> sich in der »krisis der europäischen kultur« finden und die neben
> themselves in the "crisis of the european culture" find and that next
>
> Goethes Sätzen in den Noten zum »Divan« leicht das Beste sein
> to Goethe's sentences in the notes to the "Divan" easily the best to be
>
> dürften, was in Deutschland zur Theorie der Übersetzung
> might, what in Germany to the theory of the translation
>
> veröffentlicht wurde.
> published became.

*Paraphrase*: The true significance of this freedom was flagged by Rudolf Pannwitz in some comments he made in his 1917 book *The Crisis of European Culture*—though without naming it as such, or backing it up. Those comments, along with

Goethe's remarks in the notes to the *West-East Divan*, rank among the best things published in Germany on the theory of translation.

*Commentary*: As we'll see in the commentary to #72, the actual quotation from Pannwitz reveals Benjamin's praise for it as "among the best things published in Germany on the theory of translation" to be a somewhat overblown hyperbole.

The notes to the *West-Östlicher Diwan* are another story.[61] Benjamin's motivation for praising Goethe's notes to it is so obvious that those notes may even have inspired and informed Benjamin's "Task." Goethe's remarks have to do with "three kinds of translation" (Robinson 1997/2014: 222):

"The first familiarizes us with the foreign country on our own terms" (222). His prime example of this "kind" or "epoch" is the Luther Bible; he says that for it prose is best, because "at least at first it serves us best precisely because it startles us with the wonders of the foreign right in the midst of our ordinary lives, our national at-homeness" (223). This would be more or less what Benjamin attacks as the reproduction of meaning, of course; but note how Goethe is able to find good things to say about it, something Benjamin can't manage. (Granted, Goethe also damns this epoch with faint praise, noting that "prose completely sublates every poetic property and drags poetic enthusiasm itself down to a common water-level" (222–23).

"This approach," he says next, "is followed by a second epoch in which one seeks to project oneself into the circumstances of the foreign country, but in fact only appropriates the foreign meaning and then replaces it with one's own" (223). The first clause there seems to promise the standard German Romantic theory of translation, harking back to a very young Herder in the late 1760s, and finding its fullest and most eloquent articulation in Schleiermacher's 1813 Academy address "The Different Methods of Translating" (Robinson 1997/2014: 225–38), where the distinction is between "bringing the author to the reader" (bad) and "taking the reader to the author" (good). But then Goethe snatches defeat from the jaws of victory: "in fact only appropriates the foreign meaning and then replaces it with one's own." What Goethe seems to understand there is that all translation, even the most ostensibly foreignizing, domesticates in the very basic sense of replacing the "foreign" (source) language with words from the "domestic" (target) language.

What would have been most attractive for Benjamin is that Goethe did not stop there, as the Romantics in his age did, but added a third epoch:

> But because one cannot abide long in either perfection or imperfection, and one transformation always leads to another, this second epoch brought

---

61 The *West-East Divan*, first published in 1819, with an expanded edition in 1827, is one of Goethe's last extended pieces of writing; it is a collection of lyrical poems inspired by the poet Hafez (pen-name of Khwāja Shams-ud-Dīn Muḥammad Ḥāfeẓ-e Shīrāzī, 1315–1390), who to this day is considered the greatest Persian writer ever.

us to a third, the last and highest of all. Here one seeks to make the translation identical with the original, so that the one would no longer be in the *stead* but in the *place* of the other. (Robinson 1997/2014: 223)

That already sounds quite mystical; but his final paragraph kicks even that hint up a notch:

> Let us conclude these remarks with a word on why we call the third epoch the last. A translation that seeks to be identified with the original approximates, finally, the interlinear version; in its attempt to enhance our understanding of the original it leads us onward, drives us on toward the source text, and so finally closes the circle in which the alien and the familiar, the known and the unknown move toward each other. (224)

Surely it is no coincidence that Benjamin's passing praise for the notes to Goethe's *Divan* here in #71 comes just a few sentences before his concluding line in #78 that "The interlinear version of Holy Writ is the prototype or ideal of all translation."

*Other commentators*: Berman (2008/2018: 208).

## 72 Pannwitz (2): the quotation

> Dort heißt es: »unsere Übertragungen auch die besten gehn von einem
> There goes it: "our    transpositions   even the best   go   from a
>
> falschen grundsatz aus sie  wollen das indische griechische englische
> false      principle out they want  the indian    greek        english
>
> verdeutschen anstatt das deutsche zu verindischen vergriechischen
> to germanize instead the german    to indianize    grecicize
>
> verenglischen, sie   haben eine viel bedeutendere ehrfurcht vor  den
> anglicize,     they have  a    far  weightier    awe        before the
>
> eigenen sprachgebräuchen als  vor  dem geiste des  fremden werks ...
> own     linguistic usages  than before the spirit of the foreign work ...
>
> der grundsätzliche irrtum des  übertragenden ist daß er  den zufälligen
> the fundamental    error  of the transposer  is that he the chance
>
> stand      der eignen spräche festhält anstatt sie durch die fremde
> condition of the own  language holds fast instead it through the foreign
>
> sprache   gewaltig    bewegen zu lassen, er muss zumal      wenn er  aus
> language energetically move    to let,    he must particularly if  he out

> einer sehr fernen spräche überträgt auf die letzten elemente der
> of a very distant language transposes upon the last elements of the
>
> sprache selbst wo wort bild ton in eines geht zurück dringen er
> language itself where word image tone in one goes back to press he
>
> muss seine sprache durch die fremde erweitern und vertiefen man hat
> must his language through the foreign widen and deepen one has
>
> keinen begriff in welchem masze das möglich ist bis zu welchem
> no concept in which measure that possible is until to which
>
> grade jede sprache sich verwandeln kann sprache von sprache
> degree every language itself transform can language from language
>
> fast nur wie mundart von mundart sich unterscheidet dieses aber
> almost only as dialect from dialect itself differentiates this however
>
> nicht wenn man sie allzu leicht sondern gerade wenn man sie
> not if one them all too lightly rather directly if one them
>
> schwer genug nimmt.«
> heavily enough takes."

*Paraphrase*: "our transpositions even the best proceed on a false principle they want to germanize the indian greek english instead of indianizing greekifying englishing the german, they stand far more in awe of their own usage than before the spirit of the foreign works ... the basic mistake they make is to hold tight to the state their own language happens to be in rather than letting that language be set energetically in motion, the transposer must especially when transposing from a very remote language press back to the most extreme elements of the language itself where word image tone fuse in one he must widen and deepen his language one has no idea in what measure this is possible to what degree every language can be transformed language differs from language almost as dialect does from dialect but not if one takes a language all too lightly but only if one takes it with enough weight."

*Commentary*: The Pannwitz quotation is of course German Romanticism 101—with experimental spellings and punctuation. Not only does he not capitalize nouns, as is still today customary in German, the way it was in English two centuries ago; he spells *Maß* "measure" as if it were a Polish word, *masze*. And of course that long paragraph has only two commas! Even though a paraphrase would be entirely justified in touching up the punctuation, I decided to give you a feel for the source text. It's an experience.

What makes German Romanticism unique in the history of thinking about translation is this insistence on deforming or otherwise transforming the target language through a close (literal, foreignizing) rendition of the source text. Pannwitz doesn't add much to the discussion that wasn't already there in the Schlegel brothers, Novalis, and especially Friedrich Schleiermacher's 1813 Academy address on the different methods of translating[62]—which last, surprisingly, Benjamin doesn't mention even once in the "Task." Because he takes so much from the German Romantic tradition, Benjamin seems like an honorary post-Romantic himself, and commentators like Antoine Berman (see the commentary to #1) and João Ferreira Duarte (1995: 276–77) feel justified in assimilating his thought root and branch—or, as Benjamin says in #38, *Stumpf und Stiel* "stump and stalk"—to Romanticism. But it is in fact precisely because Benjamin is so much more than a Romantic thinker that his work is so important—indeed why his high praise for Pannwitz, that these lines "rank among the best things published in Germany on the theory of translation," falls so flat. What Benjamin does, following Goethe's lead (#71)—and of course Goethe was himself a recovering former Romantic—is to *start* with the basic German Romantic position on literalism/foreignism and the deformation of the target language and retrofit it with an entire pre-Romantic and pre-Kantian and generally premodern mystical cosmogony. The Romantics were steeped in the same mystical traditions, of course—they drew on the whole dissident esoteric line of thought arising not only out of the counter-Enlightenment (sometimes called the Endarkenment) and counter-Renaissance but out of missionary/colonial translations of ancient Indian, Persian, and Chinese religion/philosophy—but they effectively secularized those traditions by psychologizing them, turning them into a figurative basis for poetics. Benjamin, by contrast, goes for broke—with the Jewish mysticism of Philo on the Logos and medieval Kabbalah. And that is why *his* essay on the translator's task, not Pannwitz's brief underpunctuated squib, ranks among the best things published in Germany on the theory of translation.

There is one moment in Pannwitz's remarks that transcends the standard Romantic view: the insistence that "the transposer must, especially when transposing from a very remote language [—as Friedrich Hölderlin was—not only] press back to the most extreme elements of the language itself" but ensure that in the process "word image tone fuse in one." That fusion does seem ontologically extreme enough to be mystical.

*Other commentators*: Bellos (2010: 216), Berman (2008/2018: 207–8), Chapman (2019: 77), Jacobs (1975: 756–57), Johnston (1992: 44–45), Kohlross (2009: 102), Menke (2002: 90), Porter (1989: 1068–69), Rendall (1997b: 178–80), Sandbank (2015: 218), Smerick (2009: np), Wurgaft (2002: 381).

---

62 For those works in English, see Robinson (1997/2014: 207–8, 212–38).

## 73 Translational fidelity (14): the translational tangent touching the circle glancingly (2): translatability (7)

> Wie weit eine Übersetzung dem Wesen dieser Form zu entsprechen
> How far a translation to the essence of this form to assimilate
>
> vermag, wird objektiv durch die Übersetzbarkeit des Originals
> is able, becomes objectively through the translatability of the original
>
> bestimmt. Je weniger Wert und Würde seine Sprache hat, je mehr es
> determined. The less value and dignity its language has, the more it
>
> Mitteilung ist, desto weniger ist für die Übersetzung dabei zu
> with-sharing is, the less is for the translation thereby to
>
> gewinnen, bis das völlige Übergewicht jenes Sinnes, weit entfernt, der
> win, until the fully overweight of that sense, far removed, the
>
> Hebel einer formvollen Übersetzung zu sein, diese vereitelt. Je höher
> leverage of a Form-perfect translation to be, this thwarts. The higher
>
> ein Werk geartet ist, desto mehr bleibt es selbst in flüchtigster
> a work disposed is, the more remains it itself in fleetingest
>
> Berührung seines Sinnes noch übersetzbar.
> touching of its sense yet translatable.

*Paraphrase*: How well a translation can assimilate itself to the Essence of this Form depends objectively on the source text's translatability. The more mired in communication the source language is, the less value and dignity it will be found to have, and the less translation has to gain from it, until its sense becomes so grossly overweight that, far from providing the leverage that a translation needs to become Form-perfect, it thwarts all salutary efforts. The higher the source text's artistic quality has become, by contrast, the more translatable it will remain—even in the most fleeting touch of its sense.

*Commentary*: This passage should be read as a further gloss on Benjamin's remarks in #8, to the effect that "A work can be translatable in either of two senses: whether among all of its readers a translator able to translate it is ever found, or, more authentically, whether its Essence allows it to be translated and its Form demands that it be translated." Here in #73 he modifies that binary choice between "whether its Essence allows [or doesn't allow] it to be translated and its Form demands [or doesn't demand] that it be translated" by giving us a whole cline of levels of source-textual quality and translatability. As I noted in the commentary to #7, if "the Essence of this Form" is transcendental, no human translation will ever fully correspond to it, in the sense of becoming *formvoll* "Form-perfect":

in Platonic copy theory every successive copy is worse than the previous one, and no earthly copy can ever attain the pristine perfection of the transcendental Form. But while recognizing that, the scalar adjectives in "the *higher* the source text's artistic quality has become, by contrast, the *more* translatable it will remain" at least allow for an infinite approach to perfected Form.

This passage also arguably explains what Benjamin meant in #12 by "Translation is built into the Essence of *certain works*." In the commentary to #12 I complained about the vagueness of "certain works"; #73 can be read as a preemptive response to such complaints, based on the infinite approach to perfection.

*Other commentators*: Cohen (2002: 102), Ferris (2008: 65), Porter (1989: 1070), Vermeer (1996: 194–95).

## 74 The translational tangent touching the circle glancingly (3): translatability (8)

> Dies gilt  selbstverständlich nur  von  Originalen. Übersetzungen
> This yields self-evidently    only from originals.   Translations
>
> dagegen    erweisen sich       unübersetzbar nicht wegen   der
> by contrast prove    themselves untranslatable not    because of the
>
> Schwere, sondern wegen der   allzu  großen Flüchtigkeit, mit welcher
> heaviness, rather  because of the all too great   fleetingness, with which
>
> der Sinn   an ihnen haftet.
> the sense on them sticks.

*Paraphrase*: This is only in force with source texts, of course. Translations prove untranslatable not because they're so difficult to write but because sense sticks to them so very fleetingly.

*Commentary*: This is a tangential reference back to #39, where the target language was wrapped loosely around *der Gehalt* "the tenor"—the kernel in the source text that when transferred to the translation became untranslatable—like the wide folds of a royal mantle. Obviously "sense" "sticking" to a translation "fleetingly" shifts the terms of the metaphor, based on #70: the language-as-mantle hanging loosely has become the sense sticking fleetingly (because the organizing image has shifted from the robed king to the tangent touching a circle), and the transferred tenor has become the translation. The sign that both are nevertheless versions of something like the same metaphysics, however, is that both explain the untranslatability of the translation. As we saw in the commentary to #39, the basic idea is that in the source text the sense and the language are both integrated closely with the source culture—the text emerges in the source author's imagination with the sense, source language, and source culture closely intertwined—but when it is translated the translator is grafting a simulacrum of the target language and target culture onto a necessarily imperfect or incomplete reproduction of the source-textual sense. That "graft" is the problem. The link between the target text/language/culture and what can inadequately be transferred from the source text/language/culture is weak, unreliable. This, according to Benjamin (#39), is what makes it impossible to translate a translation properly. Hence the unthinkability of the translation chain for him—or rather, perhaps, the impossibility of understanding the chained translations *as translations*. The very fact that each translation is a (traditional) *Umdichtung* (see the commentaries to #43 and #69), a transformative re-poeming in the target language/culture, means that, according to the notional Benjamin that I'm conjuring up here, the series of poets or other writers who participate in the translation chain are not translating but adapting.

Another way of putting all that might be that radically domesticated re-poemings and radically literalized re-poemings are the extremes that challenge the marketplace norm of striving for timid sense-for-sense equivalence. Benjamin champions radically literal re-poeming *precisely because* the greater the translations, the less translatable they are: Hölderlin's brilliant exemplars of the radically literal re-poeming would inexorably fall into the category of "untranslatable … because sense sticks to them so very fleetingly." (David Constantine's 2001 *Hölderlin's Sophocles: Oedipus and Antigone*, an English retranslation of Hölderlin's German translations of those two plays, would never have passed muster with Benjamin.)

And conversely, of course, marketplace sense-for-sense translations are infinitely retranslatable (re-mediable). The fact that a third- or fourth-generation translation of an instruction manual for a widget is often atrociously written does not prevent a fifth-generation translation from improving the quality to entirely acceptable levels. The translation histories that David Bellos (2010: 212–13) adduces—in which Gogol is translated from Russian into Japanese and from Japanese into Chinese, and *The Thousand and One Nights* is translated through a series of Middle-Eastern languages before reaching Europe and inspiring Marcel Proust—operate at a higher literary level, but for Benjamin they simply exemplify another kind of marketplace mediability. He doesn't deny them; he just doesn't like them.

*Other commentators*: Biti (2019: 249), Cohen (2002: 104), Ferris (2008: 65), Hanssen (2002: 143), Vermeer (1996: 195).

## 75 The translational tangent touching the circle glancingly (4): Hölderlin (3): the Aeolian harp

> Hierfür wie in jeder andern wesentlichen Hinsicht stellen sich
> For this as in every other essential respect body themselves
>
> Hölderlins Übertragungen, besonders die der beiden Sophokleischen
> Hölderlin's transpositions, especially those of the both Sophoclean
>
> Tragödien, bestätigend dar. In ihnen ist die Harmonie der Sprachen so
> tragedies, confirmingly forth. In them is the harmony of the languages so
>
> tief, daß der Sinn nur noch wie eine Äolsharfe vom Winde von
> deep, that the sense only yet like an Aeolian harp from the wind from
>
> der Sprache berührt wird.
> the language touched become.

*Paraphrase*: In this and in every other essential respect Hölderlin's translations, especially those of Sophocles' two tragedies, stand as proof. In those translations the harmony of the languages is so profound that their sense is touched by language only in the way an Aeolian harp is touched by the wind.

*Commentary*: As I mentioned in passing in the commentary to #45, the Aeolian harp was often invoked by Romantic poets to suggest divine or otherwise supernatural inspiration: the wind that played the harp (which in fact is a real musical instrument played by the wind) was supposedly the breath of a god.[63] Benjamin of course does not expressly deify the wind here; the hint that Hölderlin's translations of Sophocles were divinely inspired is just a hint, which is to say that I may be making this up. (See also the commentary to #55 for Berman's remarks about the Sophocles translations.) Still, considering that in #76 he calls Hölderlin's translations *Urbilder ihrer Form* "prototypes of their Form" is significant—so significant, I would argue, that it would be wrong to read that claim as casual

---

63 According to Greek mythology, the Aeolian harp belonged to Aeolus, the Greek god of wind. In Hebrew legend, King David hung his *kinnor* (harp) in a tree, and was awakened by it at midnight, when the wind would strum it. For Romantic poetic treatments in English, see Samuel Taylor Coleridge's "The Eolian Harp" and "Dejection, an Ode," Percy Bysshe Shelley's "Mutability" and "Ode to the West Wind," Ralph Waldo Emerson's "The Maiden Speech of the Aeolian Harp," and Henry David Thoreau's "Rumors from an Aeolian Harp." For Romantic poetic treatments in German, see Johann Gottfried Herder's "Die Aeolsharfe," "Die Leier des Pythagoras," and "Das Saitenspiel," Ludwig Gotthard Kosegarten's "Die Harmonie der Sphären," C.F. Schreiber's "Die Aeolische Harfe," Johann Wolfgang von Goethe's "Äolsharfen: Ein Gespräch" and two passages from *Faust*, and dozens of others (see Tenhaef 2017). Jean Paul, Clemens Brentano, E.T.A. Hoffmann, Josepf von Eichendorff, Heinrich Heine, Gottfried Keller, and dozens of others also wrote prose pieces about Aeolian harps, all collected in Tenhaef.

hyperbole (see the commentary to #76 for a fuller argument on this head). Considering also that "profound harmony" is one of the standard characteristics of the music of the spheres, and that the Aeolian harp does have that literary-historical pedigree as a spiritual and indeed quasi-divine instrument, it would be very surprising if he was referring pragmatically, empirically, to the playing of an actual musical instrument by puffs of wind.

Here's another way of putting it: if the true translation for Benjamin touches the sense of the source text the way a tangent touches a circle, the truest translation, the best and most prototypical translation, touches the sense of the source language like the wind—not a finger touch, not a geometrical touch, but a *breezy* touch—lightly strumming an Aeolian harp. Even if the wind is not the breath of a divine or quasi-divine being, it's a *lighter* touch than any other human translation can manage.

In tracking Maurice Blanchot's (1971, 1997) unpublished notes on and partial translation of Benjamin's "Task," Vivian Liska (2014) tracks a telling shift from *die Harmonie der Sprachen* "the harmony of (the) languages" in Benjamin to *l'ahmonie [sic] est si profonde entre les deux langues* (241) "the ahmony [sic] between the two languages is so profound" (242) in Blanchot's notes. As Blanchot glosses this reading, what Benjamin described in Hölderlin was

> le dessein, non pas de transporter le texte grec en allemand ni de reconduire la langue allemande aux sources grecques, mais d'unifier les deux puissances représentant l'une les vicissitudes de L'Occident, l'autre celles de l'Orient, en la simplicité d'une langage total et pur. (1971: 72–73; quoted in Liska 241)

> the intent not of transposing the Greek text into German, nor of reconveying the German language to its Greek sources, but of unifying the two powers—the one representing the vicissitudes of the West, the other those of the Orient—in the simplicity of a pure and total language. (1997: 61; quoted in Liska 242)

Liska comments:

> What for Benjamin is the lost language of paradise, an idea derived from Jewish mysticism, becomes in Blanchot's text the union of the Greek and the German. This eminently Heideggerian τόπος played a considerable role in the context of the cultural and intellectual aspirations of the National Socialists. It is clear that Blanchot's thinking is not oriented towards the claim that the heritage of Greece was destined to be realized by Germany, a claim which influenced so strongly the ultimately murderous vision of an absolutely supreme, neo-pagan Germany, opposed principally to the Jewish and, to a lesser degree, Christian tradition. Nevertheless, Blanchot's "translation" of Benjamin's pure messianic language into a pure Greco-German language, in an article in which Blanchot claims to make "some remarks" on Benjamin's essay, is surprising. (242)

Then again, Liska's translation of Benjamin's *die Harmonie der Sprachen* as "the harmony of *all* languages" is a tendentious paraphrase; the noun phrase might be translated as "the harmony of languages," which might indeed be paraphrased as "the harmony of all languages"; but it can also be translated as "the harmony of *the* languages," which might well justify Blanchot's reading as *entre les **deux** langues* "between the *two* languages." Benjamin is specifically saying that *in Hölderlin's translations* the harmony of (the) languages is profound—and rendering the definite article "the" explicitly in English would almost certainly imply that German and Greek are meant. Both readings are possible.

*Other commentators*: Baltrusch (2010: 121–22), Derrida (1985: 189), Engel (2014: 7), O'Keeffe (2015: 380), Roberts (1982: 120–21), Weber (2005: 77).

## 76 Hölderlin (4): his translations are prototypes of the Form

Hölderlins Übersetzungen sind Urbilder ihrer Form; sie verhalten
Hölderlin's translations  are  prototypes of their form; they conduct

sich · auch zu den vollkommensten Übertragungen ihrer Texte als
themselves even to the most perfect  transpositions of their texts as

das Urbild  zum  Vorbild, wie es der Vergleich der Hölderlinschen
the prototype to the exemplar, as  it the comparison of the Hölderlinian

und Borchardtschen Übersetzung der  dritten pythischen Ode von Pindar
and Borchardtian  translation  of the third Pythian Ode from Pindar

zeigt. Eben darum wohnt in ihnen vor andern die ungeheure und
shows. Even therefore lives in them before others the appalling and

ursprüngliche Gefahr aller Übersetzung: daß die Tore einer so
primal  peril  of all  translation: that the gates of one so

erweiterten und durchwalteten Sprache zufallen und den Übersetzer
widened  and transmuted  language slam shut and the translator

ins  Schweigen schließen. Die Sophokles-Übersetzungen waren
in the silence  enclose. The Sophocles translations  were

Hölderlins letztes Werk. In ihnen stürzt der Sinn von Abgrund zu
Hölderlin's last  work. In them plunges the sense from abyss  to

Abgrund, bis er droht  in bodenlosen Sprachtiefen  sich zu verlieren.
abyss,  until it threatens in bottomless language depths itself to lose.

*Paraphrase*: Hölderlin's translations are prototypes of their Form. They stand in relation to even the most perfect transpositions of their source texts as "primordial image" (*Urbild* = prototype, archetype) to "pre-image" (*Vorbild* = model, exemplar, paragon). Any comparison of Hölderlin's translations of Pindar's third Pythian Ode with Borchardt's will show that clearly. And because of that, in them lurks the most appalling primal peril of all translation: that when the gates of language have been so savagely sprung they may slam shut and enclose the translator in silence. The translations of *Antigone* and *Oedipus Rex* were Hölderlin's last work. In them sense plunges from abyss to abyss until it risks losing itself in the bottomless pit of language.

*Commentary*: As I began to suggest in the commentary to #75, Benjamin is not just saying that Hölderlin's translations are "great." In other words, it's not just that "prototypes of the Form" is a nice thing to call them. I believe Benjamin meant it literally. A prototype began in ancient Greek as a primitive or primordial form, the earliest possible image of a thing; later it became the best exemplar, regardless of primordiality. If I'm right that by "Form" Benjamin meant a transcendental prototype in Plato's Realm of Forms, then Hölderlin's translations were in his opinion the first *human* copies of the Form of translation—"first" in the displaced sense of "best," of course, but in some suprahistorical sense "first" in the temporal sequence as well. They were so great that they took their rightful place at the source—the Logos as the divine bridge between God and humans—and therefore both "above" and "before" all other human translations.

In manufacturing, a prototype can be a model, a sample built either to test a process or a concept or to be reproduced in mass production—what Benjamin calls a *Vorbild*, an exemplar or paragon—and in the second sentence of this passage he specifies that that is *not* what he means by calling Hölderlin's translations prototypes. They are qualitatively different from that kind of model-prototype: so much greater than even the most perfect translations that there is a difference in kind.

In semantics, of course, a prototype can be the most representative instance of a category, or an instance that combines the category's most representative qualities. Thus for example an actual translation can have several source texts, and can consist of several divergent target texts in the same target language or many target languages; but a prototype translation would be a single sense-for-sense reproduction of a single source text in a single target text/language. That is not what he means by a prototype translation either. One of those "most perfect transpositions of their source texts" might fit that description; but again, Hölderlin's translations stand in relation to those perfect translations as a truly mystical prototype stands to a model, exemplar, or paragon.

A factual correction: "The translations of *Antigone* and *Oedipus Rex* were [*not*] Hölderlin's last work." He finished them in 1803–4, just before their 1804 publication, and continued to write poetry for the rest of his long life, living in Zimmer's tower till he died in 1843 at the age of 73; his later work included the famous 1812 lyric "Die Linien des Lebens" ("The Lines of Life"). Sometimes after playing the piano for the tourists that showed up at the tower to see him and ask for his autograph he would write an impromptu poem for them. But it certainly makes a more dramatic story to say that "the gates of language had slammed shut and enclosed Hölderlin in silence"; that in his Sophocles translations "sense plunges from abyss to abyss until it risks losing itself in the bottomless pit of language."

As for "the most appalling primal peril of all translation," the significant commentary once again comes from Jacques Derrida (1985: 203–4). Antoine Berman had read Derrida's deconstruction of Benjamin when he wrote and delivered the lectures that were published posthumously as his commentary on the "Task" (Berman 2008/2018), and he learned from Derrida—along the way he also mentions a conversation he had with Derrida on the subject (82). Certainly there is a good deal that is brilliant in his commentary. On the essay's end-game, though, Berman's commentary can't hold a candle to Derrida's:

> The to-be-translated of the sacred text, its pure transferability, that is what would give *at the limit* the ideal measure for all translation. The sacred text assigns the task to the translator, and it is sacred *inasmuch as* it announces itself as transferable, simply transferrable, to-be-translated, which does not always mean immediately translatable, in the common sense that was dismissed [#8–12] from the start. (Derrida 1985: 203)

The idea of transferability would appear to be transposability without translation—that is, if translation means the laborious building of mediatory semantic, syntactic, and pragmatic bridges from a source text to the target language by a human translator who has studied both languages intensively and has extensive professional experience building such bridges. Transferability as what "give[s us] *at the limit* the ideal measure for all translation" would be something like what in #71 we saw Goethe calling the third epoch of translation, in which "one seeks to make the translation identical with the original, so that the one would no longer be in the *stead* but in the *place* of the other" (Robinson 1997/2014: 223)—except that in what Derrida is calling transferability one doesn't *seek* to make the translation identical with the source text, one simply *does it*. Like the interlinear version, Goethe goes on, "in its attempt to enhance our understanding of the original it leads us onward, drives us on toward the source text, and so finally closes the circle in which the alien and the familiar, the known and the unknown move toward each other" (224). It may seem as if it is "*attempt[ing]* to enhance our understanding of the original," but in fact what it is doing is "finally clos[ing] the circle in which the alien and the familiar, the known and the unknown move toward each other" (224).

Something like that ideal mystical goal seems to be what Derrida means by this next definition:

> Perhaps it is necessary to distinguish here between the transferable and the translatable. Transferability pure and simple is that of the sacred text in which meaning and literality are no longer discernible as they form the body of a unique, irreplaceable, and untransferable event, "materially the truth." Never are the call for translation, the debt, the task, the assignation, more imperious. Never is there anything more transferable, yet by reason of this indistinction of meaning and literality (Wörtlichkeit), the pure transferable can announce itself, give itself, present itself, let itself be translated as untranslatable. (1985: 203)

Transferability is the fusing of sense and word—the fusing of syntax-free meaning and the syntax-revealing letter—and that fusion itself is an untransferable event. Transferability is the untransferable. The ideal possible is the real impossible. What makes it ideal is that it is impossible for humans to achieve; it can only be achieved by superhuman forces, like the unforgetting of the unforgettable in the memory of God (#10). Because at that ideal limit the transferable is untranslatable by humans, "the pure transferable can announce itself, give itself, present itself, let itself be translated as untranslatable."

Like the holy fool, like the theia maniac driven insane by an unfiltered experience of the divine, in Benjamin's retelling Hölderlin too was driven over the edge into full-blown psychosis by the work he did translating from the ancient Greek.[64] The Logos power that made those translations quasi-divine supposedly scrambled Hölderlin's brain:

> From this limit, at once interior and exterior, the translator comes to receive all the signs of remoteness (Entfernung) which guide him on his infinite course, at the edge of the abyss, of madness and of silence: the last works of Hölderlin as translations of Sophocles, the collapse of meaning "from abyss to abyss," and this danger is not that of accident, it is transferability, it is the law of translation, the to-be-translated as law, the order given, the order received—and madness waits on both sides. And as the task is impossible at the approaches to the sacred text which assigns it to you, the infinite guilt absolves you immediately. (Derrida 1985: 203–4)

---

64 Again we should remember that Hölderlin was diagnosed with schizophrenia several years before he did his Pindar and Sophocles translations, and that during the four decades of life that remained to him after those translations he continued to write great poetry. It's not clear whether Derrida did not fact-check Benjamin on this, or knew it but decided to stick close to Benjamin's claims in his deconstruction.

On the other hand, as Hölderlin's poem "Dichterberuf"/"The Poet's Vocation" makes clear, he did conceive of the poet as someone possessed by the gods as if being struck by lightning. The theia mania implied by Benjamin is not entirely an exaggeration.

The *Entfernung* "removal" here is what Benjamin mentioned in #35: *wie weit ihr Verborgenes von der Offenbarung* **entfernt** *sei, wie gegenwärtig es im Wissen um diese Entfernung werden mag* "how far *removed* what is sequestered inside them is from revelation, and how present it might become through knowledge of the removal." There in that earlier passage the "limit" seemed to be exterior only, the temporal distance from the translation's current impact on the languages to "the messianic end of their history"; Derrida recurs to that interval of separation here in order to redouble it on the "inside" as well, as a measure of how far removed Hölderlin was from the holy madness, the theia mania, from 1800 to 1804, while translating first Pindar and then Sophocles from the Greek. So great, so mystically and transcendentally great, are Hölderlin's translations that they bring both the interior and the exterior dangerously close to that limit, the messianic history close to its end and Hölderlin close to the psychic abyss—and for Benjamin, Derrida insists, this is not a danger into the proximity of which Hölderlin stumbled by accident, but "the law of translation." The law of translation, we recall from #8, is the translatability of the source text, and it lies hidden inside the source text (*Denn in ihm liegt deren Gesetz als in dessen Übersetzbarkeit beschlossen*); the translator's law, shall we say the translator's task, is to retrieve that law from hiding, to bring it into the light—even if the light is too blinding for mere mortals, and even if "the task is [not only] impossible at the approaches to the sacred text which assigns it to you" but plunges you into the abyss of darkness and silence. And it doesn't matter that you can never translate again, never write another poem, because "the infinite guilt absolves you immediately."

Paul de Man, by contrast, debunkingly insists that for Benjamin there was no pathos in the dark Romanticism of Hölderlin plunging from abyss to abyss. It was a technical literary reference:

> The reasons for this pathos, for this *Wehen*, for this suffering, are specifically linguistic. They are stated by Benjamin with considerable linguistic structural precision; so much so that if you come to a word like "abyss" in the passage about Hölderlin, where it is said that Hölderlin tumbles in the abyss of language, you would understand the word "abyss" in the nonpathetic, technical sense in which we speak of a *mise en abyme* structure, the kind of structure by means of which it is clear that the text itself becomes an example of what it exemplifies. The text about translation is itself a translation, and the untranslatability which it mentions about itself inhabits its own texture and will inhabit anybody who in his turn will try to translate it, as I am now trying, and failing, to do. The text is untranslatable, it was untranslatable for the translators who tried to do it, it is untranslatable for the commentators who talk about it, it is an example of what it states, it is a *mise en abyme* in the technical sense, a story within the story of what is its own statement. (2000: 26)

But see Bannet (1993: 583) for a persuasive deflation of de Man's offhand attempt to deflate Benjamin's mysticism by making everything in the "Task" about either death—for de Man translations "'kill the original' (C 84) by using language 'destructively' and 'nihilistically' to plunge the original 'from abyss to abyss until it threatens to become lost in the bottomless depths of language' (C 84)"[65]—or mere technicalities "in the service of linguistic fundamentalism and an ultimate and ironic political nihilism" (Pence 1996: 85; see also Porter 1989).

Consider also that "most appalling primal peril of all translation: that when the gates of language have been so savagely sprung they may slam shut and enclose the translator in silence [*ins Schweigen*]." Appalling peril? Certainly for a writer, or a speaker. But in #48 Benjamin proclaims that "if, contrary to all common sense, there actually is a language of truth, in which, without suspense or even the spoken word [*schweigend*], the ultimate mysteries that all thought labors to reveal are kept, then that language of truth is the true language." *Schweigend* there, which I paraphrase as "without ... the spoken word," is "in silence, saying nothing, making not a noise." Peril in #76, utopia in #48. In July 1916 Benjamin wrote to Martin Buber: "Nur die intensive Richtung der Worte in den Kern des innersten Verstummens hinein gelangt zur wahren Wirkung" (Scholem and Adorno 1978: 127)"—"Only the intensive orientation of words toward the kernel of innermost falling mute attains to true operativity." That latter is Ira Allen's English translation of the letter in Hamacher (2001/2012: 540),[66] who comments: "If language thus tends, for the sake of its immanent political substance, toward 'that which is barred the word,' then translation tends, for the sake of the language of truth, toward silence." That *Kern des innersten Verstummens* "kernel of innermost falling mute" in the letter to Buber becomes in the "Task" (#38) "the kernel of *un(re)translatability in any translation*" and (#19) "the expression of *the innermost relationship among languages*": the translation as a no-longer-expressive expression of that relationship among languages. Silence.

In #0 I noted that Paul de Man and Antoine Berman are partly right and partly wrong about Benjamin's essay being about translation *and not* about the translator. The extent to which they are right is mapped in #48's celebration of silence; the extent to which they are wrong is mapped in #76's horror at Hölderlin's silencing. The "Task" is about both—and apparently Benjamin sees no contradiction.[67]

---

65  Bannet quotes from the earlier publication of "Conclusions" in de Man (1986), abbreviated "C"; the passages Bannet quotes appear on p. 24 of de Man (2000). It is of course not surprising to find a scholar like de Man eager to accuse Harry Zohn of mistranslating; what is surprising is to find his impulse to correct others' mistakes combined with an apparently gratuitous impulse to impose hostile misreadings on Benjamin's German original.

66  In the published English version of the correspondence the translation reads like this: "Only the intensive aiming of words into the core of intrinsic silence is truly effective" (Scholem and Adorno 1994: 80).

67  Fenves (2011: 150) seeks to reconcile what I read as the two contradictory stances on silence by arguing that Benjamin *does not* celebrate Hölderlin's achievement, indeed disapproves of it. In this reading his horror at silence would be a horror at a translator's failure to translate properly:

*Other commentators*: Balfour (2018: 753–54), Chapman (2019: 122), Cohen (2002: 104), Ferreira Duarte (1995: 274), Hanssen (2002: 143), Johnston (1992: 47), Liska (2014: 241), Rothwell (2009: 261), Smerick (2009: np), St. André (2011: 113–14), Vermeer (1996: 80, 92, 154), Weber (2008: 74).

## 77 Holy Writ (1): always translatable because never communicable

> Aber     es gibt  ein Halten. Es gewährt es jedoch       kein Text außer dem
> However it  gives  a   halt.    It allows   it nevertheless no   text except the
>
> heiligen, in dem    der Sinn aufgehört hat, die Wasserscheide für die
> holy,     in which  the sense ceased     has, the watershed     for the
>
> strömende Sprache   und die strömende Offenbarung zu sein. Wo    der
> streaming language  and the streaming  revelation   to be.  Where the
>
> Text unmittelbar, ohne     vermittelnden Sinn, in seiner Wörtlichkeit
> text immediable, without   mediatory     sense, in its    word-for-wordness
>
> der   wahren Sprache, der   Wahrheit oder der   Lehre    angehört, ist
> of the true   language, to the truth   or   to the teaching belongs,  is
>
> er übersetzbar schlechthin.     Nicht mehr freilich    um seinet-,
> it translatable purely and simply. No    more admittedly for   its,
>
> sondern allein um der Sprachen   willen.
> rather  alone for the languages' sake.

---

A translator who did not touch the original with a law-bound tangent line would no longer be a translator but would, instead, fall silent—or worse, become "creative." In the final paragraph of "The Task of the Translator," while drawing on both the original and the mathematical sense of *Sinn* as "direction," made even more emphatic by its association with the French word *sens* (sense, direction), Benjamin describes the situation of late Hölderlin in precisely these terms: "The Sophocles translations were Hölderlin's last work. In them, sense [der Sinn] plunges from abyss to abyss, until it threatens to lose itself in the bottomless depths of language" (4: 21). In terms of the geometric figure that describes the solution to the task of the translator, the point at which the translation touches the original turns so sharply—in the language of mathematical [*sic*], the curve would be called "pathological"—that no tangent line can be drawn. The translations of Sophocles have no regular interval Δ, hence no direction, and therefore verge on senselessness. (Fenves' insertion)

One might add that in #75 Benjamin describes Hölderlin's translations "touching" that point on the circle not with "a law-bound tangent line" but with the wind that strums an Aeolian harp. Hence, according to Fenves, the "peril" of "falling silent." This reading, of course, ignores not only Benjamin's inclination elsewhere to celebrate both silence and "verging on senselessness" but his insistence that Hölderlin's translations were prototypes of their Form. For Benjamin, near-perfection; for Fenves, failure.

*Paraphrase*: There is, however, a force that holds us back, that saves us from madness, found only in Holy Writ, where meaning is no longer the watershed in which the streams of language and revelation part ways. Where the text is not mediated by sense, but belongs immediately to true language in all its literality, indeed to truth or to doctrine, that text is unequivocably translatable. Not, to be sure, for its own, but for the languages' sake.

*Commentary*: Vermeer (1996: 80) notes that "der Infinitiv 'Halten' kann ein (mehr oder minder aktives) Anhalten und ein passives Gehaltenwerden bezeichnen" ("the infinitive 'to halt' can denote a (more or less active) holding back and a passive being halted"; by paraphrasing it as "a force that holds us back" I've obviously chosen the former.[68] That force would be the "limit" that we saw Derrida discussing in the commentary to #76. As Derrida deconstructs the image, of course, it's as much a holding back for the imperfections and incompletions of human life (and of translation) on earth as it is for sanity. In Benjamin the halt comes *after* the image of Friedrich Hölderlin teetering on the edge of the abyss, suggesting (as per my paraphrase) a force placing a limit on his suffering, and on the suffering of brilliantly extreme translators like him; but in Derrida they are the same limit, "at once interior and exterior." In Benjamin specifically what "halts" in the vehicle of the metaphor is the parting of the waters of language and revelation in the watershed of meaning: because Holy Writ categorically *does not* seek to communicate a message, because it is the pure letter of the true language, it is unequivocally translatable. The "most perfect" human translations touch the circle of sense only fleetingly on their trajectories toward Ein Sof, the Infinite; Hölderlin's translations, more perfect and more complete than the most perfect and most complete translations—so exquisitely perfected that they not only are but always have been, since the beginning of time, the prototypes of their Form—touch sense with the wind that plays the mystical Aeolian harp. But when it comes to Holy Writ, all that comes to a halt. No more touching sense, even fleetingly, because there is no sense. "What comes to pass in a sacred text," Derrida paraphrases the first clause of that second sentence, "is the occurrence of a *pas de sens*" (204): a sense-making step that vacates all sense. What that means, Derrida explains, is not a "poverty of meaning" but "no meaning that would be itself, meaning, beyond any 'literality'" (204). The unmeaning meaning; the step that steps at once decisively through and irretrievably beyond the letter. "And right there," he adds, "is the sacred. The sacred surrenders itself to translation which devotes itself to the sacred. The sacred would be nothing

---

68 Note also the appearance in *ein passives Gehaltenwerden* "a passive being halted" of the keyword *der Gehalt*, which I've followed Antoine Berman and Chantal Wright in translating "tenor." The link between *das Gehaltenwerden* and *der Gehalt* might be interpreted as having to do with the mystical power of the immediable "kernel" of the source text that every great translator seeks to translate: here at the scriptural pinnacle of all translation, "where the text is not mediated by sense, but belongs immediately to true language in all its literality, indeed to truth or to doctrine," the sacred tenor both passively is held and actively holds us back from the theia mania, because its literal belonging to true language *manages* the translation.

without translation, and translation would not take place without the sacred; the one and the other are inseparable" (204). The sacred text is not a communiqué from a personal god to humans, but an explosion of divine light, heat, energy—a mystical forge of inconceivable power that translates itself. Something like that mystical forge is most likely what Benjamin means in #36 by "the necessary mediability can be found in the growth of religions, which ripens the seed that is hidden in the languages and raises it to a higher level."

"This law," Derrida goes on, "would not be an exterior constraint; it grants a liberty to literality. In the same event, the letter ceases to oppress insofar as it is no longer the exterior body or the corset of meaning" (204–5). The law sets the letter free, in the sense that the letter (and the syntactic framework that it highlights and tropes) no longer needs to constrain meaning, as a body constrains the spirit and as a corset constrains unruly flesh. "There is [now] only letter, and it is the truth of pure language, the truth as pure language" (204).

"This situation," he concludes, "though being one of pure limit, does not exclude—quite the contrary—gradations, virtuality, interval and in-between, the infinite labor to rejoin that which is nevertheless past, already given, even here, between the lines, already signed" (205). *Even here*: here in Derrida's own conclusion, translated in the early eighties by Joseph F. Graham. Past, and yet ongoing, infinitely, in a mystical calculus that only lets itself be imagined by those who engage the Kabbalistic sacrality of Benjamin's "Task." The stopping-place translation of Holy Writ that has always been completed, always been perfected, is also always in progress, because its completion is ideal, always has been ideal, always has been an ideal toward which human history infinitely strives, ever closer and closer, boats against the current.

Carol Jacobs (1975: 765) adds one final twist: "What is it exactly that the holy scripture vouchsafes? Is it really a halt to the precipitous loss of meaning or must we translate 'Halten' rather as a holding and retaining of that loss"?

*Other commentators*: Balfour (2018: 751), Britt (1996: 52, 54), de Man (2000: 19), Fenves (2011: 150–51), Hamacher (2001/2012: 527), Johnston (1992: 46–47), Kohlross (2009: 107), Liska (2014: 243–44), Pan (2017: 42–43), Roberts (1982: 121), Smerick (2009: np), St. André (2011: 113–14).

## 78 Holy Writ (2): its interlinear is the prototype or ideal of all translation

Ihm         gegenüber ist so grenzenloses Vertrauen von   der Übersetzung
With it faced       is so borderless       trust         from the translation

gefordert, daß spannungslos wie in jenem Sprache   und Offenbarung so
required, that tension-free   as in that  language and revelation   so

> in dieser Wörtlichkeit und Freiheit in Gestalt der Interlinearversion
> in this word-for-wordness and freedom in form of the interlinear version
>
> sich vereinigen müssen. Denn in irgendeinem Grade enthalten alle großen
> itself unite must. For in some degree harbor all great
>
> Schriften, im höchsten aber die heiligen, zwischen den Zeilen ihre
> writings, in the highest however the holy, between the lines their
>
> virtuelle Übersetzung. Die Interlinearversion des heiligen Textes ist das
> virtual translation. The Interlinear version of the holy text is the
>
> Urbild oder Ideal aller Übersetzung.
> prototype or ideal of all translation.

*Paraphrase*: When it comes to Holy Writ, such boundless trust is required of the translation that, just as in the source text language and revelation are united without tension, so too must literalism and freedom be united in the form of the interlinear version. For to some degree all great writings harbor their own virtual translations between the lines—and this is true in the very highest degree of scripture. The interlinear version of Holy Writ is the prototype or ideal of all translation.

*Commentary*: In this final passage the utopian promise toward which the entire essay has been tending seems to be fulfilled. In #70 and #73 the perfected literal translation achieved almost total freedom from bondage to sense by touching it only fleetingly like a tangent touching a circle, and in #75 Hölderlin's more-perfect-than-perfect translations were even more wonderfully liberated from sense by touching it as lightly as the wind touches an Aeolian harp; here the letter and freedom are united without tension, just as language and revelation are in the scriptural source text. The implication is that the letter—i.e., fidelity to the letter, or literalism—is the translational counterpart to source-textual language, and freedom is the translational counterpart to source-textual revelation. Literal translation was for Benjamin the perfect counterpart to the language of the Bible because he believed that the Bible's language is perfectly noncommunicative: it is pure letter, pure syntax.

I say "*seems* to be fulfilled," however, because Carol Jacobs (1975: 763n9) insightfully strikes a sourer note: "In the closing passage of 'Die Aufgabe des Übersetzers,' the messianic valorization of the holy scriptures ironically serves to usher in the fundamental fragmentation which interlinear translation performs." Because it stages both the source and the target languages together, arrayed in a lattice calibrated for both horizontal and vertical (inter)linearity, the interlinear version does not in fact perfectly embody the ideal Goethe imagined for it: "Here one seeks to make the translation identical with the original, so that the one would no longer be in the *stead* but in the *place* of the other" (223; see #71, #76). In the interlinear neither the source text nor the translation is in the stead *or* the place of the other. Both line up above and below each other, like little soldiers lying prone in bunkbeds, in neat rows all the way across the concrete barracks floor. And they may *folgen* "follow" (#57) each other out on the parade ground, but never perfectly. They're always just slightly out of step.[69]

See also Christian Uhl (2012: 433) for incorporations of a series of interpretations of this passage into a brilliantly freewheeling analysis of a "translational" social formation "which produces commodities": "Pratt's [2008] 'social spaces' and 'contact zones,' Mudimbe-Boyi's [2002] 'in-between,' Emily Apter's [2006] 'translation zone,' Lydia Liu's [1995] 'middle-zone of interlinear translation,' or Bhabha's [1994] 'third space,' where 'hybridization' takes place, and 'newness' is generated." Biti (2019) also interreads Benjamin with Bhabha.

The Bible for Benjamin was of course the Hebrew Bible, which Jewish mystics have always believed to have been written in Hebrew by God himself, in his own hand. In "Midrash and the Dawn of Kabbalah" Joseph Dan (1986: 128) explains that Hebrew readings of the Bible as not only inspired but handwritten by God understand the Bible as a "total text," on the model of the Hebrew conception of the total human being who lives for a time on earth and then is "gathered to the fathers." The "body" of the Hebrew Bible for Jewish midrash included

> the sound and feel of individual words, ... the shape of letters, ... the frequency with which certain words and letters appear in a given verse or passage of chapter, ... the numerical value of textual units from individual letters to whole verses, ... the placement, shape, and sound of individual vocalization points, ... the various musical (*te'amim*) and decorative (*tagin*)

---

69 See also Bellos (2010: 217), at the end of a remarkably obtuse tissue of supercilious dismissal, for the bizarre claim that "*There are no interlinear versions of the scriptures!* Precisely because the Bible has always been translated." By "the scriptures" he means the Christian Bible, obviously, not the Hebrew Bible, which is what Benjamin would have meant; but what Bellos says of the *Qur'an* would apply to the Hebrew Bible as well: "This is not true of the Koran, of course. Precisely because it is deemed not translatable, many manuscripts exist in Farsi, Malayalam, and other languages of Islamic communities with interlinear explanations of the Arabic words. These do not count as translations, but as commentaries" (218n8). Apparently he is suggesting that these are not interlinear *translations*, but interlinear *commentaries*, so that his blanket negation should stand; but of course the interlinears that have been printed of the Hebrew Bible and the *Qur'an* have often been word-for-word translations that have simply not been *thought of* as translations by the various Jewish or Islamic communities.

And beyond that, of course, hundreds of interlinear translations have been created for the Christian Bible, beginning very early in the Christian era, with very many target languages, mostly for theology students in those various languages. A Finnish theology student once showed me his, with Hebrew, Aramaic, and Greek as its source text(s) and word-for-word Finnish as its target text. Nowadays these interlinear translations of the Christian Bible are also everywhere available for free online; I would encourage Bellos to Google "interlinear Bible" and see what turns up. My search even turned up a free online Hebrew-to-English interlinear translation of the Hebrew Bible.

"diacritics" added to letters and words,[70] ... [and] acrostics spelled out in the initial or final letters of a section (*notarikon*). (quoted in Robinson 1996: 66)

All that "body"—what Dan calls "the countless ways other than ideonic content and meaning by which the scriptures transmit a semiotic message" (128)—must be experienced by the reader of "the Bible." And obviously none of that "body" is translatable in the traditional sense, because in the West "the traditional sense" of translation was birthed and has been molded and mortified through dogmatic Christian ontology and translatology. (See the commentary to #50 for Jacques Derrida's ruminations on "materiality" as "that which translation relinquishes," but that also which, when reinstated in translation, generates poetry.)

The dualistic (Platonist/Hellenistic) Christian conception of the human being, of course, was of a spirit trapped in a body, so that death meant the freeing of the spirit from its prison; as a result, the Christian conception of the Bible was analogously that the spirit/meaning was trapped in the body/letter of the source text, and that translation freed that spirit/meaning before transplanting it into another body/letter in the target language. Total translatability—the *a priori* assumption that the spirit could be transferred unchanged from body to body—was supposedly guaranteed by the guidance of the Holy Ghost. Perhaps the deepest and most ancient reason for the sense that "we" "commonsensically" have that the claims Benjamin makes in the "Task" are counterintuitive and even bizarre is that "we" tend to take Christian body–spirit (word–sense) dualism as the "true" "nature" of translation.

In Hebrew midrashic tradition, which survives today, this focus on the "total text" has meant that any translation of the *meaning* of the Bible is to be used as a crib only, not as "the Bible," and not even as "a translation of the Bible." As a "great writing," written by the Almighty, the Hebrew Bible would certainly "harbor its own virtual translation between the lines," but it would do so mystically, and it would be experienced not on the page or the screen but in the (closed) eyes of the initiate. An interlinear version, therefore, originally worked up to teach Biblical Hebrew to the succeeding generations of the Jewish diaspora, would only be a *human* prototype or ideal of all translation.

The Christian belief in total translatability by contrast was organized by St. Paul's warning in 2 Corinthians 3:6 that "the letter killeth, but the spirit giveth life": if you free the text of its literal and syntactic backbone, you free the spirit from its prison. This is obviously the exact opposite of what Benjamin believed; and the difference lies not so much in personal opinion as in the divergence of ancient scriptural traditions, the Jews insisting that the Bible is the Bible only in Hebrew—God's language, and therefore the language of embodied

---

70 For the embodied "orality" and indeed "mouthability" of the Hebrew Bible, as marked in the *te'amim* of the Masoretic text, and the importance of translating that body, see also Meschonnic (2007/2011) and, for discussion, Robinson (2012, 2014a, 2014b).

revelation—and the Christians insisting that the Bible is the Bible no matter what language you read it in.

Benjamin's essay would have been considerably easier to read had he explained all this as he went along. As this and other commentaries on the essay show, for clarity his argument really requires a book-length exposition. Compressing it into less than 5000 words makes it vatic and mysteriously enticing, but hard to parse. But then the ideal of easy access to the sense of a text is a Christian ideal— one that is quite alien to the Kabbalistic and other Jewish mysticism in which Benjamin was steeped when he wrote the "Task." Midrash, of course, is rabbinic commentary: like Holy Writ, Benjamin's essay requires midrashic commentary to emerge into clarity.

One might add that "When it comes to Holy Writ, such boundless trust is required [not only] of the translation" but of the commentary as well—and that the tiniest feather of skepticism can derail one's grasp of the text. Some such derailment seems to have happened to Berman, in fact, and led him at the end of his commentary not only to *dislike* Benjamin's mysticism, and not only to downplay it and where possible to ignore it entirely, but to misread it, willfully, as something entirely different: Benjamin's mystical conception of pure language, for example, as not mystical at all, but a celebration of the orality of dialect. In the end he couldn't *trust* Benjamin's text.

Full disclosure: I don't trust it fully either. More specifically, I don't surrender total ontological belief to it. I don't trust it to represent the true nature of translation, or literature, or the universe. I trust it as a narrative, a story about mythical and mystical forces at work and at play in the universe. I trust it in the way I trust Lewis Carroll's *Alice in Wonderland*, or any other amazing and enjoyable story. It doesn't have to be true to be amazing. Berman's problem was that he wanted Benjamin's "Task" to be true, perhaps needed it to be true, and he couldn't swallow the Kabbalistic mysticism. Hence his disclaimer: "In saying this, I am going beyond Benjamin" (2008/2018: 209). Or, as Benjamin himself would most likely have preferred, Berman was unwilling to *go as far as* Benjamin, falling short of Benjamin, holding back from Benjamin's extremism. I don't need to go beyond him or hold back from him, because I am writing a commentary, not a credo— and a commentary on a tantalizing but cryptic story.

*Other commentators*: Balfour (2018: 753), Baltrusch (2010: 120), Bradbury (2006: 142), Britt (1996: 38, 52), Cohen (2002: 103), Engel (2014: 7), Ferreira Duarte (1995: 275), Jacobs (1975: 766), Johnston (1992: 46–47), Liska (2014: 243–44), Rendall (1997b: 181), Steiner (1975/1998: 68, 324), Sussman (2005: 108), Vermeer (1996: 80, 92, 174), Weber (2005: 76).

# REFERENCES

Annas, Julia. 1982. "Plato's Myths of Judgement." *Phronesis* 27.2: 119–43.
Apter, Emily. 2006. *The Translation Zone: A New Comparative Literature*. Princeton: Princeton University Press.
Austin, J.L. 1962. *How to Do Things with Words*. Ed. J.O. Urmson and Marina Sbisà. Oxford and New York: Oxford University Press.
Bakhtin, Mikhail. 1929/1984. *Problems of Dostoevsky's Poetics*. Translated and edited by Caryl Emerson. Minneapolis: University of Minnesota Press.
Bakhtin, Mikhail. 1934–35/1981. "Discourse in the Novel." In Michael Holquist, ed., *The Dialogic Imagination: Four Essays*, 259–422. Translated by Caryl Emerson and Michael Holquist. Austin: University of Texas Press.
Balfour, Ian. 2018. "Translating Benjamin in de Man and in Deconstruction More Generally." *MLN* 133: 743–62.
Baltrusch, Burghard. 2010. "Translation as Aesthetic Resistance: Paratranslating Walter Benjamin." *Cosmos and History: The Journal of Natural and Social Philosophy* 6.2: 113–29.
Bannet, Eve Tavor. 1993. "The Scene of Translation: After Jakobson, Benjamin, de Man, and Derrida." *New Literary History* 24.3 (Summer): 577–95.
Barnstone, Willis. 1993. *The Poetics of Translation: History, Theory, Practice*. New Haven, CT: Yale University Press.
Barthes, Roland. 1967. "The Death of the Author." Translated by Richard Howard. *Aspen* 5–6.3: 2–6.
Bartoloni, Paolo. 2004. "Benjamin, Agamben, and the Paradox of Translation." *CLCWeb: Comparative Literature and Culture* 6.2. Online at https://doi.org/10.7771/1481-4374.1231. Accessed March 25, 2021.
Bellos, David. 2010. "Halting Walter." *Cambridge Literary Review* 3: 207–20.
Benjamin, Andrew. 1989/2014. *Translation and the Nature of Philosophy: A New Theory of Words*. London and New York: Routledge.
Benjamin, Walter. 1914–15/1991. "Zwei Gedichte von Friedrich Hölderlin." In Rolf Tiedemann and Hermann Scheppenhäuser, eds., *Gesammelte Schriften* II.1: 105–126. Frankfurt am Main: Suhrkamp.

Benjamin, Walter. 1916/1991. "Über Sprache überhaupt und über die Sprache des Menschen." In Rolf Tiedemann and Hermann Scheppenhäuser, eds., *Gesammelte Schriften* II.1: 140–157. Frankfurt am Main: Suhrkamp.
Benjamin, Walter. 1923/1972. "Die Aufgabe des Übersetzers." In Tillman Rexroth, ed., *Kleine Prosa, Baudelaire-Übertragungen*, 9–21. Vol. 4, Part 1 of Walter Benjamin, *Gesammelte Schriften* ("Collected Writings"). Frankfurt am Main: Suhrkamp.
Benjamin, Walter. 1928. *Ursprung des deutschen Trauerspiels*. Berlin: Rowohlt.
Benjamin, Walter. 1935/2007. "The Work of Art in the Age of Mechanical Reproduction." In Benjamin 1968/2007: 217–51.
Benjamin, Walter. 1968/2007. *Illuminations: Essays and Reflections*. Edited by Hannah Arendt. Translated by Harry Zohn. New York: Schocken.
Benjamin, Walter. 1978/1986. "On Language as Such and on the Language of Man." Translation of Benjamin 1916/1991 by Edmund Jephcott. In Peter Demetz, ed., *Reflections: Essays, Aphorisms, Autobiographical Writings*, 314–32. New York: Schocken.
Benjamin, Walter. 1998. *The Origin of German Tragic Drama*. Translation of Benjamin 1928 by John Osborne. London and New York: Verso.
Berman, Antoine. 1986. "L'essence platonicienne de la traduction" ("The Platonic Essence of Translation"). *Revue d'esthétique* 12: 63–73.
Berman, Antoine. 2008. *L'Âge de la traduction. «La tâche du traducteur» de Walter Benjamin, un commentaire* ("The Age of Translation: 'The Task of the Translator' by WB, a Commentary"). Saint-Denis: Presses Universitaires de Vincennes.
Berman, Antoine. 2008/2018. *The Age of Translation: A Commentary on Walter Benjamin's "The Task of the Translator."* Translated and with an introduction by Chantal Wright. London and New York: Routledge.
Bernal Merino, Miguel. 2006. "On the Translation of Video Games." *Journal of Specialised Translation* 6: 22–36. Online at http://www.jostrans.org/issue06/art_bernal.pdf. Accessed May 4, 2021.
Bhabha, Homi. 1994. *The Location of Culture*. London: Routledge.
Biti, Vladimir. 2019. "Translating the Untranslatable: Walter Benjamin and Homi Bhabha." *Primerjalna književnost* (Ljubljana) 42.3: 247–66.
Blanchot, Maurice. 1971. "Traduire." *L'Amitié*, 69–73. Paris: Gallimard.
Blanchot, Maurice. 1997. "Translating." *Friendship*, 57–61. Translation of Blanchot 1971 by Elizabeth Rottenberg. Stanford: Stanford University Press.
Bradbury, Nicola. 2006. "*De cette triste plume tâtonnante*: Henry James and 'The Task of the Translator.'" *Yearbook of English Studies* 36.1: 138–44.
Brisset, Annie. 1991. "Translation and Social Discourse: Shakespeare, A Playwright after Québec's Heart." In Mildred L. Larson, ed., *Translation: Theory and Practice, Tension and Independence*, 120–38. American Translators Association Scholarly Monograph Series V. Amsterdam and Philadelphia: John Benjamins.
Britt, Brian. 1996. *Walter Benjamin and the Bible*. New York: Continuum.
Carr, David. 1986. *Time, Narrative, and History*. Bloomington: Indiana University Press.
Chapman, Edmund. 2019. *The Afterlife of Texts in Translation: Understanding the Messianic in Literature*. London: Palgrave Macmillan.
Chemero, Anthony. 2009. *Radical Embodied Cognitive Science*. Cambridge: MIT Press.
Cohen, Josh. 2002. "Unfolding: Reading After Romanticism." In Hanssen and Benjamin 2002a: 98–108.
Constantine, David. 2001. *Hölderlin's Sophocles: Oedipus and Antigone*. Hexham: Bloodaxe.
Damrosch, David. 2006. "World Literature in a Postcanonical, Hypercanonical Age." In Haun Saussy, ed., *Comparative Literature in an Age of Globalization*, 43–53. Baltimore and London: Johns Hopkins University Press.

Dan, Joseph. 1986. "Midrash and the Dawn of Kabbalah." In Geoffrey H. Hartman and Sanford Budick, eds., *Midrash and Literature*, 127–39. New Haven: Yale University Press.
de Campos, Haroldo. 1992. *Metalinguagem e outras metas: Ensaios de teoria e crítica literaria* ("Metalanguage and Other Metas: Essays on Literary Theory and Criticism"). São Paolo: Perspectiva.
de Man, Paul. 1986. "Conclusions: Walter Benjamin's 'The Task of the Translator'." In de Man, *The Resistance to Theory*, 73–105. Minneapolis: University of Minnesota Press.
de Man, Paul. 2000. "'Conclusions' on Walter Benjamin's 'The Task of the Translator.'" *50 Years of Yale French Studies: A Commemorative Anthology, Part 2: 1980–1998*. Special issue of *Yale French Studies* 97: 10–35.
Derrida, Jacques. 1972/1988. "Signature Event Context." In Derrida, *Limited Inc*, ed. Gerald Graff, 1–23. Evanston: Northwestern University Press.
Derrida, Jacques. 1978. *Writing and Difference*. Translated by Alan Bass. Chicago: University of Chicago Press.
Derrida, Jacques. 1985. "Des Tours de Babel." In Joseph F. Graham, ed., *Difference in Translation*, 165–205 (in English, translated by Joseph F. Graham) and 209–48 (in French). Ithaca: Cornell University Press.
Dilthey, Wilhelm. 2002. "Plan for the Continuation of the Formation of the Historical World in the Human Sciences." Translated by Rudolf A. Makkreel and William H. Oman. Part III of Rudolf A. Makkreel and Frithjof Rodi, eds., *The Formation of the Historical World in the Human Sciences*. Vol. 3 of *Wilhelm Dilthey: Selected Works*. Princeton: Princeton University Press.
Engel, Simone. 2014. "Walter Benjamins *Die Aufgabe des Übersetzers*: Ein philosophischer Essay über das Wesen der Sprache" ("WB's 'The Task of the Translator': A Philosophical Essay on the Essence of Language"). Seminar on "Probleme und Methoden der Übersetzungswissenschaft" ("Problems and Methods in the Science of Translation"), July 3, at the Institut für Angewandte Linguistik und Translatologie, University of Leipzig.
Felman, Shoshana. 1999. "Benjamin's Silence." In W.J.T. Mitchell, ed., *Angelus Novus: Perspectives on Walter Benjamin*. Special issue of *Critical Inquiry* 25.2 (Winter): 201–34.
Fenves, Peter. 2001. "Die Unterlassung der Übersetzung." In Christiaan L. Hart-Nibbrig, ed., *Übersetzen: Walter Benjamin*, 159–73. Frankfurt am Main: Suhrkamp.
Fenves, Peter. 2011. *The Messianic Reduction: Walter Benjamin and the Shape of Time*. Stanford: Stanford University Press.
Ferreira Duarte, João. 1995. "The Power of Babel: 'Pure Language' as Intertranslation." *Perspectives: Studies in Translatology* 3.2: 271–82.
Ferris, David S. 2008. *The Cambridge Introduction to Walter Benjamin*. Cambridge and New York: Cambridge University Press.
Flèche, Betsy. 1999. "The Art of Survival: The Translation of Walter Benjamin." *SubStance* 28.2: 95–109.
Foucault, Michel. 1969/1979. "What Is an Author?" Translated by Josué Harari. In Harari, ed., *Textual Strategies: Perspectives in Post-structuralist Criticism*, 141–60. Ithaca: Cornell University Press.
Friedlander, Gerald. 1912. *Hellenism and Christianity*. London: Valentine. Online at https://archive.org/details/hellenismchristi00frieiala/page/114/mode/2up. Accessed March 7, 2021.
Gandillac, Maurice de. 1959/1971. Walter Benjamin, "La tâche du traducteur" ("The Task of the Translator"). In Gandillac, *Œuvres choisies*, 57–74. Paris: Juillard.
Gasché, Rodolphe. 1986. "Saturnine Vision and the Question of Difference: Reflections on Walter Benjamin's Theory of Language." *Studies in Twentieth Century Literature* 11.1 (Fall): 69–90.

Gasché, Rodolphe. 1992/2002. "The Sober Absolute: On Benjamin and the Early Romantics." In Hanssen and Benjamin 2002a: 51–68.

Gelley, Alexander. 2015. *Benjamin's Passages: Dreaming, Awakening*. New York: Fordham University Press.

Gold, Joshua Robert. 2007. "'Another Nature Which Speaks to the Camera': Film and Translation in the Writings of Walter Benjamin." *MLN* 122: 602–22.

Hamacher, Werner. 1996. "'Disgregation of the Will': Nietzsche on the Individual and Individuality." Translated by Peter Fenves. In Hamacher, *Premises: Essays on Philosophy and Literature from Kant to Celan*, 143–80. Stanford: Stanford University Press.

Hamacher, Werner. 2001/2012. "Intensive Languages." Translated by Ira Allen with Steven Tester. *MLN* 127.3: 485–541.

Hanssen, Beatrice. 2002. "'Dichtermut' and 'Blödigkeit'—Two Poems by Friedrich Hölderlin, Interpreted by Walter Benjamin." In Hanssen and Benjamin 2002a: 139–62.

Hanssen, Beatrice, and Andrew Benjamin, eds. 2002a. *Walter Benjamin and Romanticism*. New York: Continuum.

Hanssen, Beatrice, and Andrew Benjamin. 2002b. "Walter Benjamin's Critical Romanticism: An Introduction." In Hanssen and Benjamin 2002a: 1–6.

Heidegger, Martin. 1916. *Die Kategorien- und Bedeutungslehre des Duns Scotus* ("The Doctrine of the Categories and of Signification of Duns Scotus"). Tübingen: Mohr.

Hodge, Joanna. 2005. "The Timing of Elective Affinity." In Andrew Benjamin, ed., *Walter Benjamin and Art*, 14–31. London and New York: Continuum.

Holmström, Lakshmi. 2006. "Let Poetry Win: The Translator as Writer—An Indian Perspective." In Susan Bassnett and Peter Bush, eds., *The Translator as Writer*, 33–45. London and New York: Continuum.

Holz-Mänttäri, Justa. 1984. *Translatorisches Handeln: Theorie und Methode*. Helsinki: Academia Scientiarum Fennica.

Homburg, Phillip. 2018. *Walter Benjamin and the Post-Kantian Tradition*. London and Lanham: Rowman & Littlefield.

House, Juliane. 2017. *Translation: The Basics*. London and New York: Routledge.

Hynd, James, and E.M. Valk, trans. Walter Benjamin, "The Task of the Translator." 1968/2006. *Delos* 2: 76–96. Reprinted in Daniel Weissbort and Astradur Eysteinsson, ed., *Translation: Theory and Practice*, 298–307. Oxford and New York: Oxford University Press.

Jacobs, Carol. 1975. "The Monstrosity of Translation." *MLN* 90.6 (December): 755–66.

Jacobson, Eric. 2003. *Metaphysics of the Profane: The Political Theology of Walter Benjamin and Gershom Scholem*. New York: Columbia University Press.

Johnston, John. 1992. "Translation as Simulacrum." In Lawrence Venuti, ed., *Rethinking Translation: Discourse, Subjectivity, Ideology*, 42–56. London and New York: Routledge.

Kant, Immanuel. 1787/1929. *Critique of Pure Reason*. Translated by Norman Kemp Smith. London: Palgrave Macmillan.

Kohlross, Christian. 2009. "Walter Benjamin's 'The Task of the Translator': Theory after the End of Theory." *Partial Answers* 7.1: 97–108.

Lachterman, David R., trans. 1996. Walter Benjamin, "The Concept of Criticism in German Romanticism." Partial translation of Benjamin 1920/1980, revised by Piotr Parlej. In Marcus Bullock and Michael W Jennings, eds., Walter Benjamin, *Selected Writings, Volume 1: 1913–1926*, 116–200. Cambridge, MA: Harvard University Press.

Lacoue-Labarthe, Philippe. 2002. "Introduction to Walter Benjamin's *The Concept of Art Criticism in German Romanticism*." In Hanssen and Benjamin 2002a: 9–18.

Lal, P. 1964. *Great Sanskrit Plays in New English Transcreations*. New York: New Directions.

Lee, Hyang, and Seong-Woo Yun. 2011. "Antoine Berman's Philosophical Reflections on Language and Translation: The Possibility of Translating without Platonism." *Filozofia* 66.4: 336–46.

Liska, Vivian. 2014. "A Same Other, Another Same: Walter Benjamin and Maurice Blanchot on Translation." Translated by Naomi Shulman. *German Quarterly* 87.2 (Spring): 229–45.

Liu, Lydia H. 1995. *Translingual Practice: Literature, National Culture and Translated Modernity—China, 1900–1937*. Stanford: Stanford University Press.

Louth, Charlie. 1998. *Hölderlin and the Dynamics of Translation*. London and New York: Routledge.

Mangiron, Carmen, and Minako O'Hagan. 2006. "Game Localisation: Unleashing Imagination with 'Restricted' Translation." *Journal of Specialised Translation* 6: 10–21. Online at http://www.jostrans.org/issue06/art_ohagan.pdf. Accessed May 4, 2021.

Marais, Kobus. 2019. *A (Bio)Semiotic Theory of Translation: The Emergence of Social-Cultural Reality*. London and New York: Routledge.

McBride, James. 1989. "Marooned in the Realm of the Profane: Walter Benjamin's Synthesis of Kabbalah and Communism." *Journal of the American Academy of Religion* 57.2 (Summer): 241–66.

Menke, Bettine. 2002. "'However One Calls into the Forest …': Echoes of Translation." In Hanssen and Benjamin 2002a: 83–97.

Meschonnic, Henri. 2007/2011. *Ethics and Politics of Translating*. Translated by Pier-Pascale Boulanger. Amsterdam and Philadelphia: John Benjamins.

Mosés, Stéphane. 1995. "Benjamin's Metaphors of Origin: Names, Ideas, Stars." Translated by Timothy Bahti. In Timothy Bahti, ed., *Jewish Writers, German Literature*, 139–54. Ann Arbor: University of Michigan Press.

Mudimbe-Boyi, Elizabeth, ed. 2002. *Beyond Dichotomies: Histories, Identities, Culture, and the Challenge of Globalization*. Albany: State University of New York Press.

Nachman of Breslov. 2006-7. "The Lost Princess." Translated by Rabbi Avraham Greenbaum. *The Essential Rabbi Nachman*. Azamra Institute. Online at https://www.azamra.org/Essential/princess.htm. Accessed March 13, 2021.

Novalis. 1965/1981. *Das philosofische Werk I* ("The Philosophical Work 1"). Edited by Richard Samuel in collaboration with Hans-Joachim Mähl and Gerhard Schulz. Vol. 2 of Samuel, Mähl, and Schulz, eds., *Historische-Kritische Ausgabe—Novalis Schriften* ("Historical-Critical Edition—Novalis Writings"). Stuttgart: Kohlhammer.

O'Keeffe, Brian. 2015. "The 'Saran Wrap' Theory of Translation: Transparency and Invisibility, or the Kernel and the Envelope." *symplokē* 23.1–2: 375–92.

Palmquist, Stephen R. 2000. *Kant's Critical Religion*. Volume 2 of *Kant's System of Perspectives*. Aldershot: Ashgate.

Pan, David. 2017. "Cosmopolitanism, *Tianxia*, and Walter Benjamin's 'The Task of the Translator'." *Telos* 180 (Fall): 26–46.

Pence, Jeffrey. 1996. Language, History, and the University: de Man on Translation." *College Literature* 23 (June): 83–99.

Pfau, Thomas. 1988. "Thinking Before Totality: *Kritik*, *Übersetzung*, and the Language of Interpretation in the Early Walter Benjamin." *MLN* 103.5 (December): 1072–97.

Phelan, Anthony. 2002. "*Fortgang* and *Zusammenhang*: Walter Benjamin and the Romantic Novel." In Hanssen and Benjamin 2002a: 69–82.

Porter, Dennis. 1989. "Psychoanalysis and the Task of the Translator." *MLN* 104.5 (December): 1066–84.

Pratt, Mary Louise. 2008. *Imperial Eyes: Travel Writing and Transculturation*. London and New York: Routledge.

Procyshyn, Alexei. 2014. "Walter Benjamin's Philosophy of Language." *Philosophy Compass* 9.6: 368–81. Online at https://onlinelibrary.wiley.com/doi/epdf/10.1111/phc3.12134. Accessed March 28, 2021.

Pym, Anthony. 2009. "On Empiricism and Bad Philosophy in Translation Studies." In Hasuria Che Omar, Haslina Haroon, and Aniswal Abd. Ghani, eds., *The Sustainability of the Translation Field*, 28–39. Kuala Lumpur: Persatuan Penterjemah Malaysia.

Regier, Alexander. 2006. "A Brotherhood is Broken: Wordsworth, Benjamin, and the Fragmentation of Language." *European Romantic Review* 17.5: 607–28.

Rendall, Steven, trans. 1997a. Walter Benjamin, "The Translator's Task." *TTR* 10.2: 151–65.

Rendall, Steven. 1997b. "Translation, Quotation, Iterability." *TTR* 10.2: 167–89.

Roberts, Julian. 1982. *Walter Benjamin*. London: Macmillan.

Robinson, Douglas. 1991. *The Translator's Turn*. Baltimore and London: Johns Hopkins University Press.

Robinson, Douglas. 1996. *Translation and Taboo*. DeKalb: Northern Illinois University Press.

Robinson, Douglas. 1997. *What is Translation? Centrifugal Theories, Critical Interventions*. Kent, OH, and London: Kent State University Press.

Robinson, Douglas, ed. 1997/2014. *Western Translation Theory from Herodotus to Nietzsche*. Third edition. London and New York: Routledge.

Robinson, Douglas. 1997/2020. *Becoming a Translator: An Introduction to the Theory and Practice of Translation*. Fourth edition. London and New York: Routledge.

Robinson, Douglas. 2003. *Performative Linguistics: Speaking and Translating as Doing Things With Words*. London and New York: Routledge.

Robinson, Douglas. 2008. *Estrangement and the Somatics of Literature: Tolstoy, Shklovsky, Brecht*. Baltimore and London: Johns Hopkins University Press.

Robinson, Douglas. 2011. *Translation and the Problem of Sway*. Amsterdam and Philadelphia: John Benjamins.

Robinson, Douglas. 2012. "Rhythm as Knowledge-Translation, Knowledge as Rhythm-Translation." *Global Media Journal—Canadian Edition* 5.1: 75–94.

Robinson, Douglas. 2013a. *Feeling Extended: Sociality as Extended Body-Becoming-Mind*. Cambridge, MA: MIT Press.

Robinson, Douglas. 2013b. *Schleiermacher's Icoses: Social Ecologies of the Different Methods of Translating*. Bucharest: Zeta Books.

Robinson, Douglas. 2014a. "Embodied Translation: Henri Meschonnic on Translating For/Through the Ear and the Mouth." *Parallèles* 26: 38–52. Online at http://www.paralleles.unige.ch/tous-les-numeros/numero-26/robinson.html. Accessed March 28, 2022.

Robinson, Douglas. 2014b. "The Inscience of Translation." *International Journal of Society, Culture, and Language* 2.2 (Fall): 25–40. Online at http://ijscl.net/article_5432_848.html. Accessed March 28, 2022.

Robinson, Douglas. 2015. *The Dao of Translation: An East–West Dialogue*. London and Singapore: Routledge.

Robinson, Douglas. 2016a. *The Deep Ecology of Rhetoric in Mencius and Aristotle*. Albany: State University of New York Press.

Robinson, Douglas. 2016b. "Pushing-Hands and Periperformativity." In Douglas Robinson, ed., *The Pushing Hands of Translation and its Theory: In Memoriam Martha Cheung, 1953–2013*. London and Singapore: Routledge.

Robinson, Douglas. 2016c. *Semiotranslating Peirce*. Tartu: University of Tartu Press.

Robinson, Douglas. 2017a. *Aleksis Kivi and/as World Literature*. Leiden and Boston: Brill.
Robinson, Douglas. 2017b. *Critical Translation Studies*. London and Singapore: Routledge.
Robinson, Douglas. 2017c. *Translationality: Essays in the Translational-Medical Humanities*. London and Singapore: Routledge.
Robinson, Douglas. 2019. *Transgender, Translation, Translingual Address*. New York: Bloomsbury Academic.
Robinson, Douglas, trans. 2020. Volter Kilpi, *Gulliver's Voyage to Phantomimia*. Bucharest: Zeta Books.
Robinson, Douglas. 2021. "Transcreating Volter Kilpi." Episode 35 of the *Feeling Bookish* podcast. Online at https://soundcloud.com/user-63759823/transcreating-volter-kilpi-episode-no-35. Accessed January 11, 2021.
Robinson, Douglas. Forthcoming-a. "The Affordances of the Translator." In Douglas Robinson, ed., *Cognition and Hermeneutics: Convergences in the Study of Translation*. Vol. 2 of the *Jahrbuch für Übersetzungshermeneutik/Yearbook of Translational Hermeneutics*.
Robinson, Douglas. Forthcoming-b. "Walter Benjamin as Translator as John Henry: Competing with the Machine." In Wang Ning and Wang Hongtao, eds., *Literary Translation in the Era of Artificial Intelligence: Challenges and its Future Prospects*. Special issue of *Babel*.
Rose, Marilyn Gaddis. 1982. "Walter Benjamin as Translation Theorist: A Reconsideration." *Dispositio* 7.19/21: 163–75.
Rothwell, Andrew. 2009. "Translating 'Pure Nonsense': Walter Benjamin Meets Systran on the Dissecting Table of Dada." *Romance Studies* 27.4: 259–72.
Ruin, Hans. 1999. "Origin in Exile: Heidegger and Benjamin on Language, Truth, and Translation." *Research in Phenomenology* 29: 141–60.
Sandbank, Shimon. 2015. "The Translator's Impossible Task: Variations on Walter Benjamin." *Partial Answers* 13.2: 215–24.
Scholem, Gershom. 1972. "Walter Benjamin und sein Engel." In *Zur Aktualität Walter Benjamins*, 87–138. Frankfurt am Main: Suhrkamp.
Scholem, Gershom. 1973. *Major Trends in Jewish Mysticism*. New York: Schocken.
Scholem, Gershom, and Theodor W. Adorno, eds. 1978. Walter Benjamin, *Briefe I ("Letters I")*. Frankfurt am Main: Suhrkamp.
Scholem, Gershom, and Theodor W. Adorno, eds. 1994. *The Correspondence of Walter Benjamin, 1910–1940*. Translated by Manfred R. Jacobson and Evelyn M. Jacobson. Chicago: University of Chicago Press.
Shapiro, Kam. 2011. "Walter Benjamin, the Kabbalah, and Secularism." In "The Secular." Special issue of *AJS Perspectives* (Spring). Online at http://perspectives.ajsnet.org/the-secular-issue-spring-2011/walter-benjamin-the-kabbalah-and-secularism/. Accessed March 13, 2021.
Smerick, Cynthia M. 2009. "'And G-d said": Language, Translation, and Scripture in Two Works by Walter Benjamin." *Shofar* 27.2: 48–68.
Spivak, Gayatri Chakravorty. 1976/1997. "Translator's Preface." Jacques Derrida, *Of Grammatology*, ix–lxxxvi. Baltimore and London: Johns Hopkins University Press.
St. André, James. 2011. "Revisiting Walter Benjamin's 'Task of the Translator' in Light of his *Concept of Criticism in German Romanticism*." *TTR* 24.1: 103–24.
Steiner, George. 1975/1998. *After Babel: Aspects of Language and Translation*. Oxford and New York: Oxford University Press.
Steiner, George. 1998. "Introduction." In Benjamin 1998: 7–24.
Steiner, Uwe. 2010. *Walter Benjamin: An Introduction to His Work and Thought*. Translated by Michael Winkler. Chicago: University of Chicago Press.

Sussman, Henry. 2005. *The Task of the Critic: Poetics, Philosophy, and Religion*. New York: Fordham University Press.
Szondi, Peter. 1986. "The Poetry of Constancy: Paul Celan's Translation of Shakespeare's Sonnet 105." Translated by Harvey Mendelson. In Szondi, *On Textual Understanding and Other Essays*, 161–75. Manchester: Manchester University Press.
Tagliacozzo, Tamara. 2018. *Experience and Infinite Task: Knowledge, Language and Messianism in the Philosophy of Walter Benjamin*. London and Lanham: Rowman & Littlefield.
Tanaka, Daniel Jiro. 2002. "Forms of Disenchantment: Kant and Neo-Kantianism in the Early Work of Walter Benjamin." Ph.D. diss., Princeton University.
Tenhaef, Peter, ed. 2017. *Äolsharfen-Romantik: Eine Blütenlese von Beschreibungen, Gedichten, Prosa, Reflexionen, Bildern und Musik* ("Aeolian Harp Romanticism: A Blossom Harvest of Descriptions, Poems, Prose, Reflections, Images, and Music"). Berlin: Frank & Timme/Noack & Block.
Thobo-Carlsen, John. 1998. "Barthes meets Benjamin? A Relating of their Views on the Conjunction between Language and Literature." *Orbis Litterarum* 53: 1–41.
Tomasello, Michael. 2008. *Origins of Human Communication*. Cambridge: MIT Press/Bradford Books.
Uhl, Christian. 2012. "Translation and Time: A Memento of the Curvature of the Poststructuralist Plane." *Frontiers of Literary Study in China* 6.3: 426–68.
Ulrich, George. 2001. "Unforgiving Remembrance: The Concept and Practice of *Eingedenken* in Walter Benjamin's Late Work." Ph.D. diss., University of Toronto.
Underwood, J.A., trans. 2009. "The Task of the Translator." In Benjamin, *One-Way Street and Other Writings*, 29–45. London: Penguin.
Vermeer, Hans J. 1996. *Übersetzen als Utopie: Die Übersetzungstheorie des Walter Bendix Schoenflies Benjamin*. Heidelberg: TEXTconTEXT.
Vieira, Else. 1999. "Liberating Calibans: Readings of Antropofagia and Haroldo de Campos' Poetics of Transcreation." In Susan Bassnett and Harish Trivedi, eds., *Post-colonial Translation: Theory and Practice*, 95–113. London and New York: Routledge.
Voloshinov, V.N. 1930/1973. *Marxism and the Philosophy of Language*. Translated by Ladislav Matejka and I.R. Titunik. New York and London: Seminar.
Weber, Samuel. 2005. "A Touch of Translation: On Walter Benjamin's 'Task of the Translator.'" In Sandra Bermann and Michael Wood, eds., *Nation, Language, and the Ethics of Translation*, 65–78. Princeton and Oxford: Princeton University Press.
Weber, Samuel. 2008. *Benjamin's -abilities*. Cambridge, MA: Harvard University Press.
Weigel, Sigrid. 2002. "The Artwork as Breach of a Beyond: On the Dialectic of Divine and Human Order in Walter Benjamin's 'Goethe's Elective Affinities.'" In Hanssen and Benjamin 2002a: 197–206.
Witte, Bernd. 1976. *Walter Benjamin: Der Intellektuelle als Kritiker. Untersuchungen seinem Frühwerk*. Stuttgart: Metzler.
Wright, Chantal, trans. 2018. Antoine Berman, *The Age of Translation: A Commentary on Walter Benjamin's "The Task of the Translator."* Translation of Berman 2008. London and New York: Routledge.
Wurgaft, Benjamin Andes. 2002. "Language and its Core: Ethical and Religious Subjects in Levinas and Benjamin." *Literature and Theology* 16.4 (December): 377–95.
Zathureczky, Kornél. 2004. "A Critique of the Messianic Theology of Jürgen Moltmann Through the Messianic Philosophy of Walter Benjamin: Staying With the Negative." Ph.D. diss., Southern Methodist University. Online at https://search.proquest.com/docview/305388638?pq-origsite=gscholar&fromopenview=true. Accessed March 31, 2021.
Zechner, Dominik. 2020. "Inventive Languages: Walter Benjamin, Ernst Jandl, and the Possibility of Back-Translation." *Translation and Literature* 29: 317–37.

# INDEX

Note: Page numbers followed by "n" denote footnotes.

**Passages**

#0 49, 87, 123, 183
#1 2–3, 19, 23, 144, 148, 172
#2 2, 4, 19–21, 23, 110, 114, 121, 148
#3 2, 19, 23, 148
#4 2, 16–17, 21, 23, 110, 114, 148
#5 2, 5, 21, 23, 148
#6 2, 19, 100, 110, 114, 148
#7 2, 5, 26, 28, 113, 173
#8 2, 16, 24, 43, 173, 180, 182
#9 2, 5, 13, 24, 43, 67, 180
#10 2, 24, 32, 43, 139–40, 180–1
#11 2, 13, 24, 43, 180
#12 2, 5, 39–40, 174, 180
#13 2, 5, 26–7, 38–40, 42, 45, 53, 61, 77, 122, 136, 139
#14 2, 5, 26, 39, 45
#15 2, 5, 26, 39, 42, 74, 144
#16 2–3, 5, 26, 37, 39, 42, 45, 71
#17 2–3, 5, 26–7, 37, 39, 42–3, 45, 53, 130
#18 2, 5, 26, 39, 42–3, 51, 53, 74, 86, 130
#19 3, 22, 27, 50–3, 55, 74–5, 118, 130, 145, 158, 183
#20 3, 22, 27, 40, 50, 51–2, 56, 88, 118
#21 3, 27, 50, 57, 76, 109, 100
#22 3, 27, 50
#23 3, 27, 50, 58
#24 3, 27, 61–2, 65
#25 3, 27, 57, 71, 148
#26 3, 13, 27, 37, 69, 71, 100
#27 3, 27, 36, 57–9, 65, 70–1, 125, 160
#28 3, 24, 27, 37, 65, 69, 71, 113, 158
#29 3, 27, 40–1, 45, 50–1, 57, 71, 73
#30 3, 27, 57, 78, 100, 145
#31 3, 27, 40–1, 75, 78, 144–5
#32 3, 27, 75, 145
#33 3, 5, 40, 75, 78, 145
#34 3, 27, 113
#35 3, 27, 57, 74, 87, 89, 113, 160, 182
#36 3, 27, 52, 74–5, 86, 89, 110, 124, 141, 151, 153, 160, 186
#37 3, 27, 86, 89, 139, 140, 150
#38 3, 19, 27, 33, 52, 86, 89, 91, 95–6, 160, 172, 183
#39 3, 19, 27, 52, 86, 89, 95–6, 100, 110, 127, 138, 154, 160, 174–5
#40 3, 19, 27, 33, 86, 89, 91, 97, 100, 105, 113, 144
#41 3, 24, 40, 81, 113
#42 3, 21, 81, 105
#43 3, 21, 24, 34, 105, 107, 111, 113, 175
#44 3, 10, 40, 107, 111, 113–14
#45 3, 111, 113, 137, 176
#46 3, 110, 114, 122, 144, 151, 153, 163
#47 3, 100, 118, 131
#48 3, 73, 144, 183
#49 3, 118, 122, 144, 156
#50 3, 5, 52, 75, 144, 189
#51 3, 9, 40, 74, 75, 87, 123–4, 131, 163
#52 2–3, 34, 127, 165
#53 2–3, 34, 165

#54 2–3, 5, 34, 40, 81, 145
#55 2–3, 34, 86, 107, 125, 128, 176
#56 2–3, 34, 40, 86, 128
#57 2–3, 34, 37, 42–3, 67, 87, 136, 138, 144, 155, 165, 188
#58 2–3, 34
#59 2–3, 5, 28, 38, 51, 90, 113, 130, 140, 156, 158
#60 2–3, 6, 34
#61 2–3, 34, 86, 128
#62 2–3, 34, 86, 100, 128, 151–3
#63 2–3, 34, 162, 165
#64 2–3, 34
#65 3, 6, 40, 144, 162, 163
#66 3, 34, 160
#67 3, 158, 160
#68 3, 144, 162, 167
#69 3, 10, 34, 107, 140, 165, 175
#70 2–3, 6, 34, 156, 162, 165, 174, 187
#71 3, 103, 170, 172, 180, 187
#72 3, 100, 103, 144, 161, 169
#73 2–3, 16, 25, 34, 61, 156, 162, 165, 173–4, 187
#74 2–3, 162
#75 3, 29, 34, 50, 100, 111, 132, 162, 165, 179, 184, 187
#76 3, 11, 25, 29, 34, 72, 91, 100, 118, 132, 176–7, 183, 185, 187
#77 3, 86, 110, 114, 128, 151, 153
#78 2–3, 5, 86–7, 121, 134, 136, 144, 165, 170

**Names**

Adorno, Theodor 31
Allen, Ira 89
Althusser, Louis 137n49
Annas, Julia 26
Apter, Emily 188
Aristotle 144n53
Austin, J.L. 5, 15, 54; on slipping and falling 125n42; on Walt Whitman 20

Baader, Franz von 137n49
Bakhtin, Mikhail 5, 13; on internal dialogism 129–30
Balfour, Ian 12, 30, 64, 86, 145, 168, 184, 186, 190; on the Tower of Babel resonances in Mallarmé, Benjamin, and Derrida 121
Baltrusch, Burghard 12, 28, 65, 140, 161, 166, 178, 190; on NOT! 147–8n54
Bannet, Eve Tavor 12, 41, 46, 47, 65; deflating de Man's deflations of Benjamin 183
Barnstone, Willis 137n49
Barthes, Roland 45
Bartoloni, Paolo 41, 53, 72, 75, 80, 84
Baudelaire, Charles 10, 88, 93, 107, 127
Bellos, David 15, 18, 19, 21–3, 25, 28, 41, 46–7, 49, 53, 58, 65, 80, 91, 93, 102, 104, 115–16, 118, 122, 125, 127, 136, 140, 146, 151, 153, 166, 172; claiming that interlinear Bibles don't exist 188n69; on pure language as "Interlingua" 73n28; on the untranslatability of translations 94–5, 175
Benjamin, Andrew 12, 18, 21, 24, 33, 41, 46, 49, 53, 64, 75, 77, 80, 86, 140, 145, 166; on the Kantian epistemological critique of objectivity 61n26
Berman, Antoine 1–2, 3, 6, 8–9, 11, 18, 21, 25, 28, 33, 41, 46–7, 49, 53, 57, 58, 60, 64–5, 67, 69–70, 72, 77, 80–1, 86, 93, 95, 98, 104, 106, 110, 115, 120, 122, 125, 128, 131, 136, 140, 142, 146, 149, 153, 159, 161, 166n59, 172, 185n68; on the aging of translations 101; on Benjamin on Hölderlin 132; on Benjamin as a Romantic 14, 87–8, 172; on Benjamin's Platonism 90–1; on Benjamin the translator *vs.* theorist 93n33, 122; on *Darstellung* as performance 51; on the endgame of the "Task" 180; on fame as "glory" 45; on *gelten* 16–17; on John's Gospel, Mallarmé, and Pannwitz 144; on literalism as maintaining ST syntax 149–50, 161–2; on meaning having weight 160–1; on Novalis on the "task" as "(re-/dis-)solving" 9, 87, 123–4; on pure language 73–5, 117n40, 144, 156, 162, 190; on reading-in-translation 4; rejecting Benjamin's messianism 144, 190; on the symbol 154–5; on the "Task" not being about the translator 8–9, 183
Bernal Merino, Miguel 166n59
Bhabha, Homi 188
Biti, Vladimir 18, 30, 65, 98, 175, 188
Blanchot, Maurice 177
Bodmer, Johann Jakob 11n3, 77
Böhme, Jakob 137n49
Borchardt, Rudolf 178–9
Bradbury, Nicola 53, 102, 120, 122, 151, 166, 190
Brentano, Clemens 176n63
Brisset, Annie 20–1
Britt, Brian 15, 18, 21, 23, 33, 41, 46, 53, 57, 75, 80, 84, 86, 88, 102, 122, 125, 151, 161, 166, 186, 190
Bruno, Giordano 42

Buber, Martin 74

Calderón de la Barca, Pedro 107
Campanella, Tommaso 42
Carr, David 39, 40
Carroll, Lewis 190
Celan, Paul 91, 102, 105
Chapman, Edmund 18, 21, 33, 42, 65, 67, 69–70, 75, 77, 80, 88, 91, 110, 140, 149, 168, 172, 184; discussed 36n14
Chapman, George 101–2
Chemero, Anthony 27
Cicero, Marcus Tullius 90
Cohen, Josh 18, 21, 41, 47, 98, 122, 174–5, 184, 190
Coleridge, Samuel Taylor 176n63
Constantine, David 175

de Campos, Haroldo 166n59
de Man, Paul 10–11, 15, 49, 64, 68n27, 70, 80, 98, 140, 157, 186; attacking Benjamin and Zohn 29–30; on Benjamin's "abyss to abyss" as a *mise en abyme* 182–3
Deleuze, Gilles, and Félix Guattari 157–8, 160
Derrida, Jacques 1, 8, 11, 21, 25, 28, 30–1, 36n14, 41–2, 49, 53, 65, 86, 102, 122, 140, 151, 157, 168, 178, 185–6; on Benjamin's theia mania 180–2; on the death of the author 45–6; on materiality and translation 189; on the royal mantle 95–8
Dilthey, Wilhelm 5, 39–40, 42, 77, 136; *see also Zusammenhang*
Dostoevsky, Fyodor 31
Dryden, John 135
Duns Scotus 77

Eichendorff, Josef von 176n63
Emerson, Ralph Waldo 176n63
Engel, Simone 21, 25, 53, 57, 60, 75, 80, 84, 86, 88, 116, 118, 127, 149, 151, 166, 178, 190; discussed 54n23
Felman, Shoshana 93, 167
Fenves, Peter 12, 57, 77, 168, 186; on Hölderlin's Pindar and Sophocles as failures 183–4n67
Ferreira Duarte, João 16, 46, 57, 64, 75, 80, 86, 91, 125, 133, 137n49, 140, 142, 149, 161, 168, 184, 190; on Benjamin as a Romantic 172
Ferris, David S. 21, 25, 30, 53, 57, 75, 80, 88, 91, 98, 102, 131, 151, 157, 161, 164, 174–5

Ficino, Marsilio 42
Fléche, Betsy 15, 41, 98, 140, 164; discussed 12–13, 36n13
Foucault, Michel 46

Gandillac, Maurice de 6, 16, 95, 150
Garneau, Michel 20–1
Gasché, Rodolphe 1, 41, 53, 57, 75, 88, 93, 98, 102, 110–11, 116, 118, 120, 168; on Benjamin on Romantic art criticism 104; on "On Language as Such" 163; on the *modus significandi* 77
Gelley, Alexander 12, 28, 31, 41–2, 46, 53, 64–5, 70, 77, 88, 98, 125, 140, 168
George, Stefan 11, 34, 88, 105, 106–8, 164–6
Goethe, Johann Wolfgang von 168n53, 168–70, 176n63, 180; on the interlinear 187
Gogol, Nikolai 175
Gold, Joshua Robert 65, 91, 140
Graham, Joseph F. 95–6, 186

Hafez 169n61
Hamacher, Werner 1, 15, 18, 25, 28, 30, 33, 42, 46–7, 49, 57, 64–5, 67, 84, 86, 88, 93, 98, 102, 114, 123, 131, 164, 186; discussed 13, 22n6, 31, 32; on immediability 110, 163n58; on "intensive" 54, 118; on "living on in citation" 38n17; on "proleptic" 50; on "protosynthesis" 73; on "wonderfully haunting" 89
Hamann, Johann Georg 11n3
Hanssen, Beatrice 175, 184; and Andrew Benjamin 104
Hartman, Geoffrey 30
Hegel, G.W.F. 162–3
Heidegger, Martin 40, 77, 107; on the union of Greek and German 177
Heikhalot (palaces) traditions 155
Heine, Heinrich 176n63
Herder, Johann Gottfried 11n3, 39, 103, 176n63
Hermans, Theo 104n37
Hesiod 107
Hessel, Franz 79–80n32
Hodge, Joanna 164
Hoffman, Eva 79
Hoffmann, E.T.A. 176n63
Hölderlin, Friedrich 3, 11, 25, 29, 34, 73–5, 87, 91, 100, 106–8, 124, 126n43, 131–3, 135, 172, 185, 177–85, 187; and the Aeolian harp 50, 111, 165, 176, 187; author of *Hyperion* 133; and

Kant 14n5; as a monstrous exemplar of literalism 131–3; as a poet-translator 105–6; and purity 73–4; pushing back the boundaries of the German language 11, 108, 164–6; and radical etymologism 72; as a Romantic 74–5; and theia mania 181–2; translated by David Constantine 175; his translations are prototypes of the Form 11, 25, 132, 176, 178–9, 183–4n67, 185; on the verge of the abyss 185–6
Holmström, Lakshmi 166n59
Holz-Mänttäri, Justa 14, 109
Homburg, Phillip 14n5
Homer 77, 101–2, 107, 166
Horace 107
House, Juliane 41
Humboldt, Wilhelm von 11n3
Husserl, Edmund 40, 76n31
Hynd, James, and E.M. Valk 6, 13, 16, 24, 26, 32, 36n14, 40, 51–3, 57n25, 61, 70–1, 73, 89, 100–1, 112–14, 116–17, 118n41, 119, 122, 126, 135–6, 150, 157–60, 166n59

Jacobs, Carol 15, 18–19, 21, 31, 47, 53, 57, 64, 67, 75, 80, 93, 98, 102, 125, 133, 159, 161, 164, 172, 186–8, 190; on the echo 111; on the tangent touching the circle 168; on the Tikkun of the Lurianic Kabbalah 138–9n50
Jacobson, Eric 31, 52–3, 84, 137n49
Jacobson, Manfred R., and Evelyn M. Jacobson 74n30
Jephcott, Edmund 52–3
Jerome 11n3, 90
Johnston, John 18, 41, 57–8, 65, 70, 75, 80, 84, 86, 123, 136, 140, 167, 172, 184, 186, 190; discussed 76n31
Joyce, James 38
Jung, Carl 40

Kant, Immanuel 14; and the epistemological critique of objectivity 61–2; on "intensive" 54; post-, 14, 61–2, 129; pre-, 15, 54, 62, 172
Keats, John 101–2
Keller, Gottfried 176n63
Klages, Ludwig 40
Kohlross, Christian 25, 33, 41, 47, 67, 80, 110, 123, 164, 172, 186
Kosegarten, Ludwig Gotthard 176n63

Lacoue-Labarthe, Philippe 53, 167
Lal, P. 166n59
Lee, Hyang, and Seong-Woo Yun 90

Liska, Vivian 12, 16, 21, 30–1, 41, 53, 84, 86, 91, 98, 102, 104, 111, 115–16, 118, 120, 123, 140, 159, 167, 184, 186, 190; on Blanchot on Benjamin 177
Liu, Lydia 188
Louth, Charlie 11n3, 77, 100, 104, 132n46, 166
Luther, Martin 11, 34, 106–8, 164, 166; his German Bible 106, 169

MacLeish, Archibald 16
Mallarmé, Stéphane 5, 107, 120–2, 165; discussed by Berman 144
Mangiron, Carmen, and Minako O'Hagan 166n59
McBride, James 137n49
Menke, Bettine 41, 46, 77, 111, 133, 140, 172; on the Romantic echo 108
Molitor, Franz Joseph 137n49
Mosès, Stéphane 77, 86
Mudimbe-Boyi, Elizabeth 188

Nabokov, Vladimir 134–5
Nachman of Breslov, Reb 140, 155
Necker de Saussure, Albertine 107
Nord, Christiane 14
Novalis 9, 11n3, 87, 91, 103–4, 137n49, 172

O'Keeffe, Brian 41, 47, 53, 91, 98, 104, 140, 164, 168, 178; on Saran Wrap 151
Ovid 107

Palmquist, Stephen 62
Pan, David 15, 21, 31, 41, 53, 75, 80–1, 86, 102, 110, 140, 161, 168, 186; discussed 151
Pannwitz, Rudolf 3, 103, 161, 168–72; discussed by Berman 144
Paul, Jean 176n63
Paul of Tarsus 150, 189
Peirce, Charles Sanders 15; on the icon-index-symbol triad 55
Pence, Jeffrey 12, 41, 115, 183
Pfau, Thomas 23, 31, 53, 64, 75, 86, 91, 93, 98, 102, 115, 131, 140, 142, 157, 164; discussed 62
Phelan, Anthony 40
Philo Judaeus 5, 28, 38, 51–2, 90, 113, 130, 137, 143–4, 156, 172, 179, 188
Pindar 11, 25, 50, 88, 91, 100, 107, 126n43, 132, 166, 181n64; *Pythian Ode* 178–9
Plato 90–1, 101–2; and the Allegory of the Cave 37; and copy theory 25, 37, 61n26, 174; cosmology of 34; and the

mystical roots of rationalism 144n53; on philosophy as the love of Sophia/Wisdom 144n53; and the Realm of Forms 5, 24, 29, 38, 42–3, 47–8, 51, 69, 113, 130, 168, 179
Porter, Dennis 15, 57, 80, 172, 174, 183; on the messianic cult of the poetic 165
Pratt, Mary Louise 188
Procyshyn, Alexei 27, 30, 41
Proust, Marcel 10, 79–80n32, 93, 127, 175
Pushkin, Aleksandr 134–5
Pym, Anthony 78–80

Rabelais, François 102
Regier, Alexander 140
Rendall, Steven: commentator 41, 69, 77, 104, 110, 123, 149, 151, 167, 172, 190; on the note Benjamin sent to the publisher of his Baudelaire translation 126n43; translator 6, 13, 16, 24, 31–2, 34, 36, 42, 51–3, 55, 57n25, 70–1, 76–7, 80, 89, 100–1, 112–14, 116–17, 118n41, 119, 122, 126, 135–6, 150, 157–60, 166n59
Reuchlin, Johann 137n49
Roberts, Julian 91, 115, 123, 164, 178, 186
Rothwell, Andrew 22–3, 53, 57, 75, 77, 140, 184
Ruin, Hans 145

Sandbank, Shimon 19, 21, 31, 80, 98, 116, 118, 140, 172
Saussure, Ferdinand de 68
Schiller, Friedrich 112, 114–15
Schlegel, A.W. 11n3, 34, 91, 103, 106–7, 172
Schlegel, Friedrich 11n3, 103–4, 137n49, 172
Schleiermacher, Friedrich 5, 11n3, 39, 64, 103, 105, 137n49, 169, 172
Scholem, Gershom 31, 54, 87, 136–8, 138–9n50
Schopenhauer, Artur 91
Schreiber, C.F. 176n63
Shakespeare, William 91, 101–2, 107
Shapiro, Kam 137n49
Shelley, Percy Bysshe 176n63
Sidney, Philip 20
Smerick, Cynthia M. 15, 18–19, 21–3, 25, 28, 31, 33, 46–7, 53, 57, 64–5, 67, 69–70, 72, 75, 77, 80, 84, 86, 88, 91, 93, 98, 102, 106, 110–11, 115–16, 118, 120, 123, 125, 127, 131, 133, 136, 142, 151, 159, 161, 164, 167–8, 172, 184, 186
Sophocles 11, 25, 50, 88, 91, 107, 111, 126n43, 131, 166, 176, 181n64

Spivak, Gayatri 36
St. André, James 15, 18, 25, 33, 98, 184, 186; discussed 36n15, 37–8
Staël, Madame de 107
Steiner, George 31, 33, 39n18, 86, 102, 137n49, 167, 190; on Celan's Supervielle 91, 102n36, 105; on pure language as "universal language" 73n28
Steiner, Uwe 15, 28, 41, 46–7, 53, 65, 75, 86
Sterne, Laurence 102
Stevens, Wallace 16
Supervielle, Jules 91, 102n36, 105
Sussman, Henry 190
Swedenborg, Emanuel 62
Szondi, Peter 110, 116, 118

Tagliacozzo, Tamara 137n49
Tanaka, Daniel Jiro 14n5
Tenhaef, Peter 176n63
Theocritus 107
Thobo-Carlsen, John 145
Thomas of Erfurt 77
Thoreau, Henry David 176n63
Tieck, Ludwig 137n49
Tomasello, Michael 55n24

Uhl, Christian 41, 65, 115, 136, 140, 142, 145; on a "translational" social formation 188
Ulrich, George 40
Underwood, J.A. 6, 13, 16, 24, 32, 34, 36n14, 40–1, 42, 51–2, 54, 57n25, 68, 70–1, 89, 100–1, 112–14, 116–17, 118n41, 119, 126, 135–6, 142, 150, 157–60, 166n59
Urquhart, Sir Thomas 102

Valéry, Paul 74–5
Vermeer, Hans J. 1, 9, 15, 19, 21, 25, 28, 33, 41, 46–7, 53, 57, 64–5, 67, 69–70, 72, 75, 77, 88, 91, 110, 116, 118, 123, 125, 136, 140, 142, 151, 159, 161, 167, 174–5, 184, 190; on Benjamin's Hegelian *Aufhebung* 162–3; on Benjamin quoting from John's Gospel 143n52; on Benjamin the translator *vs.* theorist 79–80n32, 93n33; on *ein Halten* 185; on immediability 163n57; on skopos theory 2, 13–14, 29; on translatorial action 109n38
Vieira, Else 166n59
Virgil 101, 107
Voloshinov, V.N. 148
Voß, Johann Heinrich 11, 34, 100, 106–8, 164, 166

Walpole, Horace 107
Weber, Samuel 1, 14n5, 18, 21, 23, 25, 30–1, 33, 41, 46–7, 53, 60, 65, 77, 91, 93, 98, 115, 123, 125, 127, 131, 133, 145, 149, 151, 157, 159, 161, 163, 167–8, 178, 184, 190; on the *modus significandi* 77
Weigel, Sigrid 41
Whitman, Walt 20
Witte, Bernd 1
Wright, Chantal 7, 35, 41, 49, 74n29, 110–14; on Berman's uneasiness with Benjamin's messianism 144; on *Darstellung* as performance 51; on *durchscheinend* 150; on fame 45n20; on *Gehalt* and "tenor" 95, 185n68; on *gelten* 16–18, 21–2; as translator 1, 6–7, 9, 16–17, 21–2, 24, 36n14, 41, 45, 49, 51, 57n25, 66, 70, 74, 95, 122, 124, 153, 157–60, 166n59, 185
Wurgaft, Benjamin Andes 15, 53, 98, 172

Zathureczky, Kornél 15, 18, 21, 41, 151, 164; discussed 31
Zechner, Dominik 8n1, 47, 91, 93, 102; on the affinity/kinship/relationships of languages 50; on anticipation 88
Zohn, Harry 6, 13, 16, 24, 32, 34, 51–3, 55, 57n25, 70–1, 76–7, 100–1, 109, 112–14, 117, 118n41, 119, 122, 126, 135–6, 138–9n50, 147, 150–1, 157–60, 166n59; on "afterlife" 36; attacked by de Man 29–30; dropping "messianic" 85

**Subjects**

4EA cognitive science 5

Aeolian harp 111, 165, 176–7, 183–4n67; and Hölderlin 50, 111, 165, 176
"Aeolische Harfe, Die" (Schreiber) 176n63
"Aeolsharfe, Die" (Herder) 176n63
affinity/kinship of languages 49–50, 70–3; *see also* languages
affordances 27–8
"Affordances of the Translator, The" (Robinson) 28
afterlife (Benjamin/Zohn/Rendall) 36
after-ripening 3, 27, 64–71, 148
*L'Âge de la traduction* (Berman) 6
*Age of Translation, The* (Berman/Wright) 6–7, 95
*Aleksis Kivi and/as World Literature* (Robinson) 34–5n12
*Alice in Wonderland* (Carroll) 190
analogy 55–6, 62–4

Angelic Chariot (Ezekiel) 155
*Antigone* (Sophocles/Hölderlin) 11, 132n46, 179
"Äolsharfen: Ein Gespräch" (Goethe) 176n63
aphenomenology (Hamacher) 5, 22n6
Archetypal Man (Adam Kadmon or Adam Elyon) 155
"Ars Poetica" (MacLeish) 16
Atsilut (emanations) 137, 155
*Aufhebung* (sublation, Hegel) 162–3
aura 156

Babel, Tower of 121; pre-, 122
"Bald sind wir Gesang" (Hölderlin, "Soon We Shall Be Song") 75
becoming, as movement of language 154, 160; and Deleuze and Guattari's *devenir* 157–8, 160
*Becoming a Translator* (Robinson) 129
*Begriff der Kunstkritik in der deutschen Romantik, Der* (Benjamin) 104
*Being and Time* (Heidegger) 40
Benjamin's *-abilities* (Weber) 27, 163
Benjamin's letters 54n22, 74n29, 183n66
*Beyond Good and Evil* (Nietzsche) 38n17
*Bhagavad-Gita* 107
Bible, Hebrew 5, 87, 137, 178n63, 188–9; interlinear 170, 187, 190; Luther 11, 106, 169; *see also* midrash; total text
*Brot* and *pain* 78–80

cause (Aristotle) 29
"Concept of Art Criticism in German Romanticism, The" (Benjamin) 104
constructivism *see* social-constructivism
Copernican Hypothesis (Kant) 14n5, 62
copy theory (Plato) 25, 37, 61n26, 174
*Crisis of the European Sciences, The* (Husserl) 40
*Critical Translation Studies* (Robinson) 81, 130n45
*Critique of Pure Reason, The* (Kant) 54, 61
"crudest psychologism" (Benjamin) 37, 66

*Dao of Translation, The* (Robinson) 130n45
*De Profugis* (Philo) 143
dead theory of translation (Benjamin) 36, 45, 57–9, 65, 67–9, 71, 82, 125, 150
"Death of the Author, The" (Barthes) 45
*Deep Ecology of Rhetoric in Mencius and Aristotle, The* (Robinson) 130n45
*Defence of Poesy* (Sidney) 20
"Dejection, an Ode" (Coleridge) 176n63

deterritorialization (Deleuze and Guattari) 158
*devenir* (Deleuze and Guattari) 157–8, 160
diachrony (Saussure) 57, 68, 71, 157; *see also* synchrony
dialogism, internal (Bakhtin) 5, 13, 129–30
"Discourse in the Novel" (Bakhtin) 130
*Divine Comedy* (Dante/George) 107
Divine Persona/Queen (Sophia as Malkuth) 139–40, 155
Divine Tree of Life 155
*Doctrine of the Categories and of Signification of Duns Scotus, The* (Heidegger) 77
domestication 147–8n54
*Don Quixote* (Cervantes) 15, 101

echo 10, 108–11
Ein Sof (the Infinite) 137–9, 155, 185
Elohim (gods) 137–8
emanation 5, 26–7, 39
"Embodied Translation" (Robinson) 189
emotional-energetic-logical interpretant triad (Peirce) 56
"Eolian Harp, The" (Coleridge) 176n63
epistemology, and the Kantian critique of objectivity 60–4
equivalence 36, 40, 58–65, 69, 71, 139, 153, 175; *see also* dead theory of translation; sense-for-sense translation
Essence (*Wesen*) 13, 28, 69; of certain works 33; and essentialism 14; Platonic 32, 48; vitalistic 71
*Estrangement and the Somatics of Literature* (Robinson) 130n45
etymology 57, 71; in Hölderlin 25, 50, 72, 132
*Eugene Onegin* (Pushkin/Nabokov) 134–5

fairy tale 10; Kabbalistic in #69 10, 140n51, 165
fallibilism (Peirce) 15
fame (*Ruhm*) 3, 37, 44–6
fascism, and vitalism 39–40, 42n19
*Faust* (Goethe) 176n63
feeling (*Gefühl*) 81; Romantic, for translation as a Form 105; -tone (*Gefühlston*) 5, 128–31
*Feeling Extended* (Robinson) 17, 130n45
fidelity 2–3; against the word 125–8, 165; to the form/syntax 133, 148; *vs.* freedom 4, 152, 165; in the freedom of language-movement 167; liberating pure language 164; and the tangent touching the circle 156, 165; to the word/letter 11, 147, 187
*Finnegans Wake* (Joyce) 38

*Fleurs du mal, Les* (Baudelaire) 79, 107
Foreclosing on audiences 2, 12–23
"Foreignism and the Phantom Limb" (Robinson) 147
foreignization 147–8n54
form 12, 22, 22–3n6, 58, 66, 133; of art 12; of language intentions 55, 81; of life 48–9; of literature 69; managed by the Logos 28, 38, 90, 143; Platonic Essence of 61, 134, 173–4; the poet's task as a 106–7; prototypes of their 11, 25, 132, 176, 178–9, 183–4n67, 185; of the source text's superlife 47, 49, 51; of the source text's syntax 91; translation as a 5, 23–8, 30–2, 34, 36–8, 48–9, 98, 103, 105–6, 125, 134, 156; the translator's task as a 106–7; vitalistic supplementation of 81, 130; of a word 143; *see also* Realm of Forms (Plato)
*Fortleben* (living on) 35, 44–5, 61, 64
freedom 4, 125–7; as bad translation 133–4; of language-in-motion, as fidelity 156, 167–8; from sense/meaning 164–5; as sense-for-sense translation 152; united with literalism in the interlinear version 187
"Freud and the Scene of Writing" (Derrida) 121

*Gefühlston* (feeling-tone) 5, 128–31
*Gehalt* (tenor) 93, 110, 174, 185n68
*gelten* (to be in force) 16–18
germ (*Keim*) 50–1, 120, 160
German Romantics 9, 11n3, 24, 42n19, 87, 102–4, 123, 132, 166, 171–2; and the echo 109; and Kabbalah 137n49; and literalism 107, 166; and Socratic irony 104; transcended by Goethe 169; translation *vs.* criticism 104; *see also* Romantic(ism)
Gnosticism 144n53
*Gulliver's Voyage to Phantomimia* (Kilpi/Robinson) 166n59

"Harmonie der Sphären, Die" (Kosegarten) 176n63
hermeneutics: Diltheyan 5, 39; Jewish 134, 136
*Herodias* (Mallarmé/George) 107
historicity 2, 26, 39, 121; as fame 44–7; as *Heilsgeschichte* 122; vitalistic 42–3
*Hölderlin's Sophocles* (Constantine) 175
Holy Writ 3, 165; always translatable 184–6; interlinear version of 170, 187, 190
hypercanon (Damrosch) 34

*Idiot, The* (Dostoevsky) 31
*Iliad* (Homer/Voß) 107
immediability (*Unmittelbarkeit*) 86, 87, 108, 114, 151n55, 153, 184–5; Hamacher on 110, 163n58; Vermeer on 163n57
index (Peirce) 55
*ingenium* (genius/engine), philosophical 118–20, 144n53; mystical 122, 144
"Inscience of Translation, The" (Robinson) 189
*intendendum* (*das Gemeinte*) 50, 55–6, 76, 78–81, 128–9, 145
intensive 22, 49–54, 62, 74, 83, 89, 117–18, 180, 183
*intentio* 6, 145–6, 158
intentions: of humans 55, 112; of (the) languages 3, 10, 52, 57, 62–3, 85–6, 91–2, 115, 118, 130–1, 134, 140n51, 141, 146; producing an echo 108–9; supplementation of 27, 72, 75–8, 81–2, 145, 147
interlinear version of Holy Writ 165, 170, 180; the prototype of all translation 186–8
intertwining of life (*Zusammenhang des Lebens*, Dilthey) 35, 39–41, 47–8

John's Gospel 5, 143–4

Kabbalah 37, 42, 67, 87, 136, 144n53, 162, 155, 190; Christian 5, 137n49; creation myth of 43; Jewish 5, 137–40; medieval 172
*Kategorien- und Bedeutungslehre des Duns Scotus, Die* (Heidegger) 77
Kelipot (shells) 42, 67, 138
kernel (*Kern*) 2, 3, 33–4, 52, 92–5, 99–100, 127, 160, 174; of "innermost falling mute" 183; of pure language 34, 138, 157–8; of translatability in the source text 34; of un(re)translatability 92, 96, 183
*krisis der europäischen kultur* (Pannwitz) 168

language, becoming of 154, 157–8; becoming pure language 160
languages, affinity/kinship/relationship between 3, 49–50, 59–60, 70–3; holy growth of 49, 51–2, 57; movement of 156, 167–8; and protosynthesis (Hamacher) 73; supplementation of intentions in 3, 27, 72, 76, 78, 81–2, 145, 147; and vitalistic intentions 11, 57
*Lebenswelt* (life-world, Husserl) 40
"Leier des Pythagoras, Die" (Herder) 176n63

"letter to Pammachius" (Jerome) 11n3
life: ongoing 35, 44, 61, 64; intertwining of (Dilthey) 35, 39–41, 47–8; super-, 35–6, 44
life-world (*Lebenswelt*, Husserl) 40
"Linien des Lebens, Die" (Hölderlin) 180
literalism 3–4n1, 10, 49, 86, 91–2, 130–1, 133–6; as the arcade 149–51; as a becoming-freedom 165, 181, 185–7; in Christian theology 189; and domestication/foreignization 147–8, 172; etymological 11; Hölderlin as "monstrous" exemplar of 107; interlinear 4; in Luther 11n3, 166; mystical 167; not Benjamin's problem in his Baudelaire 126n43; as reassembling the vessel 139; and re-poeming 175; and the supplementation of languages 147–8; in Voß 107, 166
Logos 2, 3, 74, 90, 142–4, 181; as theorized by Philo 5, 28, 38, 51–2, 90, 113, 130, 137, 143–4, 156, 172, 179, 188
Lord's Prayer 79
"Lost Princess, The" (Nachman of Breslov) 140, 155

Macbeth (Shakespeare/Garneau) 20–1
"Maiden Speech of the Aeolian Harp, The" (Emerson) 176n63
Malkuth (Kingdom) 139
Merkabah (chariot) mysticism 155
Messianism 29, 57; in the Philonian Logos 144; rejected in Benjamin by Berman 73–5, 144–5, 162; rejected in Benjamin by Weber 75; and revelation 62
metaphysics 14, 22n6, 34, 38
metempsychosis (Robinson) 150
midrash 190
"Midrash and the Dawn of Kabbalah" (Dan) 188–9
*modus significandi* 76–9, 81, 145
muse, of philosophy or translation 119
"Mutability" (Shelley) 176n63
Mysticism 2, 22n6, 29; Kabbalistic 190; Logos 38; and translation's task 2, 3, 27, 38, 84, 86, 88, 92, 115–16, 119–20, 146

"naïve" *vs*. "sentimental" poetry (Schiller) 112, 114–15
Neoplatonism 5, 38; Jewish, Sophia as the Divine Queen 139, 140n51, 143n52, 144; and Philo's Logos mysticism 90, 137, 143–4; Renaissance 42
"Not Ideas About the Thing But the Thing Itself" (Stevens) 16

NOT! (Robinson) 147–8

objectivity 36–7, 39, 42, 51, 63; scientific vs. mystical 59–62, 65
"Ode to the West Wind" (Shelley) 176n63
*Odyssey* (Homer/Voß) 107
*Oedipus Rex* (Sophocles/Hölderlin) 11, 132n46, 179
Ohn (spiritual light and flow) 155
Olamot (spiritual worlds) 155
"On Empiricism and Bad Philosophy in Translation Studies" (Pym) 79
"On First Looking into Chapman's Homer" (Keats) 101–2
"On Language as Such and on the Language of Man" (Benjamin/Jephcott) 52–3, 74, 83–4, 163
"On the Different Methods of Translating" (Schleiermacher/Robinson) 64, 103, 105, 169, 172
*Origin of German Tragic Drama, The* (Benjamin/Osborne) 34–5n12, 39n18
overliving (Benjamin/Spivak) 36

*Pale Fire* (Nabokov) 135n47
Partzufim (divine faces) 155
*Performative Linguistics* (Robinson) 130n45
performativism (Austin/Derrida) 21
performativity 5, 17, 20; somatic 54
phenomenology 5, 76; and aphenomenology (Hamacher) 5, 22; autobiographical (Dilthey) 39; of communication 13, 21–2n6, 130; and feeling 104, 130; hermeneutical 136; of the life-world (Husserl) 40; of slipping and falling 125n42; social 45, 54; of translation 62, 76, 81
poetic word (*Dichterwort*) 67, 93
post-Kantian 14, 61–2, 129
post-Romantic 14, 74–5, 129, 148
pre-Kantian 15, 54, 62, 172
pre-Romantic 15, 172
*Problems of Dostoevsky's Poetics* (Bakhtin/Emerson) 130
proleptic (Epicurus/Kant) 50
propagation 50–2, 57, 96–7, 157–8
proprioception 147–8n54
protosynthesis (Hamacher) 73, 91
pure language 3, 9, 73–4, 89–90, 98, 101, 122, 134, 149, 152, 186, 190; becoming-, 157, 160; as dialect (Berman) 117n40, 144, 156, 162, 190; freed from the weight of sense-making 161; as the messianic end of holy growth 5, 27–8, 49–52, 57, 74–5, 80, 87, 109, 113, 120, 122, 132, 144, 146; imprisoned in the source language 10–11, 107–8, 158, 164–5; intensively hidden in translations 117; as kernel 34, 157–8; as light source 151; movement toward 115; as the no-longer-expressive Creative Word 161; in "On Language as Such" 83; ripening the seed of 52, 74–5, 123–5, 141, 153; as spaceship 168; suspenseless and silent 117–18; as symbolized 154–6, 158, 160; through the supplementation of intentions 72, 76, 81–3; as "universal" language 73; wrapped in Kelipot shells 138
purposiveness 43–4, 46–8, 74n30
"Pushing-Hands and Periperformativity" (Robinson) 130n45
*Pythian Ode* (Pindar) 178–9

Qur'an 188n69

*Ramayana* 107
Realm of Forms (Plato) 24, 29, 42–3, 48, 51, 69, 113, 130, 168, 179; as the true reality 37
reassembling the broken vessel (Tikkun) 136–9
re-/dissolving foreignness of foreign languages (Novalis/Berman) 9, 87, 89, 124
relationship between languages see languages
re-poeming (*Umdichtung*) 164–5, 175
*Republic* (Plato) 37
"Rhythm as Knowledge-Translation, Knowledge as Rhythm-Translation" (Robinson) 189
Romantic(ism) 2, 14–15, 37–8, 74–5, 144; and the Aeolian harp 111, 176; dark 182; feeling for translation as a Form 24, 105; Nationalism 14n5; pan-, 163; post-, 14, 129, 148; pre-, 15, 172
Romantics, German 9, 11n3, 24, 42n19, 87, 102–4, 123, 132, 166, 171–2; and the echo 109; and Kabbalah 137n49; and literalism 107, 166; and Socratic irony 104; transcended by Goethe 169; translation vs. criticism 104
royal mantle, folds of 93–8, 100, 154, 174
*Ruhm* (fame) 37
"Rumors from an Aeolian Harp" (Thoreau) 176n63

sacred history (*Heilsgeschichte*) 5, 28, 80
"Saitenspiel, Das" (Herder) 176n63
*Saturday Night Live* 147–8

*Satz* (sentence), as sense-for-sense translation 149
*Schleiermacher's Icoses* (Robinson) 105, 130n45
scientism 59
seed (*Samen*) 52, 160
*Sein und Zeit* (Heidegger) 40
*Semitranslating Peirce* (Robinson) 130n45
sense (*Sinn*) 28, 58, 66, 91, 123, 131, 133, 135, 140–1, 145, 152–3, 159–65, 167, 184–5, 187, 190; -for-sense translation 11n3, 63–4, 90, 94–5, 100, 126–7, 134–5, 149–50, 152, 156, 175, 179; source-textual 4, 10, 11, 61n26, 62–3, 95n34, 110, 125–8, 134, 136, 141–2, 156, 162, 173–81; *see also Satz*; *Sinn*
Sephirot (vessels/divine attributes) 137–8, 139n51, 140n51, 144n53, 155
Shekhinah (Divine Persona/Presence) 139, 144n53
Shevirah (breaking of the vessels) 139
"Signature Event Context" (Derrida/Bass) 17
signs 55–6
silence, of the theia mania 11, 118, 178–84
*Sinn* (sense) 28, 58, 66, 91, 123, 131, 133, 135, 140–1, 145, 152–3, 159–65, 167, 184–5, 187, 190; translated into French as *sens* (also direction) 183–4n67; *see also Satz*; sense
Sitra Achra (the other side) 138
skopos theory (Vermeer) 13–14, 29
slipping and falling 125
social-constructivism 13, 129
Socratic irony (F. Schlegel) 104
somatics of language (Robinson) 130n45
sonnets (Shakespeare/George) 107
Sophia (Wisdom) 139, 140n51, 143n52, 144
source text: sense of 4, 10–11, 61n26, 62–3, 95n34, 110, 125–8, 134, 136, 141–2, 156, 162, 173–81; syntax of 10, 63, 68, 91, 127, 131, 133, 148, 149–50, 152, 165–6
speech acts 54; indirect 20
superlife (Benjamin/Robinson) 35–6, 39–40, 42–5, 51, 67, 70, 100–1; as suprahistorical 72; vitalistic Essence of 51; as vitalistically emanating the translation 47–8
supplementation: of ideal Forms 130; of intentions in languages 3, 27, 72, 76, 78, 81–2, 145, 147
symbolized *vs.* symbolizing 3, 6, 154–7; and symbolizing-becoming-symbolized 159–60

synchrony (Saussure) 57, 68; *see also* diachrony
syntax 4; -free 181; literalism as revealing 181, 187; source-textual 10, 63, 68, 91, 127, 131, 133, 148, 149–50, 152, 165–6

*Tableaux parisiens* (Baudelaire) 79, 80n32
tangent touching a circle 3, 6, 162, 167, 173–4, 176, 187; as literalism touching an infinitesimal point of sense 165, 167–8
task *see* translator's task
tenor (*Gehalt*) 33–4, 93, 100, 110, 174; -intertwinings 109
theia mania 181–2
"Theological-Political Fragment" (Benjamin) 31
theology 22n6; Christian 26, 87; Jewish 2, 52, 163; medieval 95; students and the interlinear 188n69
*Thousand and One Nights* 175
three removes 49, 51
Throne of God 155
Tikkun Olam (reassembly) 138–9n50, 139
Tohu (chaos) 139
total text (Hebrew Bible) 5, 188
transcendental idealism (Kant) 62
"Transcreating Volter Kilpi" (Robinson) 135n47
transcreation (*Umdichtung*) 107, 165–6; origins of 166n59
*Transgender, Translation, Translingual Address* (Robinson) 130n45
translatability 2, 13; of a source text 23–8, 30–4, 38–9, 61, 104, 173, 182; total (Christian) 189; of a translation 92, 96, 98, 175, 182–3
Translating *vs.* writing an original work 2–3, 92–3, 99, 102, 105–6, 110, 112
*Translation and Taboo* (Robinson) 10, 11, 95n34, 130n45, 189; on Benjamin's Kabbalistic fairy tale 140n51, 165; on "metempsychotic" translation 150
*Translation and the Problem of Sway* (Robinson) 130n45
translation chain 93, 94, 175
translation quality assessment (TQA) 59, 65, 70
*Translationality* (Robinson) 130n45
translatorial action (Holz-Mänttäri) 109
translator's task 3; awakening the echo 108–11; as giving up (de Man) 10; mystical 27, 84, 92; as responsibility (Derrida) 8; seemingly impossible 123; as (re-/dis-)solution (Novalis/Berman) 9, 87, 89, 124
*Translator's Turn, The* (Robinson) 130n45

translucence *vs.* transparency *vs.* translucidity 149–51
transphenomenology (Robinson) 5, 22n6
*Tristram Shandy* (Sterne) 102
Tzimtzum (construction/concentration) 137, 139

"Über die verschiedenen Methoden des Übertsetzens" (Schleiermacher) 64, 103
"Über Sprache überhaupt und über die Sprache des Menschen" (Benjamin) 52–3, 83–4
*Überleben* (superlife) 35–6, 44–5, 100
*Umdichtung* (transcreation, re-poeming) 107, 164–6, 175
Universal Grammar (Chomsky) 73
universal subjectivism (Kant) 62
untranslatability 27, 31–2; of the kernel in the source text 94, 96, 127; of the translation 16, 34, 75, 99, 174–5, 181–2
*Ursprung des deutschen Trauerspiels, Die* (Benjamin) 34–5n12, 39n18
Utopia 13, 29

Veil of Appearances 62
vitalism 5, 11, 28, 38, 158; of Essences 71; in fascism 39–40, 42n19; and the foreclosure on reader-response 59; and language intentions 57, 62; in Logos mysticism 39, 52, 144; of Platonic Forms 49, 56, 130; powering historicity 42; in Renaissance, Enlightenment, and Romantic esoterics 42n19; of superlife 51; transcendental 29, 34; transhuman 57; and unfolding/emanation 47

"Wayne's World" (Myers/Carvey) 147–8
*West-East Divan* (Goethe) 168–70
*Western Translation Theory from Herodotus to Nietzsche* (Robinson) 103, 166, 172n62
"What Is an Author?" (Foucault) 46
word-for-word translation 3n1, 126–7, 131, 133–4, 147, 149–50, 184, 187, 188n69
"Work of Art in the Age of Mechanical Reproduction, The" (Benjamin/Zohn) 6, 155–6
world literature 34–5n12

Zohar 6, 155–6
*Zusammenhang* (intertwining, context, connection: Dilthey) 33, 47, 71, 77, 136, 154; *des Lebens* (of life: Dilthey) 5, 35, 39–41
"Zwei Gedichte von Friedrich Hölderlin" (Benjamin) 124

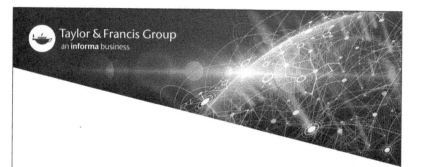